Studies in the Legal History of the South

EDITED BY PAUL FINKELMAN AND TIMOTHY S. HUEBNER

This series explores the ways in which law has affected the development of the southern United States and in turn the ways the history of the South has affected the development of American law. Volumes in the series focus on a specific aspect of the law, such as slave law or civil rights legislation, or on a broader topic of historical significance to the development of the legal system in the region, such as issues of constitutional history and of law and society, comparative analyses with other legal systems, and biographical studies of influential southern jurists and lawyers.

Tyrannicide

Tyrannicide

Forging an American Law of Slavery in Revolutionary South Carolina and Massachusetts

EMILY BLANCK

The University of Georgia Press
Athens and London

Parts of chapter 1 were published in a different form as "The Legal Emancipations of Leander and Caesar: Manumission and the Law in Revolutionary South Carolina and Massachusetts," in *Slavery and Abolition* 28.2 (2008). Parts of chapter 4 were originally published in different form as "Seventeen Eighty-Three: The Turning Points in the Law of Slavery and Freedom in Massachusetts," in the *New England Quarterly* 75.1 (2002).

Set in Minion Pro by Graphic Composition, Inc.
Printed and bound by Sheridan Books, Inc.
The paper in this book meets the guidelines for
permanence and durability of the Committee on
Production Guidelines for Book Longevity of the
Council on Library Resources.

Printed in the United States of America
18 17 16 15 14 C 5 4 3 2 1

Library of Congress Cataloging-in-Publication Data

Blanck, Emily, author.
   Tyrannicide : forging an American law of slavery in revolutionary
South Carolina and Massachusetts / Emily Blanck.
        pages cm — (Studies in the legal history of the south)
   Includes bibliographical references and index.
   ISBN 978-0-8203-3864-4 (hardcover) — ISBN 0-8203-3864-8 (hardcover)
1. Slavery—Law and legislation—South Carolina—History. 2. Slavery—
Law and legislation—Massachusetts—History. 3. Tyrannicide (Brig) I. Title.
   KF4545.S5B58 2014
   342.744087—dc23

                                                    2014005792

British Library Cataloging-in-Publication Data available

To Bill Carrigan

Contents

Illustrations

Acknowledgments

WHEN I WAS IN GRADUATE SCHOOL, my favorite place to start in any book was here, the acknowledgments. I am not sure what was so appealing about it—whether it was seeing the names that I knew from other books listed, getting a primer on the hard work that it took to write a book, or just gleaning a sense of the communal nature of research. I pictured the writing groups and interesting conversations over dinner, socks darned by wives, and libraries visited. No matter what, it is clear that although only one name appears as author on this book, many had a hand in making sure that it was done well.

For many historians, our adventure begins in a library, where we can travel back through time, touching the documents that our subjects touched, reading brilliant books by other scholars, and blinding ourselves with hours of microfilm. The librarians who helped me were invaluable. I am very appreciative of the staffs at the South Carolina Department of Archives and History, the Massachusetts Historical Society, the Massachusetts Archives, the South Carolina Historical Society, Rowan University Library, Emory University Library, Swem Library at the College of William and Mary, Yale University Library, the Harvard Map Collection, Harvard Baker Library, the South Caroliniana Library, the Boston Public Library, the Schomburg Library, the Library of Congress, especially the law library, the PVMA Deerfield Library, the Caroliniana Collection at Coastal Carolina University, the Nantucket Historical Society, the New England Historical Genealogic Society, Northampton Probate and Family Court, Hampshire Registry of Probate, the Forbes Library, the Falmouth Historical Society, the Isaac Royall House, and the Westfield Athenaeum.

All those trips to the library would not have been possible without those who funded my research. I received generous funding from the LAX fund at Rowan University, an NSFG Rowan Research grant, a research scholarship from the Colonial Dames of America, a fellowship at the Gilder Lehrman Center for the Study of Slavery, Resistance, and Abolition, Yale University, a Brown fellowship in southern studies at Emory University, a fellowship at the Institute for Constitutional Studies, and a fellowship at the Supreme Court Historical Society.

I must also thank the generations of historians who come before me. This book intersects several very large sets of historiographies, and without their intellectual and researching talents, I could not have written it. In particular, I feel particularly indebted to the early scholars of African American history such as Benjamin Quarles, George Moore, and Lorenzo Greene. While mainstream scholars insisted that we could not fully unearth the lives of slaves and African Americans, historians like these constantly proved the established view wrong.

The readers at the *New England Quarterly* and *Slavery and Abolition* as well as the many scholars who commented on my conference papers provided invaluable feedback.

I have had an incredible number of mentors from high school on. In high school, Dr. Marty Schmitz taught me to think about history, not memorize it. Professors George Wright and Jim Sidbury opened my eyes to brand-new ways of looking at the past. As a master's student at the College of William and Mary, Leisa Meier patiently took time to really teach me how to write. Michael Bellesiles, James Roark, and Leslie Harris all supported and pushed me to write a better dissertation than I thought I could write.

Colleagues have helped me succeed throughout this process. As a graduate student at William and Mary, Lily Richards, Nichole Mahoney, Dan Ingram, and others created a vibrant intellectual community that made my initiation into academia exciting. As a PhD student at Emory University, my peers Maura Farrelly, Fay Yarborough, Christopher Curtis, Rob Widell, and Brian Luskey helped me keep my focus and made me think in new ways. As a member of the faculty at Rowan, I've gained a whole new cohort of colleagues who have helped me along the way, making sure that the dissertation actually made it into book form. Between departmental "work in progress" seminars and an inspiring writing group, I did it. Thanks to Katrinka Somdahl-Sands, Lee Talley, Chanelle Rose, Kelly Duke Bryant, Melissa Klapper, Matt Karp, Katherine Gray, Elyssa Ford, Janet Lindman, Courtney Richmond, Denise Williams, and the rest of the Rowan History Department. These colleagues occasionally even included a student. Tessa Knight collaborated with me on several research trips, during which I taught her to be patient with the sources, and she provided another set of eyes that made a less than fruitful search productive enough and enjoyable.

The readers of the whole book in its various forms deserve medals, or at least a large sum of money, for the time and thought that went into their reading and commentary. This includes the anonymous readers from the University of Georgia Press, James Roark, Janet Lindman, John Bond, Michael Bellesiles, George Van Cleve, Melissa Klapper, Kerin Forsyth, Laura Shelley, and Janet Wright. Thank you to *Slavery and Abolition* and *New England Quarterly* for publishing two articles that this book builds on.

Most surprisingly, in the last phase of researching this book, I met three extraordinary historians. In particular, I had the great fortune of meeting three nonacademic historians who showed me the incredible research skills and imagination that nonprofessional historians possess. Professor Janet Wright, a retired biologist from Dickinson University, has worked with Nancy Rogers for the past eight years to uncover all of the minutiae about the *Tyrannicide* affair. As such, they have been enormously helpful in researching and imagining the events that this book revolves around. Nancy's novelistic imagination helped her give me a vivid tour around the Waccamaw Peninsula plantations. Janet's scientific mind pushed her to precisely and passionately search out every detail of this story. I am also indebted to Professor Robert Romer, a retired physicist from Amherst College. Bob parlayed a volunteer docent job at historic Deerfield into a carefully researched, locally published book that exposes the full history of this beautiful town. His book uses the words of the eighteenth-century Deerfield residents as a means of offering a view of a small town that depended on its slaves, showing that Deerfield's history belongs to African Americans as well as to white Americans, a reality that historic Deerfield buries to this day.

Last, my family has always supported my research and given it focus. My extended family has always been excited by my accomplishments, reading my work and asking questions. My mother, who passed away before I attended graduate school, always dreamed of me gaining my PhD and writing a book. Her wind has always blown my sails forward. My daughters, Julia and Sara, help me think about the future and about how our past matters in explaining the present and future. Of course, they also always remind me that the book is not the most important thing in the world; they are. I have dedicated this book to Bill Carrigan. He has traveled all these long roads right by my side, reminding me how to continue when I slip off the track and how much I have achieved. Thank you.

Tyrannicide

Forging an American Slave Law

The Commonwealth of Massachusetts, if she stood in our situation would take high displeasure at such an attack upon her spirit, freedom, dignity, independence & sovereignty; all the States [are] equally free, independent & sovereign, and no one State is to presume to assume domination or Controul over another.
—Benjamin Guerard, governor of South Carolina,
October 6, 1783

ON OCTOBER 6, 1783, as the United States was recovering from the Revolutionary War and establishing itself as a new nation, South Carolina's governor Benjamin Guerard was already threatening disunion. He believed that another state, Massachusetts, had assaulted South Carolina's independence, the very freedoms that the states had just fought for. How did they get to this point? The key to understanding this crisis begins with a Spanish privateer in May 1779.

Late that month, Don Francisco Ignatio Urezberoeta had left Charleston to sail home to Cadiz, Spain, aboard a new ship he had purchased and christened the *Victoria*. In coming to Charleston in the first place, Captain Urezberoeta probably had sought to take advantage of a chaotic situation. British privateers swarmed the region, leading the formal British invasion of the low country, and Urezberoeta perhaps hoped to attack these privateers and seize war prizes.[1]

During the Revolution, privateers from three nations and several states sailed throughout the Atlantic's western edges. Their governments had sanctioned their privateering by issuing letters of marque. The privateers attacked each other in order to disturb trade and increase their personal wealth. The war offered an enticing (and dangerous) opportunity for captains and crews of these privateers to become rich.

As Urezberoeta sailed the open ocean, an ambitious British cruiser shot at the *Victoria*. Cannons boomed between the two privateers. The British privateer had attacked in hopes of adding the freshly provisioned *Victoria* to its recent acquisition of thirty-four slaves from South Carolina's Waccamaw Peninsula. In the engagement, however, Captain Urezberoeta dominated the British privateer. He captured the ship and its cargo of valuable slaves, tobacco, wine, and indigo.

Urezberoeta now had a large number of slaves to sustain and to profit from. A few days later, however, two more British privateers attacked the *Victoria*. Captain Louis Bowen of the *Byron* led the attack. He defeated Urezberoeta and captured the *Victoria*. Rather than simply taking the *Victoria*'s stores, Bowen forced the ship to set sail for British-occupied New York.

After two weeks' slow sailing they still had not arrived in New York. Then on June 15, two Massachusetts brigs, the *Hazard* and the *Tyrannicide*, engaged the three privateers, firing two cannonballs. The brigs sailed alongside the privateers and shot at them six or seven more times, hitting once. The Massachusetts crews boarded the privateers and found that Urezberoeta was slightly injured and several others aboard were sick, but the vessel was intact. The British ships retreated, and the *Victoria* was again diverted. The *Hazard* and the *Tyrannicide* escorted their prize to Boston Harbor and docked her at Castle Island on June 23.[2]

Some very significant cargo had made this tumultuous journey from South Carolina to Massachusetts. The thirty-four slaves aboard the *Victoria* would force both South Carolina and Massachusetts to confront the meaning of the American Revolution. The discourse before the Revolution that had highlighted the concept of freedom came face to face with its "putative opposite," slavery.[3] The people of both South Carolina and Massachusetts valued freedom and held slaves, but both slavery and freedom had different meanings in each place. These words celebrating freedom had not just been bandied about as rhetorical shots in the pamphlet wars before the rebellion; they were embedded in both states' legal systems. The slaves aboard the *Victoria* experienced firsthand the differences in South Carolina's and Massachusetts' laws. They forced both states to concretely debate the boundaries of slavery and freedom, especially as they became enshrined in national law. A crisis occurred in 1783, when the owners of several of the *Victoria* slaves who were still in Massachusetts tried to recover their human property. They believed that the state of Massachusetts had unilaterally emancipated their slaves, and South Carolina was adamant that another state did not have the right to free its citizens' slaves. At that point, Governor Guerard threatened disunion.

In 1783, South Carolina warned Massachusetts that its actions concerning slavery threatened the viability of the new United States of America. The slaves never returned to South Carolina. Still, in 1788, South Carolina ratified the Constitution, binding itself even more closely to Massachusetts through a federal government that had greater power over the states than it had had under the Articles of Confederation. What had transpired during these five years to change the minds of South Carolinians about a "perpetual union" with Massachusetts and the other northern states? The answer lies, in part, in understanding the *Tyrannicide* affair, this relatively unknown story involving a band of African slaves from South Carolina's Waccamaw Peninsula.

At the crisis's height, Guerard had written Massachusetts governor John Hancock about these slaves. No doubt, Guerard's palms sweated and his heart thumped as he wrote the letter. Some of his fellow citizens had lost personal wealth at the hands of the "liberal" laws of Massachusetts. South Carolina's interest in maintaining a strong slave system required him and the privy council who ordered that he write the letter to protect their citizens' property: fourteen slaves set free by the state of Massachusetts. It probably seemed startling to these South Carolinians that slavery, an institution that all thirteen of the original states shared at the onset of the Revolution, was already dissolving in the North. Whether it was surprising or not, the consequences of northern emancipation were soon to be laid bare by the *Tyrannicide* affair. This conflict threatened to dissolve the fragile unity of the confederation of the states before it had even coalesced. The repercussions would be felt until the Massachusetts and South Carolina delegates agreed on a fugitive slave clause for the Constitution of 1787.[4]

The name of the ship, the *Tyrannicide*, represented a core idea for the white British colonists who decided to commit metaphorical tyrannicide and end the rule of their tyrant mother country. The colonists had rebelled because of the "tyranny" of British law that strove to tax them without their permission. Rhetorically, the quest to end tyranny pervaded the Revolution. Massachusetts clergyman Jonathan Mayhew introduced the idea as early as 1750, arguing that the injunction of Romans 13, to submit to one's government, became invalidated under a "tyrannical Prince."[5] Pamphlet writers in the 1760s commonly referred to the tyranny of British imperialism. As the war started, George Mason urged Virginia to choose "Semper sic tyrannis" as the state motto. The Declaration of Independence described the king's power as consisting of "repeated injuries and usurpations, all having in direct object the establishment of an absolute Tyranny over these States." Likewise, Thomas Paine urged his readers to "conquer tyranny" in the first paragraph of *The Crisis*. Where there was tyranny, the metaphor of slavery followed closely. Paine asserted that this tyranny was turning the colonists into slaves. Therefore, John Fisk's naming his ship *Tyrannicide* in 1777 reflected the deepest hopes of the American rebels.[6]

Others in the colonies—women, slaves, servants, and laborers—also wanted to end tyranny. They hoped that this revolution for liberty would give them more freedom as well—more political, personal, and economic power. Abigail Adams famously reminded her husband in March 1776 to "remember the ladies" because "all men would be tyrants if they could." Slaves, too, sought to end the tyranny of slavery. Even the slaveholding Thomas Jefferson saw the introduction of slavery in the American colonies as one of the tyrannical infractions of the British government because it violated the "most sacred rights of life & liberty."

The slaves saw the setting in which such rhetoric flourished as providing an opportunity to improve their situation and escape bondage themselves. Many of the white men seeking freedom from Britain were shocked at the extent to which women, slaves, and poorer classes sought to take advantage of the Revolutionary moment. Therefore, as they completed their tyrannicide, they turned to building their new government, mindful of the need to limit the spread of the Revolution's most radical dimensions, lest their own servants and slaves continue the movement for tyrannicide. Americans struggled in the 1780s to construct a republic that guaranteed natural rights to its citizens but at the same time qualified that citizenship. Liberty had its limits, especially for black slaves.

This story, like the American Revolution, is both a national story and a local one. It is the story of the origin of the Constitution's fugitive slave clause and the efforts of Massachusetts and South Carolina in the wake of the *Tyrannicide* incident to compromise on slavery to preserve their national unity. That story is rooted in the different local histories and experiences of slavery in each state. It is also the story of how slaves sought to take advantage of the Revolutionary moment in these two states whose societies were so different. Place and time shaped how black and white Americans moved across the continuum of freedom and slavery throughout the Revolution; slavery was fundamentally different in each state (and changed over this brief time). In Massachusetts, slaves had more freedom and could end the tyranny of slavery through legal protest.[7] South Carolinian slaves, in contrast, could not pursue such a path in a state so deeply dependent on slavery. Slaves there could not hope to end slavery; however, during the War for Independence, they were able to get closer to freedom by running away and resisting. Thousands of individual South Carolina slaves stole themselves into freedom, a number possibly exceeding the entire emancipated population of black people in the state of Massachusetts.

The Revolutionary moment and the reactionary response of the founding generation have not been lost to historians. After Edmund Morgan demonstrated that American freedom depended on American slavery and David Brion Davis highlighted *The Problem of Slavery in the Age of Revolution*, scores of historians rushed to explore the contradictions of America's founding and the important role that slaves played in both the nation's founding and their own emancipations. In examining this crucial era, a number of historians began to accentuate the existence of slavery in the North, a history that many nineteenth-century northerners worked to forget. Although many of these studies have recovered the history of northern slave owners, they have not considered the interaction between northern and southern slavery. One reason they may not have is that the colonies seemed as though they developed independently. The *Tyrannicide* affair, however, provides an opportunity to explore the interaction between northern and southern states on the issue of slavery.[8]

The war for American independence led the colonies—and then the new states—into a much greater degree of contact, collaboration, and even conflict than before. Not surprisingly, the different legal traditions of the colonies were one source of tension, particularly in connection with slavery, which was so vital to the South.[9] Many issues, including the eligibility of black troops in the Continental Army, presented themselves for debate and discussion. No issue, however, provoked more worry than that of runaway slaves. Thousands of enslaved men and women used the opportunities afforded by the war to flee their owners, sometimes to fight alongside the British, sometimes to blend in with free black communities in cities or elsewhere. As slavery crumbled in the North, the *Tyrannicide* affair made clear that defeating the British would not end the problem of runaway slaves for southern masters. The future unity of the United States depended on a satisfactory resolution to this problem created by the struggle for independence and made apparent by thirty-four black men, women, and children from the South Carolina coast.

These slaves pushed white Americans to confront at least three core questions. First, what role would slavery play in a society built on the Declaration of Independence? Second, how would white revolutionaries respond to the black freedom struggle during this period? Third, how could America secure its national unity when the states differed so deeply in their responses to the first two questions? In hindsight, we know that the tensions Guerard described in his 1783 letter were just the beginning of a persistent, increasingly virulent debate that would eventually engulf the nation.

The answers to these questions depended on local responses to broad changes in a disparate nation. Massachusetts, whose citizens generally did not rely heavily on slavery for their economic welfare, seriously questioned slavery's compatibility with a republican form of government. Many citizens of Massachusetts came to believe that the two could not coincide. The sources of this conclusion were both a genuine embrace of liberty for all and self-interest, because it was thought that the end of slavery would benefit Massachusetts' free white workers while posing no great hardship to the Massachusetts elite.

In contrast, few if any South Carolinians had reservations about slavery coexisting with a republican government and quashed any discussion of abolition in their state. The tight grip they kept on slavery proved to be a vulnerability during the War for Independence, when Britain successfully lured South Carolina's slaves to rebel and turn against their masters.

During the Revolutionary War, the desire for unity against a common foe led representatives in Massachusetts to stifle their views on slavery, and they carefully avoided pushing too hard against their southern allies. In this vein, the state moved slowly on the issue of ending human bondage, doing very little until the war reached a turning point after the victory at Yorktown. Even then, the government quietly ended slavery in Massachusetts, publicizing the decision very little, certainly less than other northern states such as Pennsylvania, which implemented a more public, albeit more conservative, plan for gradual emancipation. But to the men who operated on the national level, such as John Adams, Massachusetts' Revolutionary quest could not go too far because the disparate states were building a nation with South Carolina, and South Carolina bristled at any hint of abolition, even at an abolition movement restricted to a state one thousand miles away.

Thus, the opposition of South Carolinians and other southerners to abolition slowed the emancipation of Massachusetts' slaves. They might have forestalled it altogether if the nation's black men and women had been silent on the issue of slavery and freedom. Slave activism forced leaders from both Massachusetts and South Carolina to address whether slavery was consistent with the values of the new United States.

In South Carolina, there was a great upsurge in slave resistance in 1776 and again in 1779, when the British attacked and invaded the low country, the coastal regions of South Carolina and Georgia that included the major cities of Charleston and Augusta, where rice cultivation flourished. White South Carolinian Patriots literally battled against fugitives who joined the British army and struggled to keep their other slaves working on their plantations. South Carolina's master class emerged from the war even more cognizant of the hostility of their slaves toward their bondage and the weakness of the institution in the face of external factors.[10]

By contrast, the slave population in Massachusetts struggled to become free in concert with the white Revolutionary endeavor. Indeed, many male slaves sought to escape their enslavement by fighting alongside the rebelling Americans. Most of these men had the permission of their owners to do so. For many, this service held hopes of freedom. Other black men and women of Massachusetts fought slavery in other ways. Through their writings and petitions, they pushed Massachusetts to extend their liberatory rhetoric to include abolition. Many whites in Massachusetts responded favorably to these pleas, and throughout the war, support for slavery declined.

These two wildly divergent responses to African Americans' quest for freedom meant that Americans were already divided over one of the key institutions in the American economy and society almost five years before the Constitutional Convention. The *Tyrannicide* affair provides the immediate context for the deliberations in the convention over slavery. Historians are familiar with the many compromises regarding slavery in the Constitution, but they have neglected the fugitive slave clause. Legal scholars cite the clause often because it intersects with many aspects of constitutional law, but it is very rarely the central focus of scholarship.[11] Nevertheless, the *Tyrannicide* affair demonstrates that the Revolutionary War generation took the issue of fugitive slaves seriously. The fugitive slave issue highlights the problem that the United States was born as a nation of both freedom and slavery. Slaves may have been regarded as merely property by their owners but they regarded themselves as people of free will, and they ran away and would continue to run away from their plantations hoping to reach freedom. Historians tend to pass over the establishment of the fugitive slave clause, in part because it took little time in the convention. However, the *Tyrannicide* case, which provides the first example of the states managing the problem of fugitive slaves, proves that the issue received considerable thought before the Constitutional Convention. Massachusetts and South Carolina probably drew from the case and its legacies when helping to write the fugitive slave clause in the Constitution. In this story, therefore, we can explore how the founding generation undermined its constitutional foundation by writing the fugitive slave clause into law.[12]

The events of the *Tyrannicide* affair reveal new ways in which both the local and national experiences of the American Revolution affected the history of slavery. In both states, active black communities helped shape the local response to slavery and revolutionary change. These local responses varied, however, in part because the experience of the war for most residents of Massachusetts was different from that of South Carolinians. At the same time, the American Revolution was a national experience, which meant that each state helped shape the other's response to the major issues of the day. As I make clear, South Carolina's staunch support for slavery and the existing racial hierarchy slowed abolition in Massachusetts, while the actions of Massachusetts in the *Tyrannicide* affair motivated South Carolina to fortify the foundations of slavery at home and in the national arena. The *Tyrannicide* affair illustrates the great degree to which the law was the locus for the expressions of ideologies of race and slavery. Delegates to the Constitutional Convention underscored this when they embedded their separate and common experiences with slavery during the previous five years into the foundations of American law and, in particular, wrote those tensions into the fugitive slave clause.

CHAPTER ONE

Slavery, Rhetoric, and Reality before the War, 1764–1774

Mrs. Ann Pawley the wife of Percival Pawley was taken sick the 29th August 1773 and Dyed 4th Dec 1773 about 8 oclock in the morning, was married almost 70 years with in 25 Days to Percival Pawley.

John Pawley the son of Percival Pawley was born April 8 1776 about 11 oclock at night.

—Pawley family Bible

IN THE DECADE BEFORE the American Revolution, life went on as normal for the white members of the Pawley plantations, even as many American colonists began to reenvision their relationship to England. Percival Pawley Jr. lost his mother but soon thereafter gained a son. Historical documents do not divulge whether any of the Pawley, Todd, Lewis, or Vereen families were actively engaged in the rebellion that was brewing against Britain. More than likely, they talked about the affairs of the day, but daily lives probably changed very little. They commanded their plantations, visited the cities, and traded their goods, seeking to make their own families happier and wealthier.

Stability was fragile, however. Both the black and white members of plantations would soon find themselves at the center of a transforming storm. Between 1764 and 1774, balking at the growing demands of the British, American colonists grasped for ways to assert their will and desires, while Britain sought to shape them into more responsible (and tax contributing) members of the empire. The American colonists would draw from their own experiences for a key metaphor to explain their perceived oppression: slavery. This metaphor was potent for two reasons. First, the American colonists were familiar with the oppressive chattel slave labor on which their

9

economies depended. Second, the word helped give depth and meaning to a core value of Anglo-American identity: liberty. In associating a loss of liberty with slavery, the American colonists gave liberty a clear and emotional meaning that resonated far more than any abstract or philosophical definition of the word.

The centrality of liberty in a nation of slaveholders created intractable tensions, even in colonies that depended little on slave labor. In 1765, Peter Oliver, chief justice of the Massachusetts Superior Court, presided over the freedom suit *Slew v. Whipple*.[1] After defense lawyer Jeremiah Gridley asserted that the highest law was that which protected property, Oliver retorted, "This is a Contest between Liberty and Property—both of great Consequence, but Liberty of most importance of the two." This remarkable exchange took place in a courtroom in an Anglo-American society in the early stages of a revolution about individual rights. Over the course of the eighteenth century in England and America, the idea of freedom as a core right of human beings in civil societies had gained enormous power. Many eighteenth-century citizens had begun to declare that governments must protect their citizens' freedoms and to insist that those that did not were illegitimate.

However, these men still generally embraced a Lockean view that tied freedom to the ownership of property, making Oliver's statement truly remarkable. Oliver issued this statement in a milieu in which property could be human beings. The widespread existence of slavery in the Anglo-American world challenged Revolutionary ideas of freedom. Slavery challenged white colonists not so much because of its consistency with the discourse of liberty as because the slaves themselves usurped the language of freedom to demand emancipation. The British, the white Americans in Massachusetts and South Carolina, and free and enslaved blacks in both colonies were beginning a vigorous and dynamic dialogue over the meaning of freedom and slavery in America.

For the past forty years, historians have debated the significance of the rhetoric of slavery for the pre-Revolutionary generation. Some scholars attribute the post-Revolutionary emancipations throughout the North to the "contagion of liberty." They argue that the colonists could not help but question slavery within their communities when they themselves had complained of being enslaved. Others have suggested that this contagion was weak and that slavery did not really wane during this era but only was abolished in areas that were nominally invested in slavery. In fact, they further observe, the new nation's Constitution recognized and protected slavery. Scholars seeking to understand how the Revolutionary generation justified its rebellion and still developed complex and differing ideas of freedom have taken up this debate. Until recently, the voices of slaves themselves have been absent in the debate. Scholars now recognize that slaves engaged in the dialogue with whites and pressed the Revolutionary generation to hold true to its ideals. This chapter explores the development of the debate between freedom and slavery in two very different colonies, South Carolina and Massachusetts.[2]

The debate in the colonies in the eighteenth century over the meaning of freedom and slavery provides the immediate context for responses to the *Tyrannicide* affair. The British who captured the slaves, the South Carolinians who lost their slaves, the officials in Massachusetts who received the slaves, and the slaves themselves all made choices that cannot be understood without locating them in the context of the larger debate about liberty and slavery. Societal dialogues are rarely simply organized, and this high-stakes discussion was no exception. For all these stakeholders, freedom and slavery had a nexus of meanings, many of which contradicted one another. Each group's ideas about these concepts emerged from experiences with the others: British leaders with Massachusetts' Patriots, slaves with white South Carolinian Patriots, white South Carolinians with white citizens of Massachusetts, and so on. This web of relationships brought individuals and groups vested in pressing their own definitions of slavery and freedom into contact and conflict. The rhetoric of slavery thus became interlocked with the reality of events. In a cycle that fed on itself, the reality influenced the rhetoric, and the rhetoric then pressed and shaped the experiences and actions of the Revolutionary generation.[3]

The realities of slavery were radically different in both places, but the language was the same. South Carolinian and Massachusetts revolutionaries would both use slavery as a key rhetorical tool, but slavery meant different things to each. For Britain, the reality of slavery in South Carolina was a military tool to use. The reality of slavery would also shape the rhetoric of slavery and the course of the war.

Colonial Slavery

History of Slavery in Massachusetts

It was not a coincidence that a justice from Massachusetts concluded that liberty was more important than property. His conclusion was rooted deeply in the history of slavery in the colony. Undoubtedly, Massachusetts' inhabitants valued property greatly and tied their own freedom to their ability to freely own, buy, and sell property. Nonetheless, the history of and ideas about slavery in the colony provided a framework wherein individuals could see the humanity in their human property. To begin with, labor relationships in Massachusetts spanned a very broad spectrum of bonded and forced labor. Massachusetts depended on not only slaves but also indentured servants and enslaved Native Americans, who had a slightly different status than black slaves did. This variety provided the people of Massachusetts with a subtler picture of forced labor. And a lack of reliance on slavery paired with an evolving ideology of citizenship in Massachusetts gave slaves enough power to press for their freedom when the right moment arose.[4]

Slavery began in New England during the first years of settlement in Massachusetts, and thus, the Puritans learned how to be slave owners immediately on arrival. As white New Englanders conquered their new settlements, they enslaved Native American populations both to control them and to draw on them for labor. Although John Winthrop did not immediately see Indians as slaves, it dawned on him quickly that they could be. Winthrop recorded requests for Native American slaves both locally and abroad in Bermuda. Wars with the Narragansett and Pequot tribes garnered large numbers of slaves. The trading of Indian slaves abroad brought African slaves to Massachusetts shores. In 1645, Emanuel Downing, John Winthrop's brother-in-law and a barrister, welcomed a trade of Pequot slaves for African slaves. However, the enslavement of American Indians had a different tenor than the enslavement of Africans. The indigenous slaves represented an enemy, a conquered people, and a grave threat to their society. African slaves represented a trade transaction, laborers without strings attached. Moreover, Indian slaves were part of peace negotiations and control of the region.[5] They served as collateral with which to negotiate with Native leaders. Further, colonists could expel troublesome Native slaves out of the colony, or they could just control them as slave property.

Despite this early foray into slavery, an opposition ideology appeared in the first slave law written in the Americas, only two years after African slaves set foot in the colony. This law, appearing in Massachusetts' first legal code, the 1641 *Body of Liberties*, was unique in its proscription. Rather than legalizing slavery outright, it outlawed slavery among the Puritans. However, the exceptions of strangers (foreigners who lacked protection from the king) and war prisoners gave an opening to enslave other human beings.

The exception in the case of war prisoners gave the colonists direct permission to enslave Indians captured in war, such as in the Pequot war they had just commenced. Conveniently, the slave trade had already begun to spread strangers throughout the Atlantic world. The law, however, also protected slaves, offering them "the Libertyes and Christian usages which the law of God established in Israell." In the Bible, God instructs Moses not to enslave his fellow Israelites, inviting him instead to enslave "from among the nations around you." This Massachusetts law establishing slavery demonstrates that its version of the institution drew from a particular moral and religious place. In time, this biblical origin would provide Massachusetts' slaves with leverage over their masters, as ideas of citizenship evolved in the colony.[6]

The numbers of slaves remained small in Massachusetts, making it easier to keep these strangers under control without a harsh slave code, but most Puritans sought a homogeneous society that made any kind of stranger generally unwelcome. Puritan communitarianism depended on the maintenance of trust among the members of the community. Puritans' efforts to expunge untrustworthy members with white skin were legendary. Men and women from other cultures with different skin tones posed a more complicated dilemma. The cultural differences of Africans and Native Americans automatically made them undesirable additions to the closed Puritan societies.[7]

The Puritan aversion to difference manifested itself differently in the case of Indians as opposed to Africans. The Puritans perceived the local Native Americans as dangerous military enemies and a major competitor for land. This perception of Native Americans as dangerous led to their near eradication. Indian slaves remained a constant throughout the colonial period, but their identity frequently merged with the black population. In the Puritan imagination, Africans embodied a spiritual threat. Tituba, for instance, a West Indian African, became an important focus during the Salem witch trials. Many Puritan leaders saw her blackness as a sign of the devil. But, despite the spiritual threat, Massachusetts reluctantly became a society with slaves, enslaving those Africans that entered their society. During the seventeenth century, Africans mostly presented Massachusetts with a convenient solution to colonists' problems with local aggressive Native groups. Edward Randolph reported in 1676 that only 200 Indian slaves lived in Massachusetts, and Governor Bradstreet estimated in 1680 that even fewer did, only about 120.[8]

As King Philip's War drew to an end in 1678, Massachusetts began changing the way it approached the enslavement of Native Americans. At first, the war brought in a huge number of slaves. Hoping to socialize Indian children, Plymouth's council of war forced them to apprentice in white families. The council sold hundreds more Indians to Spain, Jamaica, and the Wine Islands. Within a decade after the war, Massachusetts officials outlawed the enslavement of Native Americans.

Three factors contributed to this first emancipation. Fears of Native infiltration into Massachusetts towns, the strategic need for peaceful relations with northern New England and Canadian Indians, and the decimation of local tribal power meant that for most New Englanders, Native Americans were better forgotten than enlisted into service. After Rhode Island banned the enslavement of Native Americans in 1652, many Massachusetts towns did so independently, and, other than in times of war, Massachusetts frowned on enslaving Native Americans and tried to prevent it through their law against man stealing.[9]

Yet Massachusetts' officials were not quite ready to accept Indians into their society and thus created a complex system of involuntary labor in Massachusetts that gave rise to a harsh legal system that sanctioned enslaving Native Americans who ran into any trouble. Judicial indentures became a common experience for Indians. The penalties for Native Americans differed from those for whites, enslavement serving as a punishment for several crimes, especially for debt. Why did officials do this? They had three reasons: to maintain laborers, to keep Indians who lived within their midst under control, and to protect themselves from what they perceived as dependent people. Puritan leaders also controlled the less threatening Indians, mostly women and children, after King Philip's War, by forcing them into enclaves that were overseen by white officials. In 1746, they would appoint guardians to represent these Indians legally, ensuring that they would remain dependent members of society. In addition, strict debt laws that were enacted after King Philip's War ensnared hundreds into indentures that became hard to escape. Last, laws were enacted that criminalized Native Americans' own cultural practices, and just as with failure to repay debts, they could be punished for engaging in their cultural practices with enslavement.[10]

As Massachusetts Puritans created a thriving commercial and shipping center, their ships began to partake directly in the Atlantic slave trade, bringing more slaves to their shores. By 1700, the reported number of slaves in the colony was 400. By 1720, it had risen to 2,000, and by 1735, to 2,600. When the colony first took an official count of black slaves in 1754, the census counted 4,489, amounting to 2.3 percent of the total population, and the next census, in 1764–1765, it reported 5,779, which equaled 2.5 percent of the total population.[11]

The rapid rise in the number of slaves at the dawn of the eighteenth century caused Massachusetts leaders to take action. Spiritually, slavery proved an obstacle for the local ministers, as some congregants began to question whether a Christian should own another Christian. In 1693, Cotton Mather took on the challenge of Christianizing the heathen population without ending enslavement. In his 1701 pamphlet *The Negro Christianized*, Mather assured nervous masters that conversion did not free the slave. He proposed a law that any slave who completed baptism could not be freed just because he or she had received that rite. Mather's vision of slavery in his pamphlet, consistent with the Hebraic model, idealized the relationship between master and enslaved, representing it as mirroring the father-child relationship in a family. Mather promised that if owners mistreated their slaves "the Sword of Justice" would sweep through the colony.[12]

In 1701, Boston, which had the largest slave population in the colony, began passing municipal laws aimed at setting many of the standard limits on slave behavior that other established societies with slaves had set. The laws were not new; they drew on existing laws for controlling other dependents within households: indentured servants and children. They could not drink alcohol, start fires, or assemble. So as not to hamper the slave owners' profits or property rights, slaves were whipped rather than imprisoned, a punishment that few whites suffered in the early eighteenth century. Bostonians specified this special punishment in the Act to Prevent Profane Cursing and Swearing and the Act for Preventing All Riotous, Tumultuous and Disorderly Assemblies.[13]

As slaves became more numerous and society became more tumultuous, the colony of Massachusetts responded in a similar fashion to Boston by passing legislation to control the behavior of African slaves. Disease, economic downturn, and unrest scared Massachusetts in the 1740s and 1750s. The growing impoverishment of the population stirred fear of irregular assemblies. The preamble of the law described the "companies of men, children, and negroes" marching through the street, "abusing and insulting the inhabitants, and demanding and exacting money by menaces and abusive language," inciting "profaneness, impiety and other gross immoralities." The legislature feared that a "turbulent temper in spirit" would grow into "an opposition to all government and order." The law targeted assemblies at night, begging, and starting fires. In the eyes of legislators, blacks, free and enslaved, posed the greatest threats to the good order of society.[14]

The culture of mastery in Massachusetts persisted throughout the colonial era and seemed to reflect an idealistic vision of slavery. Historian William Piersen calls it "family slavery." Piersen does not mean to suggest by this term that slaves in Massachusetts received fewer beatings or a lighter workload than slaves elsewhere (indeed, Puritan families beat and worked their own children) but rather that since most slaves there lived within the household, the family was a natural model. Such a model did result in slave owners' feeling a sense of responsibility for the slaves' wellbeing, however.[15]

This familial version of slavery meant that the owner intruded on all parts of the slaves' lives, but white dominance could take on an idealized form that humanized the enslaved person. An example of the ideal master-slave relationship was that between Lucy Terry and her mistress Abigail Wells. Lucy arrived in Bristol, Rhode Island, in 1728 aboard a slave ship. In 1730, when she was probably about five years old, Ebenezer Wells purchased her, from Samuel Terry of Boston, who had purchased her from Boston slave merchant Hugh Hall.[16] Almost immediately, Abigail had her baptized by Reverend Jonathan Ashley. Wells taught Lucy to read and write.[17] Indeed, in many ways, she offered Lucy an unusual degree of support. Although historians might never know why Wells lavished such attention on Lucy, it is possible Wells felt particularly strong affection for her slave because she herself was childless.[18]

By the time Lucy turned fourteen, she was entrenched in her work for the Wells family and was familiar with life in the western Massachusetts town of Deerfield. Her admission to the local church as a full member on August 13, 1744, testified to the completion of her Christianization. Two years later, she used her writing skills to memorialize Deerfield's resistance to an August 25, 1746, Indian attack in a poem entitled "Bars Fight." Although her poem is today known as the first poem written by a black American, she did not live to see it published in 1855. For one hundred years, it seems that only the oral history of Deerfield kept the poem alive. Extraordinarily, this young woman, born in Africa, had written history for a society that had brought her to America as a slave and that under most circumstances would not have allowed her to read or write. Moreover, her owners successfully raised Lucy in accordance with the ideals of Mather: she seemed to be Christian, obedient, and part of the family and community, and she had mastered English culture.[19]

With these tools, she was able to pull herself out of slavery. She married a local free black man, Abijah Prince. The two of them worked to purchase her freedom. As a free woman, she continued her remarkable life; she fought for her husband's land interests before a federal court and appeared in person to appeal her son's rejection from Williams College.[20]

However, successful stories of slaves like Lucy did not mirror the uncertain reality of day-to-day life for many slaves. Even supportive owners might lose their temper on occasion. Given the physical closeness of slaves and their masters, it is not surprising that sometimes masters and mistresses committed acts of rash violence against their slaves. For example, using her own arm, the slave Mum Bett, of Great Barrington, blocked her mistress from striking her sister with a heated fire iron. The event crippled Mum Bett but probably saved the life of her younger sister.[21]

Moreover, the circumstances of enslavement made it almost impossible for slaves to have their own family life. Marriage was legal and even encouraged by Massachusetts clergy, but marriage bestowed no rights to the married couple. Men and women frequently lived apart, and a free husband could not impart freedom to his wife, although offspring of free mothers were born free. Like whites, blacks had to abide by the many strict rules of the church if their unions were to be acknowledged. Enslaved women and men posted their intentions at the public meetings and had some of the most distinguished clergy in the colony perform their marriage ceremonies. Despite this affirmation, married life remained a challenge. The division of slave labor by sex, in particular, made it difficult to maintain a marriage. Whereas men undertook a wide variety of tasks away from the households, women were almost exclusively domestic servants. Men worked in turpentine factories, shops, distilleries, lumber mills, and artisan's shops and on ships; they even took up skilled jobs as blacksmiths, coopers, and carpenters, among others. Even if a married man worked within a master's household as a house servant, contact with his wife was severely limited. Female slaves, as household servants, worked all hours and slept in the master's house.[22] Because New England masters usually owned only one or two slaves, enslaved women or men frequently had to marry a partner outside of their homes. As a result, maintaining a marriage for most enslaved men and women meant sustaining a relationship across town or with a partner in a different town. In a sample of enslaved married men and women reported in records of vital statistics of Massachusetts towns, *one-quarter* of the couples had masters who lived in different towns.[23]

Having children was also difficult for enslaved women from New England. Not only did the restrictive nature of marriage under slavery reduce contact and hence opportunity for conception, but most masters did little to encourage reproduction. Masters found childbirth inconvenient and actively discouraged it, which contributed to the low birth rate among African Americans in Massachusetts. The vital records of Massachusetts towns reveal that during the years when slaveholding was legal, black families had an average of 2.0 children. After the courts abolished slavery in 1783, the average number of children per family shot up to 3.45.[24]

Despite the failure of most owners to remain faithful to the humanizing, if still abusive, tenets of family slavery, the law recognized many of slaves' rights as civil beings. After 1670, slaves were no longer strangers under Massachusetts law, which gave them a new status as subjects of the king. Their rank as subject was not equal to that of white, male property holders, but it was decreed that they deserved protection nonetheless. Around the same time, after King Philip's War, American Indians under English jurisdiction received status as subjects. Throughout the colonial era, white male subjects enjoyed expanding legal rights, and, in tandem, slaves earned a status as second-class subjects whose rights likewise expanded. By the time of the American Revolution, these legal rights provided slaves with unprecedented options in their society. Although no law specifically granted slaves these certain rights, no law restricted the rights of slaves. In practice, this meant that slaves in Massachusetts had the right to own property, write contracts, sue, petition, and witness. Only in some of the other New England colonies did black slaves gain these important rights of legal personhood. This acceptance of slave legal rights developed early in New England because religiously focused settlers had relatively little experience with slavery, little vision of its potential for profit, and an idealized vision of what slavery should be, based on the Bible. When human bondage expanded in the early eighteenth century, slavery in southern colonies evolved into a legal institution similar to that found in other North American slave societies, but the legal foundations of slavery in Massachusetts had already been set, and this foundation contained a tradition of basic legal rights for enslaved men and women.[25]

History of Slavery in South Carolina

The ideological bedrock of South Carolina's slave society came in part from the English philosopher John Locke. In 1669, Locke was the primary author of the Fundamental Constitutions of Carolina for South Carolina proprietor Anthony Ashley-Cooper. This framework for a government allowed men who owned only small tracts of property and asserted religious tolerance to vote, but it was also hierarchical and especially clear on the rights of masters and slaves, noting that every "freeman of Carolina shall have absolute power and authority over his negro slaves." Furthermore, this proposed constitution added that regardless of his or her religious beliefs or church membership, "no slave shall hereby be exempted from that civil dominion his master hath over him."[26] Although it was never adopted, the proposed constitution makes it clear that from a very early date southerners were attempting to balance both representative government and human bondage. The ideological difficulties that came with this balancing act increased when the South committed to an independence movement based on a Revolutionary appeal to freedom and liberty, but southerners had been thinking about this challenge for a hundred years by that time.

The proprietors of South Carolina hailed from an established Anglo-slave society, Barbados. After 1660, Barbadian noblemen, led by John Colleton, began searching for profitable commodities in their large mainland claim. They gained the capital necessary to build a plantation society in South Carolina. They hacked down the plentiful pine forests and enslaved the Native populations. Soon, however, they began looking for a more stable (and less warlike) commodity, such as "wine, oyle, reasons, currents, rice, silke &c." With that in mind, the planters soon learned from their African slaves, who had cultivated rice in Africa, that the wetlands would provide a good environment for rice.[27]

The Indian slave trade continued, even after the discovery that rice could be grown on the coast, until the Yamassee War, but it rarely depended on wars between South Carolinians and Native groups. Wars between the various Indian nations, especially the Creek, Westo, and Chickasaw, supplied Native American traders with slave property to trade for valuable English goods. This trade provided important military protection for the young colony. Desire to trade kept warring between the Europeans and different Indian groups to a minimum, and desire to acquire more Indian slaves kept wars between the different Indian nations directed at each other. The proprietors tried to keep control over the slave trade because it served important diplomatic and economic purposes for them. They sold Indian slaves, especially the most threatening male slaves, throughout the Atlantic world, even in New England. Colonists, however, also sought to exert control over Indian slaves and secure them for their own use. Thus, whenever the proprietors deemed it diplomatically important to stop the Indian slave trade, settlers would conduct the trade independently, disregarding the law. Indian nations continued the trade until the years of warring and contact with Europeans began to decimate their societies. This decimation helped provoke the Yamassee War in 1715, which brought a virtual end to the trade. Indian captures began to seem too dangerous, and most of the white slave traders were killed in the war. By this time, however, the colony had established a strong rice plantation economy using African slaves.[28]

The proprietors worked hard to attract more islanders to the vanguard of Barbadian settlers in South Carolina. They offered incentives for Englishmen from the crowded Caribbean islands to move to the seemingly open lands of South Carolina, including a headright, or settler's land grant, of 150 acres for each servant, black or white, whose transportation costs they would pay for. The Barbadian plantation owners brought over a tradition of simpler labor relations than that in Massachusetts. Within a couple of decades of settlement, involuntary labor was almost always wholly enslaved and nonwhite. The proprietors hoped to find white men to settle, not to labor. In a 1712 pamphlet, John Norris encouraged new settlers to come and build a plantation with a combination of Indian and African slaves. By 1680, the colony had more than two hundred African slaves, which was less than a third of the total population. Rice production then led to a rapid escalation in the black slave population of South Carolina; by 1708, the slave population at 4,100 outnumbered the white population at 4,080. By 1720, the number had exploded: white South Carolinians owned almost 15,000 slaves by this time. In addition, about 2,000 Indian slaves labored on the rice plantations alongside the African slaves. The slave population multiplied throughout the eighteenth century, keeping it beyond the majority mark for most of the century.[29]

The swampy land, which appeared wholly unappealing to the British noblemen, became the foundation of the South Carolina gentry. At first, most planters grew rice to feed a plantation; the English far preferred bread made with rice to that made with maize. Slave owners recognized that slaves possessed the expertise to grow rice efficiently in the swamps, and the profitability of rice became clear by the turn of the century. Slave owners began to identify which slaves had the technical knowledge to engineer the complex needs of the rice plantations. For instance, female slaves of the Senegambian region were particularly skilled at growing rice. The owners pressed slaves to escalate production.[30]

Rice's success stemmed from slaves and slave owners developing a variety of innovations in production and labor organization. Slave owners had great expectations for their unimproved lands, and the satisfaction of those expectations depended greatly on their slaves. The early years of rice cultivation focused on the need to grow food and settle on the land effectively. The harsh demands of rice plantation cultivation led slaves to insist on a more productive and manageable labor system, the task system. This system, under which slaves remained responsible for most of their own food production, benefited slaves as well as masters. For most crops, like tobacco and, later, cotton, slave owners employed the gang labor system in which the slaves worked in large groups, doing moderately grueling labor such as picking and hoeing from dawn to dusk. But under the task system, slaves had to accomplish a list of tasks for the day, and if they completed the tasks, their work was complete, at which point they could attend to their own needs. Slaves used this time for various activities, such as leisure, food production, and household maintenance.[31]

Using the knowledge of their slaves, especially their female slaves, whites by the 1830s had begun to harness the power of tidal plantation techniques, which transformed rice production. Before 1730, rice crops had been at the mercy of weather and tides that could flood or dry out the swamps that they depended on. Perhaps drawing from Senegambian women's experiences, slave owners learned how to control the waters and tides. The tidal plantations on the rivers used complex canal systems to draw water in and out of the rice fields, protecting them from the whims of weather and controlling the cycle of the tide. Slaves and slave owners had to resculpt the landscape completely. This massive reengineering of the landscape led to large-scale agricultural production that made plantation owners very wealthy.[32]

Rice encouraged South Carolina slave owners to distance themselves emotionally and physically from their slaves, just as they had in Barbados. Months of odiferous standing water and malarial mosquitoes chased away most slave owners, who spent a large part of the year enjoying the urban comforts of Charleston while their slaves toiled with minimal supervision.

This combination of distance, fear, great wealth, and power led to the creation of a restrictive slave code. Slave laws reflected the practical protections that plantation owners needed. The first slave code, issued in 1690, drew primarily from the Barbadian code. Plantation life was a regime that expected the law to coerce through control and severe punishment. The code restricted slave movement, denied due process, allowed all citizens the right to punish slaves, harshly punished any disruptive behavior by slaves, and provided only a minimal amount of legal protection for the enslaved. The code was adjusted nine more times before 1740.[33]

South Carolina in 1740 clearly directed all elements of its twenty-page slave code toward one purpose: avoiding insurrection. In 1739, a literate slave born in the Congo led some eighty other slaves to rebel. During their march, beginning at the Stono River, they killed more than twenty whites and forty slaves. This terrifying revolt, known as the Stono Rebellion, propelled into law a slave code that had been lingering as a bill in the assembly for years. The code's tone was even harsher toward blacks than earlier laws. This code, for example, stipulated death not only for slaves participating in rebellions or homicide but for "any slave, free Negro, mulattoe, Indian or mustizoe" that was found to have "willfully and maliciously set fire to, burn[ed] or destroy[ed] any sack of rice, corn or other grain."[34] The primary goal of the new code was to force slaves into "due subjection and obedience" to save the "public peace and order of this Province."[35]

The code added legal protections for the enslaved and justified itself, not only in an effort to preserve slavery but to create legitimate rule. It guaranteed slaves basic protections from their owners and strangers. Owners could not cruelly punish their slaves, had to provide basic needs, and could not overwork them.[36]

Enacted by white fear and in an effort to appear more legally sensitive to the needs of a plantation society, law in this evolving slave society now differentiated the crimes of slaves from the crimes of other colonists. The law justified this distinct treatment by claiming that it was beneficial for the slaves, since "natural justice forbids that any person, of what condition soever, should be condemned unheard." Magistrate courts made up of local slave owners tried slaves accused of a crime. Slaves could not testify against any white citizen. This version of the code endured throughout the colonial and into the early republic period.[37]

After acknowledging the importance of "the labor and service of negroes and other slaves," lawmakers described slaves as enemies with "barbarous, wild, savage natures" that could not be governed by the general laws of the colony. Legislators explained further that special laws were necessary to control their "disorders, rapines and inhumanity." This vision of blacks underpinned the legislators' decisions to exclude slaves from their legal society.[38]

The law explained why people of color needed special treatment. The

Stono Rebellion inspired lawmakers to pass laws grounded in clear racial terms that would solidify and increase their control over a slave population that was now deemed hostile and dangerous. "The people commonly called negroes, Indians, mulattoes and mustizoes, have been deemed absolute slaves," the law read, "and the subjects of property in the hands of particular persons." The law enslaved them based on two basic principles: skin color and ethnicity. Tethered to blacks, Indians were tarred by a particular physiognomy that includes darker skin, which became by 1740 an indicator of slave status.[39]

South Carolina's legal structure differed greatly from that in Massachusetts. For most of the history of England's colonies in North America, these differences mattered little. However, as tensions with Britain spurred more intercolonial travel, these differences became more apparent. Josiah Quincy, a Massachusetts lawyer, traveled to South Carolina in 1773, and as he dined in the finest Charleston homes, he learned how different the systems were. In a discussion about a recent slave-stealing case, he learned that South Carolinians were more worried about the theft of their human property than the killing of their slaves. In his journal, he recorded that in South Carolina to steal a slave was punishable by death but "to *kill him* only finable." He was surprised that blacks and mulattoes did not receive a jury trial. He saw the root of this law in the planter dominance of the colony. Coming from New England, where the democratic town hall meetings were such a critical part of political life, he felt that there was no true representative body in the colony: "It is true they have a house of Assembly, but whom do they represent? The labourer, the mechanic, the tradesman, the farmer, or yeoman? No,—the representatives are almost wholly rich planters." Conflicting bodies of law were merely a curiosity before the Revolution, but once Massachusetts and South Carolina sought to join as one nation, these ill-aligned laws fomented interstate conflict.[40]

After handling the challenges of the 1739 slave rebellion, slave owners faced another problem, the plummeting price of rice. The solution, indigo, proved to be advantageous on several levels. The famously industrious and scientifically minded Eliza Pinckney, with help from a West Indian dye maker of African descent, had begun experimenting with the indigo plant in 1739 and soon discovered that indigo grew well on the uplands of the Carolina coastal regions. This added to the productivity of the land and provided planters with more stability during market dips in rice. The production of indigo skyrocketed. Indigo was nonexistent in 1740 in the colony, but by 1747, South Carolinians were exporting 138,000 pounds a year. In 1757, slaves loaded 800,000 pounds of indigo cakes onto ships leaving the colony.[41]

Just as white slave owners adapted to the changing economic situation, slaves worked to create full lives for themselves under oppressive circumstances. African inhabitants designed and constructed their own spaces and leisure lives. With very little spare time, they built homes out of the local materials. These dwellings, which were semi-temporary huts, merged English and African styles. Observers commented that the housing for the slaves had an open structure and palmetto roofs rather than the traditional wooden and shingled roofs.[42]

Similarly, along with this physical space, South Carolina slaves created a cultural space separate from the white world. One distinctive aspect of this autonomous slave lifestyle was a flourishing slave economy. Slaves bought and sold goods that they had grown themselves and owned, sold, bought, lent, and even inherited property, which could include substantial assets such as livestock. They would frequently sell their goods to urban slaves, who would take the goods to the streets. Grand juries complained in 1772 about "the great number of NEGROES who are continually passing and re-passing, selling vegetables, etc. without tickets" or permits to sell. Black female vendors dominated the city markets. An account of a Charleston market recorded as many as sixty-four women out on one day. In the imagination of whites, many of whom saw the presence of these vendors as economically threatening, their numbers were even larger.

Not only were women selling goods, but they were also buying them. Urban mistresses relied on their female slaves to do the everyday household purchasing. Their trust in their servants was limited, however. Store records reveal that although slaves made daily purchases, mistresses made special purchases, especially for expensive goods, on their own.[43] A newspaper report complained of the "disorderly negro women" who spent their entire day, "morn 'til night," swindling their customers by buying goods from "country negroes" at low prices and reselling them throughout the day for "100 or 150 per cent" profit. What particularly vexed the author of this report was that these women seemed to have exclusive access to plantation goods. Whites had no wholesale access; these black women monopolized the goods until the retail stage. This report not only shows the strength of the trade by these women but also demonstrates the strong ties that existed between urban and plantation slaves. The role of women in marketing goods in the colony was probably connected to a tradition in many African societies that assigned the task of trading goods for the household to women.[44]

In addition to economic freedom, African slaves in South Carolina often had power over their cultural lives. Ironically, Native American slaves, residing closer to their ancestral lands than any of the other populations, had little cultural power on the plantation. Within one or two generations, American Indian slaves lost many of the outward signs of their culture and began adopting African and European cultural mores. Religion proved to be an important part of slave life. Although slaves were exposed to Christianity, slave owners were still unsure about its effect, so slave quarters maintained traditions of African religious practices. Most slaves lived in communities of Africans with differing traditions, but they found ways to bring their cosmologies together to express their spirituality. Their beliefs regarding connections between the dead and the living and believed religion pervaded all aspects of life translated into practices that divined or conjured spirits, and they used artifacts, known as minkisi, to express these beliefs. One archaeologist found a cache of these minkisi in bowl form in riverbeds. These objects of material culture tied African religious beliefs to the practices of South Carolina low-country slaves.[45]

Another factor that would improve the lot of slaves in the colony was South Carolinians' engagement with the Atlantic world discourse extolling human rights, encouraging them to improve the treatment of their slaves.[46] Much of this emerging concern focused on maintaining family ties. Henry Laurens, an elite South Carolina planter who was intimately aware of international happenings, was one of the first South Carolinians to express a serious desire to maintain the family ties of his slaves. He wrote to Elias Ball in 1765 about the "inhumanity of seperating & tareing asunder my Negroe's several families." He regarded the slaves in these families as among his "best Negroes." Laurens claimed that effort to keep families together was purely an ethical decision, one that he would "pay well for." Two years later, however, he acknowledged the financial advantages of the natural reproduction of slaves. He valued one of his enslaved women above others, because she was "a breeding Woman & in ten Years time may have double her worth in her own Children."[47] Over time, more South Carolinians would follow and then surpass Laurens in their advocacy of a paternalistic system that produced more slave children for their plantations.

Despite the emergence of varying ownership styles, involuntary labor in South Carolina was fairly monolithic compared to that in Massachusetts.

Native American slavery provides an enlightening example in this case. Both colonial powers saw their Native American slaves differently from their African slaves because of the threat that relationships among tribes posed to the colonists. In Massachusetts, this threat led the colonists to increasingly use Indians not as slaves but as indentured servants. South Carolina Native American war captives, in contrast, became slaves. There were no indentures. However, diplomatic necessity could trump ownership of these slaves. South Carolina, for example, freed dozens of Tuscarora slaves working on plantations as part of a peace treaty. Nonetheless, the condition of involuntary labor—slavery—whether in Massachusetts or South Carolina was a wholly degraded and separate status from the status of the free English colonists.

Slavery on the Waccamaw

Although the thirty-four captive slaves on the *Tyrannicide* all came from the Waccamaw neck in the Georgetown district of South Carolina, they had varied lives. These slaves were owned by five individuals, Thomas Todd, William Vereen, William Henry Lewis, and Anthony and Percival Pawley, each of whom owned plantations that varied in size, status, and use.

Seventy miles north of Charleston, the Waccamaw Peninsula stretches for about seventy miles and has a few subregions. It is formed where the Winyah Bay opens its mouth to the ocean's tides that push and pull the water up the Waccamaw, Peedee, and Black rivers. Farthest east, the Waccamaw River has the widest opening into the bay, creating a neck of land that points southward, called Waccamaw Peninsula or Waccamaw Neck. At the head of Winyah Bay and the beginning of the river sits Georgetown. The river flows southward to Georgetown from the southernmost regions of North Carolina. The river splits after about twenty miles around Sandy Island. After Sandy Island, the river becomes less navigable by larger vessels. Along the seacoast of Waccamaw Neck, barrier islands protect the land and plantations from the harsh waves. This open area was used for roads and fishing. In the interior, Waccamaw Neck is sprinkled with forests and swamps. The Socestee swamp was so large that planters could not settle it; however, they were able to grow rice at its edges.[48]

The Waccamaw was at the frontier of colonial South Carolina settlement. William Vereen, Henry Lewis, and Thomas Todd had smaller plantations on the upper Waccamaw River. Because the tides could not assist in

Map of Coastal South Carolina, Thomas Jeffreys, 1776. Courtesy of the David Rumsey Map Collection.

expanding their rice production, they grew rice only in the swampy areas of their plantations. Each man owned about five hundred acres that included some swampland, but they did not have enough swampland to grow rice for a profit. Most of their slaves labored, instead, at growing indigo. The sandy, "moderately fertile" uplands grew a variety of indigo known at the time as "false Guatemala."[49]

They did grow rice to feed the members of the plantation. A visitor to William Vereen's plantation, Johann Schoepf, recorded eating a South Carolina staple, rice bread. Vereen served rice compacted to make a loaf as a replacement for bread. Schoepf described the rice loaf as the only bread available in South Carolina and as the primary form of food for the slaves. In the unusual landscape of coastal South Carolina, wheat was not readily available, and rice was preferable to corn.[50]

Although we do not have many details about upper Waccamaw plantations, we do know that they were isolated in many ways. Since the closest city, Georgetown, was at least a twenty-mile trek, slaves rarely visited it. Given that Charleston was even farther away, it too was not a destination for slaves. The slave quarters of these plantations were small, making it harder to have the same familial and cultural lives found on the large plantations. Nevertheless, there may have been interplantation connections to add richness to the slaves' lives. For example, Lewis and Vereen lived near each other and were brothers-in-law.

The Pawley family had a much larger operation on Waccamaw Neck. George Pawley Sr., among the first settlers of South Carolina, had settled in Charleston in 1694, and his son, Percival Pawley, pioneered in the Waccamaw region. Grandfather to Percival Pawley Jr. of the *Tyrannicide* affair, he acquired hundreds of acres by grant and purchase beginning in 1711. The son of Percival the elder and father to Percival Jr., Colonel George Pawley expanded the Pawley family lands. By 1730, Pawley lands included thirty-five hundred acres on Waccamaw Neck and additional acreage along the Peedee River. The Pawley plantations grew a combination of rice and indigo. When he died, Colonel George Pawley willed six thousand acres to his children. When rice fell on hard times in the 1740s owing to global conflicts that disrupted shipping, they were among the early adopters of indigo.[51]

Their large and sprawling plantations meant that life was more complex for their slaves than for the slaves belonging to Vereen, Todd, and Lewis. The slave quarters were larger and closer to Georgetown. The Pawley slaves were consequently less isolated, had more complete family structures, and perhaps led a stronger independent economic life. However, the size of the Pawley empire meant that as slaves were transferred between family-owned plantations throughout the Waccamaw and Peedee River basins, families suffered.[52]

Although the Waccamaw was on the margins of colonial South Carolinian society, the Pawley family, being one of the most prominent in the region, maintained ties to the center, Charleston, and therefore had more power than other families on the peninsula. Members of the family owned houses on Broad Street in Charleston that permitted them to remain connected to the markets where they sold their goods and purchased their slaves.[53] The closest port to the Pawleys, Georgetown, transported crops to Charlestown before they traveled across the Atlantic.

Planters controlled Charleston's rice markets. Charleston's plantation owners could sell their rice in Charleston and receive immediate payment rather than have to wait for the shipment to reach England. This allowed them to haggle directly for the highest price, using the knowledge they had of the many shifting factors that shaped the price of rice. During the agricultural season, merchants would visit rice fields, learn about the season's crops, and oversee growing techniques. In the storehouses along the Cooper River, the planters collectively hired and observed a few dozen agents sell their products to 230 mercantile firms.[54]

Likewise, these slave owners purchased their slaves in Charleston. Merchants such as Henry Laurens brought their captives to the large market complex between Chambers and Queen Streets. When a planter such as Percival Pawley needed to expand his labor force with a strong and skilled slave, he would inspect the captured men and women and purchase those who looked capable. Laurens reported, unsurprisingly, that harvest conditions and the prices of indigo and rice determined whether slave owners purchased new slaves. When economic times were flush and labor demands increased, Laurens had a hard time keeping slaves. In depressed periods, he had to transport his leftover slaves northward to find owners.[55]

The Pawley homes in Charleston asserted the family's status to those who mattered the most. South Carolina's elite gathered in Charleston for most of the summer. This was their primary community. For example, John LaBruce, whose family lived on Waccamaw Neck, probably courted Martha Pawley in Charleston before the two married and merged their fortunes back on the Waccamaw. Families usually married into other local families, even though there was opportunity in Charleston to meet members of families from other areas. This maximized the value of the marriage, making it easier to concentrate their plantation holdings.[56]

Back at the plantation, the rice culture created a dangerous and laborious environment for slaves; slave owners, inclined to protect their property above all and yearning to continue their ascent from frontier farmers to landed gentry, sought to exploit their slaves without limits. But slaves found ways to make life bearable. Family ties made escape and revolt less attractive and life more tolerable. The task system allowed the slaves some control over the pace of their labor. Distant slave owners and leisure time provided cultural space in which slaves could express their separate identities.

Metaphor of Slavery

The ideas that whites in Massachusetts and South Carolina had regarding their own slave owning shaped metaphors of slavery they invoked during the Revolutionary era. White Patriots in Massachusetts would perceive slavery as a form of personal oppression by Britain in its trampling on the rights of individuals within society. Moreover, because whites in Massachusetts believed that they treated their slaves well, white writers could suggest that blacks' enslavement was due to deficiencies within the character of the slaves themselves. For many in Massachusetts, slavery was not a physical state but a mental one. A person was a slave because he or she did not fight for freedom but instead accepted submission to another. White South Carolinian Patriots, in contrast, had a visceral understanding of the oppression of slavery. When they used the term "slavery," it evoked a very guttural response to a sense of political and economic oppression. When South Carolinians began to see themselves as being enslaved, they imagined themselves being whipped, forced to labor, and separated from their families. South Carolinians feared not only the degradation of slavery but also the potential disorder a fight against slavery might bring forth. These fears radicalized their rhetoric, but their responses would work conservatively toward maintaining order in their society.[57]

The colonists' metaphorical understanding of slavery was not just influenced by the nature of literal enslavement in each region but also by the very nature of a metaphor such as slavery. Metaphors are inherently relational. They describe the relationship of one state to another. The concept of slavery is also relational. It describes the relationship between a master and one or more slaves. Further, because power also informs the concept of slavery, it implicitly suggests positive and negative states. The slave owner has power, and the slave does not. Slavery as a concept of white disenfranchisement gains ascendancy because the concept of freedom becomes an essential quality of Anglo-American identity. It becomes powerful because these Americans, who began to cherish freedom as a core value in the mid-eighteenth century, owned slaves who, by definition, lacked freedom. These two realities made the metaphor of slavery very potent in the 1760s and 1770s.

Black and White Enslavement in Massachusetts

In Massachusetts, much of the anger against Britain was initially directed against Britain's local political officers whose families were from Massachusetts. Many felt betrayed as their neighbors and respected leaders enforced unpopular British policies. Governor Thomas Hutchinson, who was from an old family, became a particular target for this sense of betrayal. A moderate stuck with tough imperial policies, he worked not so much against the rebels as for good order. He insisted on a trial for the soldiers involved in the Boston Massacre and tried to move the governor's council out of Boston, across the river to Cambridge, so as to be able to conduct business with fewer rebellious disturbances. The sense that local leaders betrayed them provoked Massachusetts Patriots' feelings of personal oppression. The excitement over local politics was the first step in an emerging radicalism that would move beyond Massachusetts politics to challenge the British government. First, it was easier to conceive of toppling Governor Thomas Hutchinson, a man whose family was from Massachusetts, than Parliament or the king of England. Moreover, this perceived personal oppression reflected the rebels' ideas of slavery as being a relationship between two humans in close proximity. Slaves in Massachusetts were held in small aggregations and within colonists' households. This reality of slavery shaped the rebels' notions of personal slavery. Of course, their disruptive behavior resulted in the British government punishing Massachusetts in particular, further inciting feelings of personal enslavement. The wide spectrum of involuntary labor in Massachusetts also made devolving into enslavement a gradual slope of degradation. Any slipping, even in small events, could be the beginning of transforming white colonists from free to slave. The leading Patriot newspapers portrayed events such as the Boston Massacre not as a scuffle but as an unprovoked attack, which pressed the people of Massachusetts to feel particularly persecuted.[58]

This sense of enslavement provoked a rhetorical war against Britain, in which slavery was a central metaphor, one that emerged early. In 1765, Joseph Warren of Massachusetts called out, "Defeat the designs of those who would enslave us and our posterity."[59] Enslavement was a favorite trope of Samuel Adams. For example, he extolled the colonists' success against the Stamp Act as a blow "against that slavery with which they were threatened."[60]

This idea of slavery and their experiences with black slavery led some whites in Massachusetts to recognize their contradiction and to begin to question the institution of slavery and promote antislavery ideas. Individuals made the connection between black slavery and the metaphor illustrated by the British leadership. Despite the growth of antislavery sentiment among many in Massachusetts, outward antislavery thought was rare among the Patriot leadership. Only James Otis, who grew up in a household with slaves, pressed abolition in writing. As early as 1764, he asserted that the colonists, "black and white, born here are free born British subjects, and entitled to the essential civil rights of such." He went on in *The Rights of the British Colonies Asserted and Proved* to explain that slavery was "directly opposite to the temper and courage of our nation."[61]

Others in Massachusetts also saw the contradiction in Anglo-Americans' identities as free people who owned slaves. Although not all New England clergy during the Revolutionary era sermonized against slavery, those who did were the most outspoken leaders against the institution. Rooted often in New Light theology, antislavery ministers defended the humanity of the enslaved and condemned the institution's inhumanity. The Reverend Samuel Webster, for example, declared in 1769, "let these oppressed ones *go free without delay*." Benjamin Colman described the enslavement of blacks as "God-provoking and wrath-procuring sin."[62]

Secular writers mirrored these arguments. Nathaniel Appleton pressed to end slavery for political, economic, and social reasons. He believed that ending slavery would strengthen the Americans' case against the British. America would truly be a country of liberty if it would "show the same regard to all mankind." He also argued that slavery prevented white immigration, took jobs away from whites, and even promoted prostitution. In 1774, "A Watchman's Alarm" mirrored the clerical arguments. The author, John Allen, writing under the pen name of "a British Bostonian," criticized the Revolutionary movement for "trampling on the sacred natural rights and privileges of the Africans" at the same time that "you are fasting, praying, non-importing, non-exporting, remonstrating, resolving, and pleading for a restoration of your charter rights." This hypocrisy, Allen argued, undermined the Revolution.[63]

Most Patriots used the multiple meanings of "slavery," which reflected their experience of involuntary labor in their colony, for their own purposes. The metaphor justified the enslavement of blacks' and whites' right to fight their own oppression. Whites in Massachusetts frequently referred to slavery as a degraded mental state. Most American colonists agreed with the perception that the liberties of Englishmen surpassed those of all other peoples. These liberties, they believed, rested on the vigilant protection of and constant struggle to maintain virtue.[64] Sam Adams expressed this concern in a letter to James Warren. "It is the Disgrace of human Nature that in most Countries the People are so debauched, as to be utterly unable to defend or enjoy their Liberty."[65] He related this to the problem for the black slaves: "I Believe that no people ever yet groaned under the heavy yoke of slavery, but when they deserv'd it."[66] For some in Massachusetts, nonetheless, the rhetoric of slavery as white oppression continued to strike a tone of contradiction, and antislavery thought grew.

The Patriot newspapers of Boston, however, continued to depict blacks in ways that served this idea of black degradation. These derogatory depictions of black slavery gave the colony's leadership cultural justification to exclude blacks from the republic. They could not be respectable citizens if they were only criminals, runaways, and objects for sale, which was how blacks were primarily depicted in the press. For instance, Patriot newspapers covered carefully the story of Mark, Phyllis, and Phoebe, slaves from Charleston, who murdered their owner. For the crime, Phyllis was burned at the stake and Mark was executed. These depictions gained further support as the papers offered detailed accounts of slave rebellions and riots in other colonies. The paper ran a constant stream of ads that reported runaways or slaves for sale. These two consistent features reminded readers that the slaves were, above all, property. At the same time, these kinds of ads testified to qualities of slaves that belied their status as desirable property. The runaway ads emphasized the slave as disobedient and lazy, whereas the sale ads focused on the obedience of the slave. Both, however, were informed by the same ideal: that black slaves ought to be obedient servants.[67]

The events not covered in the newspapers also remind us of this bias. Blacks in Massachusetts had accomplished plenty that deserved column space. The annual election of their own governors in the center of the city was never covered. Whites did watch the event. Many town histories and personal diaries document the rituals and celebrations. The newspapers ignored the free and enslaved blacks who wrote legislative petitions to demand slavery's end, and the role of black soldiers did not receive print space.

Even the *Somersett* decision, which ruled that slavery was not legally supported in England, was inaccurately and anemically covered.[68] Although the Loyalist papers, the *Massachusetts Gazette* and *Boston News-Letter*, gave a lot of factual and editorial coverage of the case, the Patriot newspaper, the *Boston Gazette*, gave the shortest coverage of all the newspapers in Boston and misrepresented the case as wholly emancipating slaves in England. The *Massachusetts Gazette* and *Boston News-Letter*, in contrast, supplied specific accounts of the case, recording the nuanced and relatively conservative decision of magistrate Lord Mansfield as a London reporter recorded it. In many ways, the freedom-seeking activities of slaves and free blacks became invisible.[69]

Public discussion of slavery—of both the reality and the metaphor—mobilized the black population in Massachusetts. Although some blacks worked toward individual freedom by suing their owners for freedom in cases called "freedom suits," others worked collectively through petitions to demand an end to slavery. They made some of their demands in self-published pamphlets. The responses of whites to these public actions reflect their evolving attitudes toward slavery.

Between 1764 and 1774, seventeen slaves appeared in Massachusetts courts to sue their owners for freedom. These freedom suits drove a wedge into the wall of slavery, creating an opening for slaves to escape from their bondage. Although there were a few freedom suits in the first part of the eighteenth century, the vast majority were brought during the 1764–1774 period.[70] This escalation was especially dramatic considering the interruptions that the Intolerable Acts and the war itself brought to the orderly administration of justice. In addition, although most slaves lost those early cases, the cases that date from the pre-Revolutionary era were decided in favor of the slaves except when the lawsuit hinged on ideological claims such as that slavery was immoral rather than wrongful enslavement. That would change in 1780 when lawyers would argue that slavery was unconstitutional based on human rights ideology.[71]

Only eleven cases in the Revolutionary era offer enough documentation to divulge the basis of the slave's claim that he or she was illegally enslaved. Of those, six claimed to have made contracts of emancipation with dishonest owners, two claimed free parentage, and three argued that slavery was illegal in Massachusetts. Massachusetts was one of the few colonies that supported a slave's right to enter into a contract, which explains why more freedom suits were brought on the grounds of alleged breach of contract. In contrast, in Virginia, which had a flurry of freedom suits after the war, almost all the suits were brought on the grounds that the plaintiff's parents had been free.[72] Virginia's law clearly stated that a mother bestowed her status on her child. Massachusetts had accepted this idea in custom but not in law, which was probably the reason fewer slaves argued free descent as grounds for emancipation.

The juries in freedom suits demonstrated how deeply antislavery sentiments pervaded the white population. The environment of the pre-Revolutionary era made it easier for the general white population to free individual blacks. These cases are interesting because juries usually determined their outcome. When asked in 1795 about the demise of slavery in Massachusetts, John Adams, a frequent lawyer and note taker of these cases, explained, "I never knew a Jury by a Verdict, to determine a Negro to be a Slave. They always found them free."[73] The jury proved especially important in *James v. Lechmere*, in which a weak legal argument blended with growing popular sentiment against slavery, compelling the jury rule in favor of freedom.

Nevertheless, with the exception of *James* and *Newport v. Billing*, these litigants did not fight to end slavery for all, just for themselves. In the earliest Revolutionary-era cases, slaves sued because of personal illegal enslavement. In 1766, Benjamin Kent, the lawyer who took on most of these cases, began his argument on behalf of Jenny Slew's illegal enslavement by stating explicitly that he would not "enter into the Right of some Men to enslave others."[74] By avoiding questioning the validity of slavery and by suing based on an *illegal* enslavement, cases in the 1760s and 1770s bolstered the *legality* of enslavement. Declaring the existence of an *illegal* form of slavery implies an understanding that there is a *legal* form of slavery.

During this period, Sewall and Bliss represented the leading edge of antislavery activism among whites. Pre–Revolutionary War freedom suits reflect a shift in thought among Massachusetts' population. Although, presumably, many enslaved blacks supported abolition, the slaves in these cases generally sought a less radical goal: emancipation from illicit enslavement. Nonetheless, in the history of slave societies, very few slaves outside of New

England felt empowered even to challenge their own enslavement, but the Revolutionary era heightened slave confidence. Likewise, except for a brief moment at the beginning of the eighteenth century, whites in Massachusetts rarely questioned slavery. The dissemination of Enlightenment thought in the Anglo-American world encouraged more white men to embrace anti-slavery ideas. Of course, these men had the luxury to consider ending slavery because whites in Massachusetts did not rely too deeply on slaves' labor. In this milieu, men such as Bliss, Oliver, and Sewall could assert radical ends for their community: the end of slavery.

Another form of formal black protest, petitions, explicitly contested slavery. In January 1773, claiming to speak on behalf of the "many slaves living in Boston," black Bostonian Felix Holbrook sent the first petition to the governor, the colony council, and the legislature. This petition and the six that would follow tested the rhetorical boundaries of antislavery in Massachusetts. Holbrook tried many approaches in an effort to convince white officials that Massachusetts had to free its slaves. The text overflowed with Christian language that highlighted the commonality of slaves' humanity before God. "Bless God," Holbrook wrote, "who loves Mankind, who sent his Son to die for their Salvation, and who is no respecter of persons." The petition attempted to raise the character of African Americans; Holbrook observed that "some of the Negroes are vicious" but also noted that many were also "discreet, sober, honest, and industrious . . . virtuous and religious." Living life like "Beasts" had pressed their patience, he warned. He followed by adding that slaves were denied basic human needs: "We have no Property! We have no Wives! No Children!"[75]

Holbrook's petition, however, illuminated how other states, especially South Carolina, served to circumscribe antislavery thought in Massachusetts. The petition was read and advanced to a committee, where it stalled. John Hancock, a slave owner, and John Adams, a man who had misgivings about slavery, quashed the discussion. But, as leaders on the national Revolutionary scene, they had nationalistic concerns that ending slavery in Massachusetts would create division between the colonies.[76]

Holbrook was not to be deterred; he sought to expand the ideas of "True Liberty" in Massachusetts. He followed the petition with another petition, signed by Peter Bestes, Sambo Freeman, and Chester Joie. This petition had a more international focus and attempted to shame the legislature into emancipating the slaves by noting that "the Spaniards" offered their slaves the right to hire themselves out, "to purchase the residue of their time." Holbrook stated that they would save "from our joynt labours . . . to transport ourselves to some part of the Coast of *Africa.*" Again, the petition did not go far in the Massachusetts General Court. This petition, however, would be printed and distributed as a pamphlet written by "a Lover of True Liberty."[77]

White interest in antislavery ideas came to a halt with the beginning of the war, but blacks would continue to press the issue with petitions. They kept up the broad rhetorical assault on slavery, infusing their language with even more Revolutionary-era republican rhetoric. Various groups of Boston slaves and free blacks came together to petition the legislature five more times. The petitioners included future leaders of the free black population such as Prince Hall. After 1774, these petitioners invoked concepts such as "natural rights," "justice," and "liberty" to support their arguments. They became more demanding by pointing out the inconsistency between slavery and the Revolutionary cause.[78]

African Americans began to publish other kinds of antislavery writings. Caesar Sarter, a free black from Newburyport, wrote a piece entitled "Essay on Slavery" that appeared in the *Essex Journal and Merrimack Packet* in 1774. His column urged proslavery advocates to live up to their own rhetoric. He reminded them of the "absurdity of your exertions for liberty, while you have slaves in your houses." Like Holbrook, he reminded readers that slaves were denied basic family lives and could be bought and sold. He also challenged the prevailing white idea that Africans were happier enslaved in Massachusetts than free in Africa, reminding them that they could not know another person's happiness.[79]

Blacks' use of petitions, freedom suits, and published tracts to contest freedom in Massachusetts brought radical changes in the whole community. Pamphlet writers in Massachusetts such as Sam Adams had claimed that one must fight to be worthy of freedom. Slaves and free blacks in Massachusetts had begun to assert that they sought the freedom that whites in Massachusetts were crying for. This change compelled whites to begin ending slavery. However, as the people of Massachusetts veered toward abolition, the significance of slavery one thousand miles away in the southern colonies prevented any legal change. The rhetoric and slaves' responses to the rhetoric would not have the same effect in South Carolina as in Massachusetts. More than in any other state, whites in South Carolina refused to give in to ideological pressure to extend the slavery metaphor to their black slaves.

Black and White Enslavement in South Carolina

Whites in South Carolina certainly vigorously employed the metaphor of slavery in reference to themselves, but their use of the metaphor was almost always enhanced and narrowed by their sense of ownership. White South Carolinians defined freedom as the "undoubted right to think and act for" oneself and believed that they possessed a particularly strong sense of freedom.[80] Their sense of freedom developed out of their relationship with England, the freest country in the world, the independence and great economic success of the South Carolinian settlers, and their own remoteness from the British government. South Carolinians such as David Ramsay believed that this love of freedom existed well before the Revolution. The Revolution, in fact, stoked South Carolinians' ardor to a dangerous degree. Ramsay pointed out that the youth of South Carolina had developed a "repugnance to subjection" that threatened the social order in the colony. Relics of black slavery were apparent in the rhetorical enslavement of white colonists. Unlike in Massachusetts, where slavery was a gradual slope to oppression, slavery in South Carolina was an unfathomably terrible fall from whites' free status to the dark abyss of slavery. Despite the tone of this antislavery rhetoric, it was virtually impossible for a white person to speak publically against black slavery. The black community, free and enslaved, also found it difficult to challenge slavery but would take advantage of every opportunity it was presented with.[81]

South Carolinian leaders, like their Massachusetts counterparts, frequently used the word "slavery" to describe Britain's oppressive policies. In 1769, a writer to the *South Carolina Gazette* argued that England sought to "keep Us in abject Slavery."[82] Rusticus, an anonymous poet, expressed his unhappiness over the colonists' position in his poem *Liberty*. The poem, dedicated to South Carolina's Sons of Liberty, complained that they were "the Sons, not Slaves of Briton."[83] William Henry Drayton explained to a 1776 grand jury that the colony had to choose between "Slavery or Independence."[84]

When South Carolina leaders invoked slavery, they referred to more than the mere political oppression about which the British Whigs wrote. Their vision of slavery was rooted deeply in their experience with black slaves. Hints of physical torture, unequal labor relationships, total subjugation to another, and blackness defined their fears in the face of British oppression. The denial of rights by Britain, in the minds of the South

Carolinians, degraded them to the level of "galley slaves"; they were being "insulted—bullied—treated like emasculated eunuchs."[85] The physical castration of dangerous male slaves found its rhetorical counterpart in white South Carolinians' fear that political oppression would symbolically castrate them. Their rhetoric made connections between political enslavement and blackness. Hugh Alison feared the "native horror and deformity, black with ignorance, wickedness, and misery" that would ensue. His intimate knowledge of slavery also allowed him to recognize the "apprehension of violence" and the "lingering dread of a premature death" with which slaves lived.[86]

Whites primarily perceived their enslavement in economic terms, echoing their perception of slaves as property. British oppression took the form of their mother country controlling their purse strings. South Carolina's engagement with the Wilkes affair reflects the colonists' economic interpretation of their persecution. John Wilkes published attacks on King George III and was exiled to France. He was popular with American revolutionaries as a champion of expanding civil rights, supporter of the American cause, and critic (and target) of the king. As a response, the legislature passed a bill to grant money to help with John Wilkes's debt after the Townsend Acts, a move no other colony had yet made. When Parliament prohibited the colony from giving Wilkes the money, South Carolina's leaders immediately proclaimed that England was unjustly interfering with their colony's finances and suddenly counted themselves direct victims of British tyranny.[87]

They felt enslaved by Britain's tax policies, and their complaints resonated with their own slaves' lives. Henry Laurens complained in a letter to Jonathan Bryan that he feared being "doom'd to Labour in the Planting & Watering without hopes of reaping the Harvest."[88] His property was jeopardized, and he worried that his labor and the wealth that it created would not remain his. Some thought this enslavement so unbearable that an "autonomous freeman would not prefer [slavery] to death"; he would rather die than become a slave and be "sold like a stock of sheep."[89] To the Revolutionary South Carolinian slave owners, the metaphor of slavery had a practical meaning that they fully understood and lived with daily; it gave voice to a reality that they all sought to avoid.

Because of the danger of this metaphor in South Carolina, few men followed Henry Laurens's path toward antislavery. Henry Laurens built his wealth not only on slavery but also on the slave trade. He was one of the leading South Carolina slave traders, bringing more than five thousand souls to South Carolina's shores. In the 1760s, when Enlightenment consciousness spread throughout Anglo-American culture, he gave up the slave trade. He quit largely for business reasons but later stated that he had done so because he had developed a moral dislike for the trade. By 1769, the vociferousness of his misgivings about the slave trade led a British official, Egerton Leigh, to attack him in public. Leigh's pamphlet "unmasked" Laurens as an opponent of slavery and implied that his ideas posed a danger to South Carolina. Laurens immediately understood the financial repercussions of alienating his peers and backpedaled publicly. He denied any moral repugnance against the trade or the plantation economy.[90]

Henry Laurens's doubts grew as his freedom-minded son, John, pressed him to explore his conscience further. Henry first criticized slavery in a 1776 letter to a Moravian missionary; his criticism mirrored language heard farther north. Like Jefferson and Adams, he worried about the damage that slave ownership inflicted on the owner, not the slave. It made masters lazy and dependent. In a well-known letter to his son in 1776, Laurens expressed his personal feelings about slavery more explicitly: "I abhor Slavery."[91] He repeatedly told his son about his hopes to manumit their slaves gradually. Certainly, his ideas were not extreme; he had not even suggested that others free their slaves. As in his relinquishment of the slave trade, he only questioned mastery for himself, not for others. However, in South Carolina, even such modest proposals passed for radicalism.

Although few South Carolinian slaveholders shared Laurens's views, they did worry about the disorder that revolution might bring. They had nightmares about insurrections. In 1775, Lord Dunmore issued a proclamation in Virginia that declared martial law and invited slaves "that are willing and able to bear Arms" to join the king's army. Lord Dunmore's proclamation, although applicable only in Virginia, convinced the South Carolinian planters that the British sought to instigate rebellion. In addition, the idea of separation from England did not sit easy with South Carolinians. They had tight cultural relationships with the mother country. Most young wealthy men from the South attended school in England, and throughout their adult careers, they fostered the strong networks they had established as schoolboys. Merchants frequently visited England and relied on strong personal ties with the English to preserve their credit. Likewise, colonial political leaders had to maintain a strong relationship with England to lead the colony. Not surprisingly, Charleston's large merchant class cultivated business and personal connections with their mother country. Therefore, when rebellion seemed imminent, independence was a difficult decision for South Carolina's citizens. It was not surprising, therefore, that when a relatively small British contingent demanded the surrender of Charleston in 1779, more than half of the Charleston elites pledged neutrality in order to prevent a destructive invasion.[92]

Personal relations with the British did not inspire rebellion in the colonists of South Carolina as it did in those of Massachusetts. Rather, their intimate relationship with abject slavery did. They felt they were being threatened with the loss of their wealth. When they perceived that Britain was trying to control their property, they quickly adopted the metaphor of slavery. The enslavement they described was not like Massachusetts' mental or spiritual enslavement; rather, it was a slavery of the body, the inability to reap what one sows. They began to envision themselves as slaves, whipped bloody, gaining nothing for their backbreaking labor. South Carolina whites, therefore, sought to keep a tight hold over their property.

The oppressive environment of South Carolina slavery limited the colony's black population from responding to the Revolutionary situation with anything like a petition. Slaves in South Carolina had no right to petition and, indeed, very limited rights of any kind in the colony's courts. Nonetheless, they used the resources they did have to disengage from their bondage. Beginning in 1766, they would take part in increasingly rebellious activity. Without legal means to express their ideas, they had to use illegal means such as running away and revolt. White elites in South Carolina would not accept any open expression of those ideas they themselves were voicing with respect to their rhetorical enslavement.

Slaves in South Carolina tested the boundaries of public protest early in the era of Anglo-American tensions. Enslaved men and women in South Carolina made their desires clear on a New Year's morning in 1766. Most owners and employers gave free blacks and slaves in Charleston New Year's Day off. On that cold morning, black men and women gathered in the streets that they normally dominated on business days as sellers of goods. Even without their goods, this gathering of blacks, who were perhaps dressed in slightly finer clothes than normal, probably did not alarm many white Charlestonians. Almost spontaneously, however, the black crowd, mirroring the recent Stamp Act demonstrations by whites, began marching through the streets crying, as their white counterparts had, "Liberty!" This action demonstrated that they understood the rhetoric of liberty emanating from their owners' pens and speech and that they were demanding it for themselves. Although the demonstration included no violent behavior, white Charlestonians feared rebellion, and so they cracked down. The colony eventually banished one black because of the incident. This response seemed to work. In the ensuing years, most enslaved and free black South Carolinians refrained from demonstrations or even rhetorical expressions of their desire for freedom, relying instead on alternative, subtler methods such as insubordination, negotiation, and work slowdowns.[93]

Although we do not have many examples of slaves speaking publicly against slavery, slaves did speak out, and South Carolina experienced a rise in emancipation that reflects an equivalent rise in the number of freedom suits filed in Massachusetts. Slaves pressed their masters, who were somewhat softened by their own cries for liberty, to free them. These negotiations appear in the colony records of manumissions. South Carolinians recorded all legal deeds, including manumissions, with the secretary's office. For a small fee, usually five shillings, a clerk would create a public record of a private transaction. Between 1737 and 1785, 379 men and women recorded their emancipation. Most of them, however, emancipated themselves in the last decade of that era. Between 1775 and 1785, the secretary's office recorded 199 manumissions.[94]

Nevertheless, no freedom-hungry slave could free himself. It required a willing master. The manumission records do not shed much light on why masters freed their slaves during the Revolutionary era. No one attributed emancipation to humanitarian sentiment—quite the opposite. Masters in South Carolina seemed compelled to give practical reasons for emancipating their slaves. Many owners cited the exceptional "Fidelity, Care, and good Service" that their slaves gave them. Others offered financial reasons. Slaves who purchased themselves or contributed toward their freedom supplied an automatic justification for emancipation, but usually that was not enough. Most added a vague statement, such as "for divers other considerations." Benjamin Clifford gave no specific reasons but relied on the stock phrase "for divers good & Lawful Causes." The addition of "Lawful Causes" hints at the potential danger in emancipating a slave without sufficient reason.[95]

Some slaves had to enter into complex negotiations through many channels to gain freedom during this era. Leander, a South Carolina slave, worked hard to negotiate his freedom and registered it in 1770. Leander and his owners, William and Susanna Mason, lived in Charleston, where Leander was a successful butcher. The Masons were not comfortable with allowing Leander to purchase his freedom. Therefore, he made a deal with Jacob Willeman to purchase him and then free him.[96]

Leander's work as a butcher brought him extra money, and over several years, Leander was able to pay Willeman "from time to time as monies" became available from his "dilligence and industry." On October 8, 1770, Willeman paid the Masons the £900 he had received from Leander to purchase him. Willeman accompanied the Masons to the secretary of state's office to legalize the deed of sale. Three days later, Willeman returned to the secretary of state's office, where he submitted an official deed that he would "hereby Enfranchise, manumise and let Free the said Mustee or Negro Fellow Leander."[97]

Not all slaves, however, got to the secretary of state's office to register their freedom. The law could not protect slaves beyond recording the emancipation at the secretary of state's office. Had either Willeman or the Masons decided to withdraw, Leander would have had virtually no recourse, as suggested by the fact that several slaves in Massachusetts sued their owners for their freedom because they did not uphold their side of the bargain with a slave. Owing to the provisions against blacks testifying in courts against whites, a slave, to be a plaintiff, had to find a white representative. Therefore, it is not surprising that only four slaves brought cases before the court in South Carolina.[98] Free blacks could only testify if the court gave special permission.[99] These restrictions severely limited the number of freedom suits.

The first documented case demonstrated how dangerous coming before the court could be. A black woman, Clarinda, did not sue but was brought forth as a runaway slave. Clarinda claimed to be free, having recently left Spanish America. However, she had no evidence of her free status. A white man claimed her but had no proof of his ownership. Faced with an unresolvable situation, the presiding judge, in a brash act of judicial tyranny, claimed her as his own property.[100]

Many more blacks challenged their enslavement, but they would have to suppress their desire to be free until the chaos of war afforded some opportunities, when the British would take advantage of the South Carolinian dependency on slavery and lure slaves their side. Slaves ran away, hoping that the British would offer them more than the rice and indigo plantations where they toiled.

British Ideas of American Enslavement

British rhetoric challenged the hypocrisy of the liberty-loving slave owners. Because Britain had already ended slavery within England, Loyalists and

This print, *A View in America* (1778), by Mattias Darly suggests the hypocrisy of American slave owners conducting a war in America based on liberty. Courtesy of the Library of Congress.

British critics used slavery as a tool to show the superiority of Britain and the hypocrisy of Americans. This moral superiority gave them ideological power over the Americans, especially with their own slaves. Samuel Johnson deflated the colonists' rhetoric, bitingly pointing out, "How is it that we hear the loudest *yelps* for liberty among the drivers of negroes?"[101] Samuel Johnson was not the only one who recognized the American paradox; British political cartoonists also highlighted the contradiction of slave owners fighting for liberty. Mattias Darly's *A View in America in 1778* captured the hypocrisy of the Patriot cause. In this etching, freezing American soldiers at Valley Forge carry away the liberty cap of a black soldier who has been knocked to the ground by a cannonball that is emblazoned with "Liberty or Death."[102]

The critique of American hypocrisy traveled across the Atlantic, where Loyalists frequently led the antislavery cause. Loyalists, especially in Massachusetts, stretched the metaphor of slavery to include slaves, as evidenced by the fact that the Loyalist newspapers were more willing to print antislavery commentary and gave the *Somersett* case full coverage. Loyalists' clearer understanding of British events, especially in relationship to slavery, strengthened their claim that the real nation of freedom was Britain.

Although most lawyers in the freedom suits did not take these cases for ideological reasons, the few who attested to embracing antislavery ideas were Loyalists. Loyalists Daniel Bliss and Jonathan Sewall, the plaintiffs' lawyers in *Newport v. Billing* (1768) and *James v. Lechmere* (1769), used these cases as a forum to end slavery. Bliss represented Newport in the lower court, and Sewall represented him in the superior court. Sewall and Bliss sought to topple slavery by appealing to Enlightenment ideals. The case of *Newport* was particularly weak and would be the *only* freedom suit to lose in the Massachusetts Supreme Judicial Court after 1763. No one claimed that Newport was illegally enslaved; he just claimed that his master beat him. Bliss chose to build his argument on moral, religious, and historical grounds.[103] John Adams documented that Sewall's argument in the superior court for freeing Newport drew on the new Enlightenment humanitarianism. Sewall questioned the basis of Newport's enslavement and a master's right to injure his slave by citing Montesquieu and Voltaire and by reviewing the history of slavery. This philosophical approach did not succeed in the case of *Newport*, but Sewall's second effort in *James* did. In this case, Sewall drew on ancient English law and the lack of positive law, foreshadowing the arguments made in *Somersett v. Stewart*.[104] Last, Loyalist Peter Oliver, chief justice of the superior court in 1764, showed an openness to end slavery in the *Slew v. Whipple* case and challenged Americans' affinity for holding human property above the ideal of liberty.

These rhetorical battles had an impact on the reality of the pre-Revolutionary era. Missives between Britain and the colonies racheted up the tensions. The use of slavery as a metaphor fired the imaginations of blacks and whites in South Carolina and Massachusetts in different ways. Their own experiences with slavery, and the legal and political structures that supported it, shaped their understanding. It became a rallying cry with which whites fought British oppression. For some whites, the calls for freedom made them begin to question slavery as an institution. This questioning was sparked by African Americans who, inspired by the freedom talk, then demanded their own emancipation. The British, too, heard this dialogue and would use it directly against the Americans, especially in the South. Rhetorical attacks on slavery would become physical attacks on the institution when the cannons began to rumble.

The distinctive history of slavery in each constituency meant that they developed their own definitions of slavery, freedom, and, eventually, anti-slavery. As the American Patriots sought to assert their freedom and prohibit their own enslavement, the slaves and the British would challenge their notions and push them to ask how free their society would be and whether property and liberty could be separated. Although very few Revolutionary-era leaders dismissed property ownership in favor of black human and civil rights, and even though eventually the founding generation chose to protect slavery rather than end it, the rhetoric of slavery had great implications. It focused attention on actual slaves and gave their actions greater power. Although rhetoric influenced reality, once the war had ended the abstract virtue of liberty began to recede. Economic and political realities superseded ideological ones, protecting slavery and suppressing black citizenship.

CHAPTER TWO

Slavery and the Start of the Revolution, 1775–1779

This day I fell in with and took the bark John *from London for Antigua, William Barrass, master, with a cargo of King stores, English and India goods. . . . I have taken another ship loaded with lumber from Pensacola for Grenada; she is not worth sending home, and therefore shall detain her with me for the present.*
— Capt. John Fisk, commander of the Brig *Tyrannicide*

BY NOVEMBER 27, 1776, the Massachusetts privateer *Tyrannicide* had embarked on its mission to attack the king's supply lines and trade. As a privateer, the captain, John Fisk, and its crew would profit personally from the attacks on British ships. No longer was Massachusetts simply accusing the king and Parliament in pamphlets of corruption and unjust occupation. The war to commit political tyrannicide had begun. By November, the Americans had not only fought militarily with the king's troops for more than a year, but they had declared their independence from the British monarchy. They had taken the first steps to sever ties with their mother country. They were now independent states at war to maintain their own sovereignty.

By November 1776, the Pawley plantation had settled down. South Carolina's troops had repelled an invasion attempt by the British. William Pawley, brother to Percival and Anthony Pawley, had contributed potatoes grown by his slaves to the troops, but whites and blacks on Waccamaw peninsula had resumed their familiar routines. Still, whispers throughout South Carolina's plantations told slaves that the king, who had always been the supreme power over their society, now wanted them to leave their plantation and join him against their masters. They, like loyal white colonists, could free themselves from their oppressors. However, the British had abandoned their shores, and all authority seemed to rest with their owners once again.[1]

As America moved toward a hot war with Britain, the rhetorical war faded for whites. Throughout the states, African Americans set their targets on fighting, hoping thereby to gain more freedom. They would take advantage of the disruption of the Revolutionary War. For the first four years of the war, the white leaders of Massachusetts and South Carolina, who had approached slavery differently on a rhetorical level, began to view the nation through the same lens as they fought a common enemy. Although many Massachusetts leaders felt uncomfortable with slavery, they worried that taking action to end slavery would risk alienating the lower South and South Carolina in particular, a wealthy state that weakly supported independence. In other words, the national effort to create a union stymied the efforts of blacks and whites to dissolve slavery within Massachusetts. In the end, the Revolutionary leadership from Massachusetts supported maintaining slavery during this era and quashed any efforts to end it, even within their state. Despite the general sense of historians that the American Revolution accelerated freedom for all, the efforts toward union might have retarded it. The Patriots had decided. It would be a nation with slavery.[2]

Although national leaders united over slavery, on a local level whites in South Carolina and Massachusetts drifted apart. South Carolina's white citizens worked to maintain and protect slavery during wartime. Despite a tumultuous period while the British attempted to invade Charleston in 1776, slave owners spent most of these four years trying to profit from the war and to sell their rice and indigo crops to the world market. After Massachusetts expelled the British from its shores in 1776, the white population likewise struggled to rebuild a strong economy. However, in deep contrast, more and more whites in Massachusetts favored ending slavery for economic and ideological reasons.

African Americans' experiences of the war in South Carolina and Massachusetts could not have been more different. Different ideas of slavery and race, in combination with the varied strategies of black activists, shaped these experiences. During the war, slaves and free blacks had opportunities to control their own lives in ways that forced whites to see them in new ways. Race has always been a fluid concept, but the multitude of activities free blacks and slaves participated in demonstrates how racial ideology not only ran a spectrum within the nation but even within a single state. Throughout these four years, slaves and free blacks in Massachusetts had more options than ever before to protest slavery and take action against it. For them, freedom came by aligning with the American side. As they fought their own enslavement with the Americans, whites became more open to seeing African Americans in more humanistic ways. South Carolina slaves and free blacks found themselves presented with new, although typically illegal, ways to fight their enslavement. In addition, the British and Patriot leadership in South Carolina used slavery as a weapon early in the war. In this battle, the British supported the slaves, so slaves and free blacks in South Carolina aligned with the British. This alliance created an even greater rift between white South Carolinians and slaves than had existed before, intensifying white South Carolinians' perception of slaves as less human.

The War Begins in Massachusetts

Massachusetts took up arms against Britain before any other state. Britain was uninterested in using the small slave population in Massachusetts to destabilize society. Without a large slave population inside its borders or large Native population outside its borders, Massachusetts' war focused on fighting Britain. As a result, the military war in Massachusetts fit the schoolbook narrative of the British redcoats versus the Patriot bluecoats. For the most part, whites in Massachusetts did not see the colony's slaves and free blacks as menacing turncoats. Instead, they saw them as potential soldiers to fill the ranks against Britain. Many blacks had hopes that they would prove they were equal men by joining ranks against the British and that that would lead to their own freedom.

The African American community sought to fight for the side that would bring freedom. Very early in the conflict, a group of black men urged the Loyalist governor of Massachusetts to enlist black men to fight in return for freedom. Abigail Adams reported that the governor gave the request little notice. This incident reminded Adams of why she was so uncomfortable with slavery in her colony. She felt it wrong to "plunder from those who have as good a right to freedom as we have."[3] Without the promise of freedom from the Loyalists, the black community quickly sided with the Patriots.

The early military engagements gave African Americans in the state an opportunity to make their choice quickly, before too much thought went into the makeup of the military forces. A great number of New England

African Americans joined local militias and the Continental army to fight against the British. Massachusetts' slavery ideology offered slaves a stronger sense of personhood. Slaves and free blacks had a history of fighting in Massachusetts wars, and whites in Massachusetts would accept blacks as soldiers during most of the Revolutionary War. Although not officially sanctioned early in the war, slaves and free blacks joined Massachusetts' military ranks enthusiastically. Many of the most prominent black Patriots hailed from Massachusetts.

Before the war, there was a fear of slave insurrection in Massachusetts just as there was in South Carolina, but this fear waned once the war began. In 1768, the *New York Journal* reported that British general James Wilson told slaves that "the Negroes shall be free, and the Liberty Boys slaves" if the slaves murdered their owners. This story stunned Boston, whose judiciary filed a charge against Wilson. John Adams also played on these fears in 1770 during the Boston Massacre trials. To delegitimize a slave witness, he asked in the newspaper whether the slave witnesses, Andrew and other slaves, had "been familiar with the soldiers" and whether some of them had been coaxed into "cut[ting] their masters' throats." The message that a slave who cavorted with the enemy would turn on his owner revealed the racist fears of people in pre-Revolutionary Massachusetts. This fear, however, subsided because the British became the literal foes of the Massachusetts Patriots, not just a rhetorical device.[4]

The Massachusetts government sought initially to limit the number of blacks in the military. The legislature passed laws exempting blacks and Indians from service. Apparently, some muster masters did not interpret these exemptions as barring blacks from service; they happily enlisted blacks from many Massachusetts towns. Fourteen blacks from Lancaster volunteered, for example. In 1778, the legislature relaxed its restrictions and allowed blacks to enlist and to be drafted. Blacks were not to have their own regiments. Perhaps whites in Massachusetts were more comfortable seeing blacks dispersed among other regiments, which is how Massachusetts had assigned blacks to duty in the past, rather than seeing a large group of armed blacks. In addition, as the war wore on, whites could pay blacks, especially slaves, to fight in their place for less than they could pay poor whites.[5]

Serving in Massachusetts' militias or in the Continental army brought many benefits to the slaves and free blacks. Owners offered slaves emancipation in return for their pay or as a reward for replacing a white man called to join. Military service allowed black men to gain respect as well. By fighting in the war, they could prove both their manhood and their dedication to the Americans' cause. As low-level enlisted men, they had experiences alongside white men: training, fighting in battles, and standing watch. They sought to prove themselves worthy of being granted the status of a full man in Massachusetts' society. Black women, who could engage in the rhetorical battles, could not take advantage of this opportunity to gain communal respect.

Military service had more tangible benefits for black servicemen than for whites, so blacks were willing to endure more than their white counterparts. Often slaves were promised freedom after fighting the war until its end, not for a prescribed period, so their service tended to be longer. Despite their long service, black men rarely rose up the ranks to command other soldiers. Enslaved blacks might have been more content as soldiers than as servants. They tended not to desert the army at the same rates as white soldiers. Perhaps they were able to adapt to the soldiers' life more easily; certainly, they realized that running away could lead to enslavement or could count as breach of a contract for freedom. Nathanael Greene and Alexander Hamilton both believed that offering freedom ensured loyal and enthusiastic black soldiers.[6]

The promise of respect and freedom drew a large number of black men into service. Despite the danger of war and the discrimination they faced, black men obviously saw the American armies, militias, and navies as attractive options. The exact number of black soldiers and sailors is unknown because the race of enlisted soldiers was not always identified on musters. In 1778, the Continental army had registered at least 775 black men throughout the colonies. This number probably grew as the war progressed; the army depended more and more on substitutes to fight. Massachusetts regiments in particular had "a lot of Negroes."[7]

This high degree of participation meant that all of Massachusetts' important battles had black participants. Peter Salem fought in both the Battle of Lexington and at the Battle of Bunker Hill and then negotiated with his master for freedom. At Concord and Lexington, at least five other blacks served, with one, Prince Eastabrook, losing his life. Along with Peter Salem, another contingent of at least six blacks participated on Bunker Hill. Scipio Pernam received a pension after the war for his service, and Barzillai Lew, who had war experience from the French and Indian War, served with distinction in the Battle of Bunker Hill. In the battle at Charlestown, Massachusetts, Salem Poor conducted himself with distinction. Fourteen Massachusetts officers petitioned the Massachusetts General Court to recognize his service, which they compared to that of "an experienced officer: he was "an excellent soldier . . . brave and gallant." He would continue to fight for the Continental army in White Plains and Valley Forge. Likewise, the siege at Boston included a scattering of blacks.[8]

Despite these early contributions, George Washington worried about the addition of black soldiers. Washington was particularly concerned that the Continental army was not professional enough. He had famously described the Americans' dependence on militias as "resting upon a broken staff," and undoubtedly, seeing militias of black and white faces would have unsettled him even more. Indeed, after he first saw Massachusetts' integrated militias, he insisted that black soldiers no longer be recruited. Massachusetts acquiesced to Washington's request and suspended recruitment of black soldiers. As time passed, Washington and the Massachusetts legislature would reinstate black recruitment. As Washington gained firsthand experience of what black soldiers were capable of by working with stellar black military forces such as Rhode Island's all-black First Regiment, his opinions would change. Rhode Island's black regiment fought alongside Washington at Yorktown.

The story of a very young man, Peter Brooks, shows how hard black men worked to be a part of the war effort. Brooks, who was from Lincoln, Massachusetts, enlisted in the militia for the first time at the age of twelve in 1775 to prove his manhood. During his first enlistment, he marched to Boston and participated in the Battle of Bunker Hill under the command of John Nixon. This diverse and disorderly regiment was among those that George Washington first saw, and he described them as an "exceeding dirty and nasty people," "a mixed multitude of people . . . under very little discipline, order, or government." In the eyes of a professional soldier such as Washington the novice regiment had mistakenly equalized its enlistees. Brooks and his comrades, black and white, learned discipline and gained experience as they improved fortifications, sat on watch, and engaged in skirmishes with the British. When his family needed him home to bring in the harvest, he slipped away from the front. By early 1776, Massachusetts and the Continental army had decided against enlisting blacks, and so although Brooks wished to reenlist, he was forced back to his owner's home. The restrictions were soon lifted because soldiers were desperately needed. Brooks managed to reenlist in the militia in late 1776. His regiment, under the command of Benjamin Lincoln, marched to the center of British engagement, New York, and fought the British. Brooks would reenlist repeatedly and fight through to the Battle of Yorktown. At the end of the war, his service and that of his father earned both of them freedom. He was also able to purchase the freedom of his mother and sisters with his reenlistment bonus, although his father died only one year after gaining his freedom. Peter too died at a young age, in 1792, at the age of thirty.[9]

Boston had its own black unit called the Bucks of America, but very little is known about it. There were only three black Patriot units. The Bucks were a force whose job was to protect the "property of Boston merchants." Colonel Middleton was the black commander of the unit. When the unit stopped at John Hancock's mansion, Hancock and his son recognized the black "protectors" by giving them a silk banner with his initials and those of George Washington with a "device of a Pine tree and a Buck." This flag is prominently displayed at the Massachusetts Historical Society today, given to the organization by the first black historian, William C. Nell. The best known black unit was the First Rhode Island Regiment, regarded by George Washington and Nathanael Greene as among the best in the Continental army because they fought with such distinction. Haiti also had a military force that fought as part of French support of the American cause.[10]

Black men could be found more frequently in the navies. Men of African descent were ubiquitous on ships before the war. Historian Jeffery Bolster estimates that about 20 percent of mariners were black. The undesirability and danger of the work on a ship gave blacks many opportunities to serve in the Continental navy and state navies and on privateers. On ships, the Americans often captured blacks fighting for the British. Rather than make them prisoners of war, naval officers insisted that they would serve the Americans. These commanders obviously assumed that the black sailors had no real Loyalist conviction. As in the army, blacks mostly served at the lowest ranks. Captains usually assigned blacks as captain's boys and cleaners of the ships as well as powder carriers. Occasionally, blacks rose up in rank to become watchmen or gun operators.[11]

Clearly, African American men in Massachusetts sympathized more deeply with the rebellious Americans' calls for freedom than with the king's army that appeared to oppress its people. Several factors were at play in the clear decision of most blacks to remain loyal to the Americans. The king's promises of freedom must have seemed disingenuous to blacks, as they witnessed and participated in the mob activity and British occupation before the war. Furthermore, aside from the promises issued in 1775 and

1779 in Virginia and South Carolina, the British made no effort to bring Massachusetts' slaves to the king's side. Therefore, records of black Loyalists during the initial British occupation of Boston are virtually nonexistent. In state records, only one black Loyalist emerges, and Massachusetts could not build up a case against him. Thomas Nichols was brought to the attention of the Committee of Safety for suspicious behavior. It recommended that Congress decide whether he should be prosecuted for treason. The congressional committee, however, had "nothing proved against him" and sent him back to the selectmen of his town. This case highlights the deep differences between South Carolina and Massachusetts. Whites in Massachusetts recognized Nichols's presumed activity as treason, an act in favor of the British and against the American cause. In South Carolina, whites perceived slaves' and free blacks' pro-British activity as slave rebellion, an act against slavery, not against the American cause. When the British evacuated the United States in 1783, only twenty-three of the three thousand black Loyalists came from Massachusetts. The slaves in South Carolina would perceive the British in a wholly opposite fashion.[12]

The War Begins in South Carolina

At the beginning of May 1775, five days before news of Concord and Lexington hit Charleston, a report flew in that the British intended to free slaves who joined the British military. As early as March 1776, Henry Clinton had noted that "upon news of the affair at Lexington which arrived about the beginning of May the people of Carolina were thrown into a great Ferment" because they feared that a British official planned "to Employ the Indians and to Arm the negroes for the Service of the Government."[13] Soon, Charlestonians searched for affirmation that their worst fears might be realized. They found it in John Stuart, the British Indian superintendent of the southern district. General Gage wrote Stuart in February or March 1776 and warned that if South Carolinians did not temper their "hot" dispositions in the Philadelphia Continental Congress, "your Rice and Indigo will be brought to market by negroes instead of white People." The British general Henry Clinton recorded much of this uproar and witnessed how white South Carolinians began to fear that the world was being turned upside down.[14]

As the Revolution turned hot, white, elite South Carolinians had plenty to worry about. As a colony, South Carolina had already dealt with friction between different groups. The poor white, western settlers of South and North Carolina felt disenfranchised and had led a rebellion known as the Regulator movement. Despite structural changes that the colony made in 1769 to appease the instigators of the Regulator movement, South Carolina was still wracked with class tensions in the backcountry. In addition, Native American nations, the Creek and Cherokee, were constantly hostile and challenged the colony's western frontiers. The Carolinians also did not know what to expect from them. Moreover, inside and surrounding many homes, black men, women, and children toiled as slaves.

The slaves heard these stories that rumored the British might grant them their liberty, too. They gained hope that the king, whom their masters had marked as the ultimate authority in the land, now called them to service and might free them. They now seemed to have monarchical permission to escalate resistance against their slave owners. With the king's support, they hoped to become free or at least to live freer lives. The chaos of the war and British intervention made this possible.

While Patriots took advantage of African Americans' service to aid their cause in Massachusetts, the British sought to use the slaves against white slaveholding South Carolinians. The fear at the onset of the war was palpable. This real fear became a tool that both sides used to draw support for the war. Loyalist Thomas Knox Gordon argued that the revolutionaries had "propagated a Report that the Negroes were meditating an Insurrection" as a "plausible pretence for arming with great industry."[15] Royal governor William Campbell believed that the colonists had purposely implicated the British in "agitation . . . to instigate and encourage an insurrection amongst the slaves."[16] Despite Campbell's stated concern, the British generally encouraged such rumors because they disrupted southern society. Loyalist William Bull wrote to Lord Dartmouth that "a counterbalance in the hands of the white men against the superiority of strength and numbers of the Slaves" could benefit their efforts.[17] Despite rumors of dozens of rebellions, only three suspected uprisings warranted action during the era.

In July 1775, magistrates accused John Burnet, a white minister, of encouraging a slave named George to distribute an unnamed book that would "alter the World, & set the Negroes Free."[18] George was executed. Burnet, who had first been admonished for ministering to the slaves in August 1773, denied instigating rebellion. This plot was reported to the Council of Safety, but unlike the other two plots it did not become a central bone of contention between the revolutionaries and the royal government.

The second plot revolved around a free mulatto, Thomas Jeremiah, whose fate became the center of dispute between Britain and South Carolina in August 1775. The conflict over Jeremiah's case reflects a tug-of-war for power: Britain tried to use Jeremiah's trial as proof that the British government stood for justice and rule of law, while the nascent South Carolina leadership used it to propel itself into power. By protecting white South Carolinians from a perceived threat, the leadership proved that it understood the real needs of South Carolina in a time of crisis.

In summer 1775, widespread fear and rumors of insurrection, paired with an overheard conversation among several slaves, implicated Thomas Jeremiah in a slave rebellion. Jeremiah was a very successful harbor pilot who owned slaves and might have been one of the wealthiest black men in the American colonies. The conversation revolved around an impending armed rebellion by slaves. Authorities immediately questioned the slaves, who had been overheard, and they began pointing fingers elsewhere, particularly at Jeremiah. The key witness was a slave named Sambo, who accused Jeremiah of urging slaves to run away to the British, of running guns to other black South Carolinians, and of having ambitions to take control as the commander of this slave army.[19]

The South Carolina court system immediately went into action. The magistrates and freeholders interviewed several slaves and found sufficient evidence to implicate Jeremiah as the ringleader of the plot.[20] They had not considered whether the informers might be "terrified at the recollection of former cruelties" and "easily induced to accuse" others, as the royal governor had suspected.[21] Jeremiah refused to confess to having a role in the plot. Even after Reverend Smith used "every argument every art to draw him to confession, endeavoring to make him contradict himself," Jeremiah held his ground.[22] The justices and freeholders took two months to gather what they believed to be sufficient evidence against the free black man. Although there were many reasons to question the evidence, Jeremiah's fate was sealed in the minds of the white magistrates.[23]

The court sentenced Jeremiah to death, a decision that took some maneuvering on the part of the court. They had to sentence him based on the "Negro Act," but not on its literal words, because the act listed insurrection as a capital crime only for slaves. Loyalist judges and the attorney general reported to Governor Campbell that he should not be executed even if he was deemed guilty, for the penalty did not apply to him as a free black. They could not conceive that a successful free black who owned slaves would try to raise the slaves up in arms against whites, and the royal Governor, William Campbell, agreed.[24]

Challenging the power of the royal government, the Patriot justices and freeholders of the court held their ground. For decades, South Carolina's whites had grappled with royal authorities overstepping their local rights. In 1751, for instance, the king had angered the locals when he disallowed two popular laws that Governor Glen, a royal appointee, reluctantly had signed. In this case, the royal governor had, according to South Carolinians, impinged on their authority over the free and enslaved black population. They argued that "the Justices and Freeholders have a power to try and convict all free Negroes for any crime which a slave under this Act can be tried or convicted."[25] They added that the fact that free blacks were not mentioned in the section of the act that covered insurrection had to be an error. They could not imagine that a free black man could be tried as a white man. Moreover, and perhaps most important to the South Carolinians, the notion that the law did not apply to Jeremiah and other free blacks would have the "most fatal consequence to the lives and properties of the white Inhabitants." As black men became greater threats to society, whites pressed race as the primary category of law, not slave status.[26]

These two interpretations of the law formed the grounds of a contest for legitimacy between the royal and Revolutionary leaders at a time when power over South Carolina was in contention. Local leaders, including those who constituted the magistrate court, tended to be Patriots, and they began challenging the royal government, which held colonial offices such as governor and attorney general. Both sides used the conviction of Thomas Jeremiah for their own purposes. The revolutionaries used Jeremiah's suspected plan to tie the British to the slave insurrection and established themselves as the better government for South Carolina, and they garnered slave-owner support by asserting the existence of such an alliance between the British and the slaves. Their government sought above all to protect society and property, disregarding the letter of the law. The royal government tried to use its superior powers to delegitimize the Revolutionary government through a critique of its interpretation of the law. Campbell and the royal judges used law in a distinctly impartial way, trying to prove the blindness, and thus the superiority, of their justice. In contrast, the South Carolinians' new governmental organization, the Council of Safety, sought safety above justice.

The South Carolinians knew that their fellow citizens did not want blind justice. That the royal judges and attorney general had decided to review the case "raised such a Clamor amongst the People, as is incredible."[27] South Carolinians used this review of the case to bolster their accusation that the royal government supported insurrection. To accentuate this connection and assert their power, they built the gallows for Jeremiah in front of Governor Campbell's house.[28] Although Campbell was suspicious of the South Carolinians' effort to execute Jeremiah and thought the Patriots propagated "the most notorious falsehoods . . . to work up the people in every part of America to that pitch of madness and fury," he quickly saw that the mob would take control of the situation, and he did not pardon Thomas Jeremiah.[29]

A month after the execution of Thomas Jeremiah, Campbell moved his administration to a naval ship in Charleston's harbor. He believed that he could no longer "support the King's authority" in the colony and felt powerless to protect his "faithful and Loyal subjects," black or white.[30] South Carolina's Patriot leadership had wrested control of the state from their colonial oppressors. Jeremiah's execution was the beginning of the Patriots' tyrannicide of the monarchy. Unlike Massachusetts, South Carolina had concerns about ending its relationship with Britain. Although Massachusetts did accept the king as the primary authority for most of its history, it also always was more egalitarian and was far more independent of and antagonistic toward the royal government. In the more hierarchical society of South Carolina, Campbell's evacuation ushered in an era of disorder in South Carolina. The highest colonial authority in South Carolina had fled, and that flight automatically disrupted the social order because it was through the authority of the king that South Carolinian slave owners had "become accustomed to proclaiming and legitimating their own authority" over their slaves.[31]

In Charlestonians' minds, the British withdrawal from Charleston strengthened ties between slaves and the royal administration. Many perceived the government that floated in the Charleston harbor to be a goal for runaway slaves, and this perception was strengthened by the significant presence of the British navy in the harbor. The popular support that the revolutionaries assembled to successfully condemn Jeremiah to death, despite the findings of royal officials, demonstrated the hold that the revolutionaries had over white inhabitants of the low country and the law, but the South Carolinians' case against Britain was not yet complete. Another situation was brewing that worked to convince whites that the British sought to pit the slaves against their masters. Rumors of Dunmore's proclamation in Virginia in November 1775 and the presence of the British Navy in Charleston's harbor drew slaves off the plantations and into boats on the rivers. A fairly large contingent of runaway slaves sailed across Charleston's harbor to Sullivan's Island, where they gathered and created a maroon community. For many, this place of freedom was probably familiar because it was the same place, ironically, where slave traders held newly imported slaves before taking them to market.[32]

Only a month after Dunmore issued his proclamation, the Council of Safety began hearing stories about slaves running to the island. John Ash's overseer reported that a "man-of-war boat with a number of armed men, blacks as well as whites," had plundered Ash's plantation, taking at least one of his slaves to the island.[33] Other reports of missing slaves boarding "the King's ships" and living on Sullivan's Island continued to flow into the council. Observers spotted houses in increasing numbers on the island, suggesting that the slaves were organizing. The council suspected that the Sullivan's Island slaves had, "in armed parties, committed several robberies and depredations on the people of the colony." Moreover, Henry Laurens, the president of the council, received a report that the British governor's ship had helped runaway slaves. Because getting across the harbor undetected would have been difficult, the Americans assumed that the British had aided the slaves.[34]

These various reports compelled the council to resolve to "apprehend and disperse the runaway slaves" on Sullivan's Island.[35] South Carolinians were not just concerned about recovering their lost property; they also feared that these slaves were "under the protection of the men of war" and had become armed and would attack Charleston.[36] The slaves, the council maintained, had joined the British and planned to upend white society through armed resistance. Henry Laurens described the British support for the slaves as a serious betrayal: "What meanness! what complicated wickedness! . . . O England, how changed! how fallen!"[37]

This sense of betrayal and fear ignited the first low-country bloodshed, as the colonists launched an attack on the island in an attempt to obliterate the maroon community that slaves had created.[38] Colonists invaded the island in the darkness in December 1775, "disguised as Indians," just as the Boston Tea Party's Revolutionary leaders had been when they boarded ships loaded with tea in Boston Harbor.[39] To quell the community of slaves, whom they expected to be armed, fifty-four foot rangers attacked. They did not find what they expected. Their fears had outpaced reality once again. The South Carolina soldiers raided a community that had fewer than ten runaways. Interestingly, instead of a maroon of slaves, it appeared to be an integrated community of whites and escaped blacks. Four blacks were taken prisoner, and, according to Laurens, "three or four" were killed. At least seven of the white Loyalists they found were women and children. The rangers took the whites prisoner and "destroyed everything in sight."[40]

The action on Sullivan's Island started the war for Charleston. Largely a civil war, it pitted Patriots against the Loyalist South Carolinians and black slaves and the white Patriots who owned them. According to a Patriot source, the Sullivan's Island attack had "serve[d] to humble our negroes in general and perhaps mortify his Lordship not a little."[41] This assault helped them solidify their aims for the war: to reassert control over their slave population and replace the British government in South Carolina.

South Carolina and Massachusetts on the National Scene

Soon after the Sullivan's Island raid, South Carolina and Massachusetts delegates to the Continental Congress in Philadelphia began deliberating their decision to declare their independence from Britain. The delegates from both were of the opinion that in attacking their states' towns and slaves the British had clearly overstepped their power. In the wake of Thomas Paine's *Common Sense*, which urged Americans to focus on building a new nation, both states set out independently to declare independence from England. This act of fully expelling the British from their states unified South Carolina and Massachusetts, despite their wholly different experiences in the war.

Many colonists believed that one aspect of becoming independent of England was eliminating the unwanted vestiges of British rule, including ending the slave trade. In April 1776, they rejected nearly a century of trade regulation and taxes, asserting that England had no power over colonial trade. They also declared that "no slaves be imported into any of the thirteen United Colonies." This decision was not new; many colonies—Maryland, New Jersey, Virginia, Pennsylvania, and others—had already begun controlling the trade through the imposition of higher duties. Nonetheless, the colonies had begun to see ending the slave trade as an element of ending their enslavement to Britain.[42]

South Carolina set out not to sever its ties with England forever but to establish a temporary, legitimate, and independent government. The wealthy and successful South Carolinians had long sought a great deal of control over their own affairs. As events such as the Jeremiah affair attested, South Carolinian elites generally agreed that the royal government no longer served the people. In April 1776, Chief Justice William Henry Drayton handed down a decision stating that South Carolina must write a new state constitution, "independent of Royal authority." The way Britain had overstepped its power was evident, and relying on William Blackstone's constitutional thought, he justified separation from England. The state, however, was hesitant because the elite had had close relationships with British traders for generations, and they possessed a strong sense of English identity as "Carolina Englishmen." The 1776 state constitution that passed about six months later hoped for reconciliation with Britain, announcing that the state would be independent "until an accommodation of the unhappy differences between Great Britain and America can be obtained."[43]

Massachusetts hoped to lead the colonies toward independence. In late 1775, the General Court attempted to write an instruction for its delegates to vote for independence. Massachusetts hoped that if it sent its delegates with an instruction, an official statement of how to vote on a bill, other state legislatures would do the same. This strategy was not very successful. The representatives of the towns, fearing the repercussions of treason and the loss of their country, did not support it heartily. The General Court did not get unanimous support for the instructions until July 3, 1776.[44]

Nonetheless, movement toward independence proceeded in Philadelphia. The Philadelphia delegates wrote a document, both practical and idealistic, declaring independence. The convention had appointed Thomas Jefferson, Benjamin Franklin, John Adams, Robert Livingston, and Roger Sherman to the committee to write the document. Jefferson, in consultation with the committee and other Revolutionary-era documents, drafted it. The sentiment expressed in "We hold these truths to be self-evident, that all men are created equal, that they are endowed by their Creator with certain unalienable Rights, that among these are Life, Liberty, and the pursuit of Happiness," emblematic of American ideals, was the least important in their minds. As significant as these ideals were, they were part of the intellectual air the Patriots breathed and not the document's central purpose. The Congress intended, first and foremost, to use the document to declare independence, and the statement of rights was merely one part of its justification for declaring independence. The specific injustices took much more space and were more significant in the minds of the men at the Congress. In fact, Jefferson borrowed much of the language from prior documents such as George Mason's Virginia Declaration of Rights. The core parts of this document for those who wrote and signed it were the sections outlining the "causes and necessity of their taking up arms"—the declaration of independence, the justification of revolution based on the usurpations of power by Britain, and the establishment of a new nation. Although the language of these parts was not always heady, the ambitions they voiced were. Nevertheless, these goals were tentative for many. Most, especially the men of South Carolina, hoped for reconciliation.

A very strong argument was required to support the radical decision to declare independence, and slavery was a part of this argument. Slavery was such a significant trope of oppression throughout the pre-Revolutionary era that attacking the king for imposing slavery in various forms on the Americans helped define independence even more strongly. This support came in the list of grievances included in the petition. In the original version of the declaration, Jefferson castigated the king for "waging a cruel war against human nature" by imposing slavery and the slave trade on the American colonies. Although Jefferson had exaggerated the extent to which Britain forced the colonists to own slaves, the Crown valued the revenue from trade in tobacco and rice. It had fostered slavery through specific readings of common law and in its imperial trade policies and also by militarily supporting the trade. It is possible that some delegates refused to sign the declaration because they recognized that the clause was disingenuous; they were wholly aware of the extent to which they were responsible for and dependent on slavery. The petition held little back, alerting the king that he had "prostituted his negative [veto]" to block legislation against the slave trade. Then Jefferson turned the rhetorical tables and accused the king of using that slave population to his own advantage by "exciting those very people to rise in arms among us."[45]

The delegates held a wide range of opinions regarding the abolition of slavery and the slave trade, and those opinions changed over time. Many more delegates supported abolishing the slave trade than supported slavery. A few people on the furthest end of the spectrum, such as Massachusetts abolitionist John Bacon, argued that upholding Revolutionary ideals necessitated a rapid emancipation. But most abolitionist schemes pressed for a gradual emancipation. Thomas Jefferson, for example, consistently supported the abolition of the slave trade but had varying and complex ideas about abolishing slavery. A few years after writing the Declaration of Independence, Jefferson simultaneously advocated abolition and upheld a racist ideology based on biology. In *Notes on the State of Virginia* (1781), he proposed a gradual emancipation act, one aspect of which would be to educate the former slaves, but he also insisted that the former slaves be exported out of the country because "the real distinctions which nature has made . . . will divide us into parties, and produce convulsions, which will probably never end but in the extermination of one or the other race." In the light of a potential American race war, the Virginia legislature did not seriously consider his proposals to end slavery. Like Jefferson, those sympathetic to abolition favored a gradual emancipation, and this legislation would pass in Pennsylvania, Rhode Island, and Connecticut during the 1780s; New York and New Jersey would follow at the turn of the nineteenth century. Nevertheless, others, such as the men from South Carolina and Georgia, occupied the other end of the spectrum, opposing abolition of slavery vehemently and regarding the abolition of the slave trade as a states' rights issue.

The passage in which Jefferson proposes gradual emancipation illuminates the central role slavery played in preserving American unity in the face of ideological diversity. The founders were trying to construct a workable form of government. The issue of slavery was one of many the delegates deliberated on in an effort to secure consensus and maintain a strong moral center. An earlier draft of the Declaration of Independence contained one of the Revolutionary period's clearest statements about the immorality of slavery, but it was removed at the insistence of the delegates of South Carolina. Their votes were important. The South Carolinian delegates, Edward Rutledge, Thomas Lynch Jr., Arthur Middleton, and Thomas Hayward Jr., had not yet decided to vote in favor of independence. In fact, they would reject the declaration on its first vote. Edward Rutledge, a supporter of independence, talked his fellow South Carolina delegates into voting in favor for the second vote. Jefferson felt compelled to take the passage out, but in his journal, he excoriated South Carolinians for "never attempt[ing] to restrain the importation of slaves" and for "wish[ing] to continue it."[46]

Given the acceptance of antislavery talk in Massachusetts, one might naturally assume that its delegates would have supported this attack on slavery and the slave trade. However, they did not. They supported South Caro-

lina's insistence that this section be removed. Although many in Massachusetts questioned the morality of slavery, the leadership did not do so publicly.
The merchants of Massachusetts and Rhode Island depended on the slave
trade. This point was not lost on Jefferson. He noted that "their people have
very few themselves yet they had been pretty considerable carriers of them
to others." The founders could not afford to include a statement in the declaration that questioned the morality of some of the most successful inhabitants among the colonies, so the revised versions of the document would
continue to support the slave trade into the Constitutional Convention.[47]

Massachusetts' national leaders were much more concerned about securing independence and preserving unity among the leaders of the states
than they were about eradicating slavery. John Adams, whom many cite as
detesting slavery and who had no personal slave-trade ties, led the effort
to have the antislavery and anti–slave trade clause removed from the declaration in order to placate his southern colleagues. Adams, like Jefferson
and Franklin, thought in continental terms and put national interests before
states' ones, whereas many other Americans had a local focus.

In his quest for national unity, Adams was not content to merely sac-
rifice mention of abolition in the Declaration of Independence but also
sought to quell abolitionist activity within Massachusetts. When Felix Holbrook's petition to end slavery ended up in a committee in the General
Court, John Adams urged the committee to table the petition because of
national interest. He argued that slave-owning states such as Virginia and
New York would object to the emancipation of slaves in Massachusetts.
Revolutionary leader James Warren agreed that the antislavery act in Massachusetts would "have a bad effect on the Union of the Colonies." More
important, Warren stopped the representatives from sending a letter to the
Continental Congress about abolishing slavery, prevented them from, as he
put it, "embarrass[ing]" themselves. Although he did not mention South
Carolina in this instance, he pointed to South Carolina's concerns on other
occasions. John Adams expressed the concern well in his objection to the
recruitment of black troops. He said, "We have Causes enough of Jealous
Discord and Division." He pointed directly at South Carolina in a letter
to Jonathan Dickinson Sergeant, telling Sergeant, a New Jersey delegate,
"your Negro Battalion will never do. S. Carolina would run out their Wits
at the least Hint of such a Measure." Their fears appeared to be warranted. A
month after the signing of the Declaration of Independence, South Carolina's Thomas Lynch began to worry that if Congress taxed slaves as property,

it would be "an end of the Confederation." These threats to national unity would continue to be posed into the Constitutional Convention. The leadership, however, could not control a drift *within* Massachusetts toward ending slavery. Massachusetts' black and white population had already begun to let go of slavery, but when national unity was at stake, Massachusetts would acquiesce to the idea that the United States was a nation that condoned slavery rather than one that embraced universal freedom.[48]

Writing State Constitutions

When the Massachusetts delegates gathered to write a new state constitution in 1776, many in the state would press for a document that would form the basis for a more radical new nation, a nation in which slavery was no more. Although Massachusetts' revolutionaries began constitutional debates earlier than any other state, it took them six years to arrive at a satisfactory document. Following Governor Gage's 1774 dissolution of the General Court, the legislature sought "explicit advice" from the Continental Congress on how to proceed in establishing a legitimate government.[49] Like leaders in South Carolina, Loyalists such as Thomas Hutchinson believed that the state would devolve into anarchy without a constitution. The citizens did not have that worry. In 1775, in response to the beginning of the war, the citizens ratified the Massachusetts charter in a convention, and in 1776, they voted against drafting a new constitution. In 1778, the legislature convened a convention to write a constitution that would be free of the stain of British origins. Written in haste, this constitution proved wholly unsatisfactory. When the proposal was sent to the towns, they soundly defeated it and responded with lengthy disquisitions criticizing the document. These criticisms provoked yet another attempt at a constitution. In 1779, Massachusetts leaders convened, and this time the convention included more prominent thinkers such as John Hancock, Samuel Adams, and John Adams. John Adams took on the task of drafting the document. Keeping the advice of the towns in mind, he required the towns' approval for ratification. It passed, and the new constitution went into effect in 1780.[50]

The 1780 Massachusetts constitution reflected the idealistic opinions the towns had expressed in 1778. The long history of Massachusetts' town governance and new Enlightenment ideals informed freeholders' debate of fundamental issues of representation, governance, power and authority, taxation, individual rights and collective interests, and slavery.[51] Their discussions often foreshadowed those of the Federalists and anti-Federalists a decade later. *The Essex Result*, for example, a critique of the 1778 constitution by the towns in Essex County, examined all aspects of the 1778 constitution, recommended changes, and ruminated on the nature of government and man.[52] The 1780 constitution, according to its enthusiasts, protected both individual and collective rights, provided moral and educational aid for future citizens through public schools and public churches, and balanced power between the legislative, executive, and judicial branches.[53]

Constitution making in Massachusetts did not ignore issues of slavery and race. The 1778 constitution did not abolish slavery, and it made racial distinctions that disenfranchised blacks in Massachusetts. The towns' responses to the 1778 document demonstrate that the people of Massachusetts had begun to see racial hierarchies in new ways and to question slavery in the state. Their particular concern was a suffrage restriction in article 5: "Every male inhabitant of any town in this State, being free and twenty-one years of age, excepting negroes, Indians and mulattoes, shall be entitled to vote for a Representative." Of the twenty-three towns that offered explicit details of their dissent, seventeen listed this article as unacceptable. Some towns protested because they hoped for universal suffrage, and still more disagreed with the property requirement for suffrage. The denial of voting rights to black inhabitants did not go unnoticed in the town assessments of the constitution. The people of Charlemont, Boothbay, Westminster, Upton, Blanford, Essex County, Sutton, and Spencer expressly challenged this article for both its establishment of a racial hierarchy and its implicit approval of slavery.[54] The people of Spencer, for instance, pointed to exclusion on account of race as an "Infringment upon the Rights of Mankind, if so be they are freed by Law and pay their full proportion of taxes."[55] These complaints hearkened to the Americans' own grievance against Great Britain of taxation without representation. The town of Sutton made more direct links between article 5 and an implicit acceptance of slavery. They not only argued, like Spencer's inhabitants, that the article was "diametrically repugnant" to "Human Rights" but also characterized it as "wear[ing] a very gross complexion of slavery." These townspeople had grown to accept a society without slavery and so now expected full rights for blacks.[56]

Historians have wondered why Massachusetts' citizens were willing to end slavery. Although the 1778 constitution did not abolish slavery, a significant number of Massachusetts' citizens had begun to embrace a more egalitarian society. This reflects a deep change in the social order. Historians weigh whether this societal choice was pragmatically or ideologically motivated.[57] For citizens to consider ending an institution so entrenched in Western culture, no doubt both ideology and pragmatism were factors. Slavery and other forms of involuntary labor had been identified as a foundation of the European social structure justified by core texts such as the Bible and Plato's *Republic*. This brief moment constitutes a point when ideology gave the people a new vocabulary to question slavery. Historian Chris Brown has also demonstrated that this new moral righteousness with respect to abolition matched the colonists' indignation over their own "enslavement." Pressing for abolition became a tool with which to prove that their emancipation from tyranny was morally justified. The beginning of the war also brought a relatively new economic reality to the white citizens of Massachusetts: recession. Even before taking up arms, Massachusetts and Britain had begun fighting an economic war. Britain blockaded Boston, and the colonists boycotted British goods. The fighting itself exacerbated the effects of these economic disruptions. The first two years of the war divided the economic fortunes of the people. Some were hurt deeply by increasing state taxes, a miserable labor market as the laborers fought in war, and rising prices on food. After the war, John Adams would attribute the abolition movement to the growing sense by "labouring white people" that slaves harmed their economic well-being. Others profited. Merchants, in particular, flourished; they could now trade freely with the world and militaries needed supplies. The economic insecurity brought on by the war made human property, which was not essential in such circumstances, seem frivolous and a burden to an open economy. Since slavery came to be regarded as both immoral and an economic burden, few saw reason to maintain it.[58]

Nonetheless, the 1780 Massachusetts constitution did not free the slaves, in large part, because some worried about what the national reaction would be to such a move. At the convention, the delegates debated the exclusion of blacks and Native Americans from full citizenship rights. Antislavery delegate John Bacon reported that "great and important" men had argued that if they did not limit rights on the basis of race, it would "greatly offend and alarm the Southern states." Like Adams, the delegates were aware of the tensions that might arise if one state favored freedom over slavery. Bacon rejected that argument as "ridiculous and absurd." He insisted that Massachusetts should press southern states to test their own mettle against the "most essential Human rights."[59]

It is at this moment that a broad spectrum of racial ideas emerged in Revolutionary-era Massachusetts. A significant number of white men spoke out to insist on equal treatment of blacks. In his speech at the Massachusetts convention, Bacon had avoided using racial titles for the slaves and had referred to them as if they were full members of Massachusetts' community. He noted that they were born in America and "were forced here by us." He contended that they were due "the same privileges with any of their fellow-subjects." Underlying Bacon's speech was the hope for a color-blind society. Despite this tremendous shift in thinking about race, most people in Massachusetts were uneasy with the idea of a society that ignored race. Many accepted the racial designations of article 5, even though they would eventually be cut. They did not feel comfortable living in a society in which black men and women stood equal with whites. Despite a growing acceptance of the idea of abolition that became evident in the 1780s, the vast majority of people from Massachusetts did not see their new society as a multiracial paradise. They hoped to scrub slavery and black people from their society.[60]

South Carolina legislators wrote a constitution in 1776 as a temporary fix to compensate for the absence of legitimate authority. The legislature, not a convention, passed this provisional constitution, just as it would an ordinary law. In fact, South Carolina avoided even calling it a constitution. Instead, the legislature proposed "some mode . . . for regulating the internal polity of this colony." The main goal of legislators was to regain control over the state governmental offices. Many South Carolinians still believed they would reunite with Britain. Historian Max Edelman notes that at the time of the Revolutionary War, South Carolina had reached a pinnacle as a representative of Britain, having widely disseminated British material and social culture within its state. The war had the unfortunate effect of disrupting the cultural networks that South Carolina had worked for decades to foster. It had to create a society that would weather this storm and, it hoped, maintain its cultural superiority. The preamble also proclaimed that the document should provide guidance for maintaining "'good order' . . . during the continuance of the present dispute between Great Britain and the colonies." Like New Hampshire's legislature, which two months earlier in January had written a constitution, the South Carolina legislature decided to create a temporary order.[61]

South Carolina's lawmakers wrote a constitution that would restore a strong sense of order in the face of the loss of the highest authority, the king. This political tyrannicide left them feeling lost. Therefore, in contrast to Massachusetts, South Carolina created two more constitutions between 1778 and 1790 to update earlier ones and maintain that strong sense of order. The 1778 South Carolina Constitution was not the product of such temporary intentions but still amounted to little more than a "series of laws," published in pamphlet form, that could be repealed or changed at any time. The new constitution was different from the 1776 version but retained many of the democratic measures from the 1776 version, such as the extension of suffrage, which prior to 1776 had not been extended since 1721. The document lacked a lofty declaration of rights that expressed the ideals of the state. This constitution stood until 1790, when South Carolina revised it again.[62]

South Carolinians did not debate slavery or race in their discussions about the new constitutions. They assumed slavery would continue and wrote the constitution to buttress the power of those who owned slaves. Very high property requirements for elected officials came close to guaranteeing that those elected would own slaves. Likewise, the writers assumed that electors and the elected would be white. No one debated the appropriateness of excluding blacks from either the vote or public office.[63]

The War Moves Away

Massachusetts

After the British had retreated from Boston in March 1776, some African Americans remained in the military, but many turned their attention toward their personal fight. Service to the nation gave these men even more confidence in their ability to fight their enslavement. Free and enslaved blacks submitted four out of the seven petitions demanding an end to slavery after the war started. Still other slaves and free blacks pressed authorities to end slavery either individually or wholesale. Slaves continued to sue their owners for freedom, despite disruptions in the legal system. In the meantime, many whites accepted these abolitionist demands because it seemed morally right and economically beneficial. Nonetheless, at bottom, Massachusetts' white population viewed slaves and free blacks of Massachusetts as outsiders, although they suppressed such ideas during the liberal era of the late 1770s.

Three free blacks—Prince Hall, Phillis Wheatley, and Lemuel Haynes— offer insight into this era of openness. These individuals took advantage of the liberal environment to change how whites perceived blacks and how blacks perceived themselves. As they took the stage and tried to explain their identities as both members of the community of Massachusetts and men and women from Africa, they began to construct the double consciousness that Massachusetts-born W. E. B. Du Bois would eloquently describe more than a hundred years later. They sought to impress whites and thereby establish their belongingness. However, having come from Africa, they also sought to define themselves as separate in their experiences. They were constructing an African American identity that would prove that they deserved the legal rights of full citizens, even if their skin was a different color.

Prince Hall began his work to create a strong and activist community in Boston at the beginning of the Revolution. Many of his undertakings reflect his desire to assert his ability and right to be a full-fledged man. Hall's early background is murky and the subject of much debate because there were more than a dozen Prince Halls in the city. Several black Prince Halls had enrolled in the military. We are uncertain that he was one of them, but it seems likely that he was. Military service fit into his ideological trajectory of seeking to prove himself as a man and establish himself as an important citizen.

We know more about what he did after he was denied admittance to the Boston St. John Masonic Lodge in 1775. He became determined to join the Masons, for they asserted that they valued "liberty, equality, and peace," and becoming a member of a lodge would accord with his aspiration to establish himself in the mainstream as a middle-class man. We do know that a growing empowerment among the black community during the war allowed him to establish a separate black unit of the Masons. He contacted the Irish military lodge stationed near Boston. This Irish Mason lodge agreed to initiate them. Like many African Americans during this period, he found an alliance in the complex nexus of participants in the Revolution; he would go to the enemy to get the legitimacy the Americans failed to offer. This lodge, African Lodge No. 1, would be formally recognized in England in 1787 and would initiate the Prince Hall Mason lodge.

He and the other Freemasons insisted through this organization that black men should be treated as the equals of white men. He petitioned the Committee of Safety to allow black men, like the other men of Massachusetts, to enlist. His request was refused at first by the committee, which was led by two Masons, because of fears of insurrection. Once George Washington gave recruiters the go-ahead to enlist free black men if they wanted, many black men joined up, including six men named Prince Hall, one of whom was quite possibly the Prince Hall who founded the black Masonic order. Likewise, his name and that of his son, Primus Hall, appear on some of the petitions to end slavery. After the war, Hall organized four hundred black men to fight against Shays' Rebellion, although the governor denied his petition to aid in that cause.[64]

Lemuel Haynes, of Grenville, Massachusetts, shows how service in the name of the American cause could translate into subtle and overt challenges to slavery. Haynes was born in Connecticut to a black father and white mother but was given to Deacon Rose, who served the Massachusetts Congregationalist church. Haynes came to the family as an indentured servant and adopted son. The ideals of the Revolution inspired Haynes, and he wrote and published a patriotic ballad. He subsequently served for twenty-four days in the militia, helping expel the British from Boston. When his service was over, he joined the Continental army. A bout of typhus ended his service only a month later.[65]

Far exceeding white expectations of what blacks were capable of, Haynes became a respected clergyman who worked for the next five years toward becoming an ordained Congregational minister. His outward demonstration of Christian character, through his gentleness, humility, and sobriety, matched his hard work, intelligence, and charisma and encouraged whites to support his ministry work, at which he excelled. His talent, careful presentation of his character, and hard work had convinced whites that his soul was "white, all white!" The designation of him as a white soul demonstrates the situational and complex construction of race in this era. It was not wholly a biological construct. He could, in their eyes, improve himself and become effectively white through exceptional behavior. He also was raised in the same milieu as the white congregants. His ministry spoke to their condition well. The exoticism of seeing a black man who appeared to be "the *whitest*" man in the room made his ministry famous. To these New Englanders, Haynes's success also reassured them that Christianity had a transformative effect. This reassurance meant more during the brief idealistic era when New Englanders sought to create a free society. It appears that he lost status along with all other African Americans in the 1780s. Nonetheless, perhaps many of the Congregational communities were still not ready for him to be their own minister; his most permanent ministerial position was on the frontier, in Vermont, where he became a beloved minister.[66]

As a minister, Haynes published several sermons, of which his most famous was *Universal Salvation*. In it, he challenged the idea that all men are universally saved. He believed in a benevolent God who exercised divine judgment of sinners, and so although the sermon does not explicitly address slavery, one might infer that on his view, serious sins, such as slavery, could bar one from salvation. Later, when his Vermont congregation would become more classically liberal, valuing individualism over communal values, he would exhort them not to abandon "benevolence," "family," "virtue," and community for ambition and pride. His Federalist point of view frustrated his congregation, and they dismissed him in 1818.[67]

In 1776, however, Haynes wrote but never published a very assertive forty-six-page antislavery tract defending the abolition of slavery on the grounds that slaves and free blacks had proven themselves worthy of inclusion in the new American society. "Every son of freedom" had to end all tyranny, he maintained, including the "oppressive and tyrannic power" of the slaveholders. His argument stands as the most thorough call to end slavery written by a black person up to that point. The surviving copy appears to be a revised draft, painstakingly written and revised with an intent to publish. Haynes probably recognized the challenges of confronting the white community with his ideas of freedom. Given that he had high ambitions to minister to blacks and whites, he might have felt in the end that it was too dangerous to publish a tract emphasizing his blackness.[68]

The text shows that he read about and listened carefully to the slavery debate. He methodically refutes the proslavery arguments. He begins the text with the Declaration of Independence. Whereas the white Revolutionary population read the Declaration of Independence primarily as a text that justified their rebellion against Britain, Haynes read it in a more modern way, as an assertion of rights. Few viewed the declaration as a document that granted rights, but African Americans seemed to hear that meaning early. Soon thereafter, a slave named Mum Bett would also cite it as a motivator for her freedom suit in 1781.[69]

Haynes's theoretical discussion is in part an exegesis on the declaration's inalienable right to liberty. He explains that God determined that human beings possessed equal rights, not necessarily equal abilities. He then seeks to prove that an "affrican has Equally as good a right to Liberty in common with Englishmen." He asserts with scientific confidence that all men "are of one species" and that citizenship has no connection to race. Perhaps his favorable environment was the source of this viewpoint. He was raised like a son in a white family, in a state that recognized wider rights than most American states, even for slaves. He identified himself as mulatto, a person that bridged black and white identities. Despite and because of his comfortable upbringing, Haynes was able to recognize that racial discrimination and oppression were un-Christian and un-Republican.[70]

Other African Americans used less formal means to press whites in Massachusetts to see African Americans in a new way. Although most of her work did not explicitly participate in the Revolutionary dialogue, leading some scholars to dismiss her work as imitative, Phillis Wheatley became known worldwide for her poetry. People throughout the Atlantic world—including those from Europe, Africa, and Latin America who depended on Atlantic trade and shared knowledge through Atlantic networks—knew of her. She may be the first literary example of Du Bois's idea of double consciousness. Wheatley had to write to a white audience but use her own black voice and experiences to express ideas. Even though Thomas Jefferson would deride her style as derivative, her distinctive and adept use of the language and literary forms surprised many citizens of the Atlantic world. Seeing a woman who had been born in Africa and educated as a slave in America write good poetry must have challenged the prejudices of many. We know that Wheatley's writing impressed many of the intellectual elite. The members of the Paris salons read Wheatley's works, and Voltaire described her work as "good English verse." Her work represented a "literary watershed" in the Atlantic world.[71]

She did express her disdain for the oppression of African Americans, although she tempered her tone. Her best-known and most direct statement against slavery comes in a letter, not a poem. The letter was published in the *Connecticut Gazette*, and so Wheatley had to navigate difficult linguistic terrain, seeking approval from whites while at the same time remaining true to her own opinions. She wrote a letter to a close acquaintance, Reverend Sansom Occom, a Mohegan Presbyterian. She expressed her gratitude for his comments against slave-owning Christians. She complimented him on his well-argued remarks and said that the human heart was naturally "impatient of oppression, and pants for deliverance." Again drawing back from confrontational speech, Wheatley told Occom that she did not desire God's vengeance against Christian slave owners but bemoaned the "strange Absurdity of their Conduct whose Words and Actions are so diametrically opposite."[72]

Her poetry expressed her themes more subtly. In her poem to the Earl of Dartmouth, she praises liberty and scorns tyranny. The poem follows the rhetoric of freedom and enslavement that the Patriot camp used, but it ends by underscoring her love of freedom, drawing on her blackness, her experience as a slave taken from her home, to authenticate its grand emotions: "I, young in life, by seeming cruel fate / Was snatch'd from Afric's fancy'd happy seat." Likewise, she uses religious imagery to warn her audience against elitist and abusive behavior and describes Christ as a "divine racial leveler," crediting him with freeing her from her ignorance in Africa.[73]

Phillis Wheatley, like Haynes, did not challenge the social order but, impelled by the rightness of the Patriot cause, tied abolition to the Revolutionary cause. Although her poetry generally did not seek radical ends, she reached out to the Revolutionary luminaries. She faced the challenge of being a young African-born woman in a white community. In gaining recognition from this community, she helped those outside it become more accepted. Many of her poems drew from events around her and the inspirational individuals who took part in them, such as the Earl of Dartmouth, who rescinded the Stamp Act, and the Reverend Sansom Occom, who had written an eloquent antislavery news article. When the war began, her focus moved to Revolutionary-period figures. In 1775, she mailed a letter and poem to George Washington: "Proceed great chief," she wrote, "with virtue on thy side." George Washington received it and responded graciously by complimenting her "great poetical Talents." He hoped that they might meet at some point, and eventually they did, in March 1776. Thomas Paine published the poem in the April issue of the *Pennsylvania Magazine*. In addition to urging Washington on, this poem extolled America's fight for "the land of freedom's heaven-defended race" and, like Haynes's service to the Patriot cause, it did not speak specifically to the interests of abolition but to freedom generally. However, in referencing the common cause of blacks and whites, the poem helped bridge the chasm between the races and thereby challenge ideas about race that white Americans held at the time. It also humanized Wheatley and proved to a broad audience that African Americans were allies more than threats to the new nation. For some members of the white audience, it legitimized the radical nature of the cause: even the lowliest (an enslaved woman) supported their efforts to be free.[74]

Black Patriots such as Wheatley, Haynes, and Hall sought to topple an institution that was clearly eroding by 1779. The General Court revisited and failed to pass legislation ending slavery twice between 1775 and 1779. In fact, the state had begun to take more interest in the citizenship status of free blacks than in the status of slavery. Even though in the debates over the state's constitution several towns had asked that the document grant suffrage to blacks and Native Americans, and even though there were observers outside Massachusetts who believed the state had abolished it, the state did not end slavery until 1783.

South Carolina

After the British withdrew from Charleston in November 1776, white South Carolinians sought to create a stable society on the plantations. The war sparked slaves to push for more freedom. However, with the withdrawal of British forces, slaves did not make radical choices to secure their freedom, such as running away permanently or revolting. White South Carolinians, as the Thomas Jeremiah example makes clear, kept a tight grip on their plantation society, although they could not always maintain control on their plantations from day to day. Many slaves used this quieter period as an opportunity to wage a subtle war on their enslavement.

Even after Britain withdrew, rumors of freedom spread across the plantations, and slaves pressed for more autonomy and less work. Slave communities had developed excellent networks through which rumors spread. As they spread, slaves interpreted these messages in ways that served their own needs. Many felt that the king wanted them to be free. Although their day-to-day existence might not have changed much, many slaves became more impertinent. When British officials reported about slavery in South Carolina, they not only mentioned the rumors of slave insurrection and murder of masters but also noted that masters had complained that their slaves stopped working. Some slaves might have just defied the authority of their owners by pausing "a moment longer than usual before obeying" or speaking with less deference. Whites noted the challenge of asking slaves to obey when the white slave owners themselves challenged the authority of the king.[75]

Nonetheless, between the two British invasions in 1776 and 1779, few owners complained of serious affronts to authority. This thirty-month period of stability gave South Carolina whites false confidence. Because the state offered a relatively stable environment in a world wracked by war, South Carolina planters flourished, and immigrants flowed in. Moreover, the Continental Congress passed legislation that opened up American trade, which meant that low-country rice now flowed directly to Europe without stops in England. The planters were preoccupied with taking advantage of these opportunities. David Ramsay, a late eighteenth-century historian, described South Carolina before the invasion as a profit-driven society. "A spirit of money-making," he stated, "has eaten up our patriotism." When the war returned to the low country in mid-1779, the question of slaves' loyalty ceased as they began to run away, take up arms for the British, and stifle crop production.[76]

The low-country planters shared a rigid slave system that refused any extension of rights to blacks or any softening of the slave regime. Therefore, with the rare exception of those with national exposure, white South Carolinians resisted the proposition that abolition extended Revolutionary-era ideology. They sought freedom for whites and regarded absolute control over their property as part of their rights as white men.

One elite South Carolinian who resisted the slavery regime, calling for a complete end to it, was John Laurens, Henry Laurens's son. Very few others followed his example. David Ramsay, who moved to South Carolina during the war from Pennsylvania, shared his antislavery ideas, but Ramsay was an outsider, which highlights the marginality of his point of view. During the war, John Laurens recommended the creation of a black regiment as the most practical way to begin emancipating slaves. Like the handful of men who supported this plan, he had experiences that were more cosmopolitan. His antislavery ideas may have developed during his extensive European education in Geneva and London. There, he engrossed himself in the growing romantic movement that would take hold of England and America in the nineteenth century. In the 1770s, upper-middle-class men began to adhere to the culture of sensibility, which argued that virtue resided in charity and fighting for the oppressed. This virtue was still regarded as masculine because men saw themselves as protectors. These ideas grew out of Enlightenment ideals of equality but were augmented by sentimentality and a romanticization of the oppressed. This ethos, as captured by Henry Mackenzie's book, *The Man of Feeling*, enveloped Laurens and his comrades. One of his friends in London, for instance, published an antislavery poem entitled "The Dying Negro." Another friend, Thomas Dey, published *Fragment of an Original Letter on the Slavery of the Negroes*, which argued for an end to slavery, not because of its effect on the slave owner but because it denied the slave, as an individual, the right to happiness.[77]

As the war progressed, John pestered his father with his ideas on emancipation. Henry was unreceptive at first and urged John to consider the poverty that would ensue if they emancipated their slaves immediately. However, the war soon provoked conflicted feelings. On the one hand, the rise in reports of slave insurrection at the beginning of the war persuaded Henry that South Carolina had to reclaim order over its slaves. On the other hand, reports probably exaggerated the number of insurrections and kindled a contradictory feeling that slavery had pressed slaves to act in such danger-ous ways. Henry Laurens did not blame himself or his compatriots but, like Thomas Jefferson, blamed England for inflicting the slave trade on the colonists. His feelings became so strong that he promised his son that he would free £20,000 worth of his own slaves. At the same time, he realized that "great powers oppose me, the laws & Customs of my Country, my own & the avarice of my Country Men."[78]

Henry Laurens's abolitionist sympathy developed as he considered John Laurens's solution to the problem: the creation of a black regiment. To John, it appeared beneficial to all involved; the black regiment would prove the loyalty of the slaves to white South Carolinians and would offer the men in the regiment a "proper Gradation between abject Slavery and perfect Liberty."[79] Although the slaves' participation in the military would mean a loss of revenue for the slave owners, their service would ensure victory.

To propose such bold policies in South Carolina, one needed a per-sonality like John Laurens's—passionate, bold, and romantic. These same characteristics led to his rapid rise to the rank of lieutenant colonel in the Continental army, made him recklessly engage in battles, and enabled him to defend with little regard of its reception a proposal not only to arm slaves but to use military service as a way to end slavery in his home state.[80] John Laurens believed that black regiments would work for the greatest good of society. He saw this mission as personally necessary for his romantic self-image "as a Soldier, as a Citizen, as a Man."[81]

At first, Henry discouraged John from pushing for a black regiment. He believed that slaves would not wish to trade their current way of life for that of a soldier. He also worried that such a scheme would cast a deep shadow over his own public image. In 1778, the elder Laurens tried to bring this matter before the Continental Congress, but he could not even find support there. This rebuke by his father convinced John to retreat temporarily from pressing the issue further.

The war changed dramatically for the Laurenses in 1779, when the Brit-ish began focusing their attention on the low country, spurring John to pro-pose his plan again. He received support from some unlikely sources. Con-cerned that without black regiments, the British, who had already captured

Savannah, would take Charleston, John announced that he would lead such a regiment and pressed his father and his commander, George Washington, to support his plan. Although Henry was no longer president of the Continental Congress, he used his influence to get John's proposal heard. In a surprising move, the other South Carolina delegate, William Henry Drayton, agreed with John's plan. Perhaps the most significant endorsement came from Brigadier General Isaac Huger, a South Carolinian who relayed how difficult it was to raise men because most wanted to stay "at home to prevent insurrections among the negroes, and to prevent the desertion of them to the enemy."[82] When the proposal was brought before Congress, Laurens's, Drayton's, and Huger's endorsements carried enough weight to pass the plan. Congress recommended that South Carolina and Georgia should raise "three thousand able bodied negroes" with white commanders and grant freedom to all slaves who served until the end of the war and returned their arms.[83] John Laurens was commissioned to execute the plan.[84]

South Carolina's leaders did not receive Congress's recommendation positively. They were angry that Congress sent them this plan instead of Continental army reinforcements. David Ramsay, who saw the plan as their last hope ("ultima spes"), stated that they "received" it "with horror" and thought that they would see "terrible consequences" from it. They were so angry that they offered to surrender to Britain in return for South Carolinian neutrality throughout the war, but the British rejected their offer.[85] John Laurens continued to press the South Carolinians to accept the plan in the face of repeated refusals and even disgust. Laurens persevered and, after being elected to the South Carolina House of Representatives, submitted a bill that included the black regiment plan; it failed resoundingly. David Ramsay counted twelve favorable votes, only 17 percent of the house.

South Carolinians would not arm their slaves, deal with the resulting free black community, or give up their property. Laurens's only supporters had extensive experience in national and international politics. Men such as the Laurenses, Drayton, and Ramsay saw the late 1770s in terms of a national war that needed to be won. They worried less about the loss of property or profits. They had heard the complaints of Northerners such as James Lovell of Massachusetts that South Carolina had "neglected themselves" because they would "not raise *black regiments*." John Laurens made another unsuccessful effort on the eve of the 1780 invasion of Charleston.[86]

Even though South Carolinians did not support arming the slaves, they were not shy about using them. As early as November 1776, the South Carolina Navy Board commissioned eight black boatmen, including Thomas Jeremiah, to support the navy. In fact, South Carolina would impress more slaves into nonmilitary service than any other state. Congress paid masters ten shillings per slave a day to help build fortifications and transport goods and services. Slaves served as spies on a couple of occasions. It was a black man, Antigua, who alerted American general William Moultrie about an attack on Charleston. At the behest of John Rutledge, the South Carolina legislature recognized Antigua's service as a spy in 1783 by freeing him, his wife, and their child. Of course, personal servants of Patriot soldiers served the militias and Continental army, sometimes giving their lives.[87]

In 1782, John Laurens was reelected to the house and pressed South Carolina to consider the proposal again, though this time with a difference. He proposed that the state should force slaves from Loyalists' confiscated estates to work on behalf of the Patriots, so that no true South Carolinian would lose his property. This proposal failed, although not without some debate. White South Carolinians were still uncomfortable with arming and emancipating slaves, even those belonging to Loyalists. Instead, they pressed the confiscated slaves into service in support roles without any promise of freedom. Slaves never received any official sanction to fight for South Carolina.[88] Henry Laurens's own dedication waned when the war destroyed much of his property and killed his radical son. It was hard for Laurens to take an ideological stand because he was economically devastated by the time the war was over. In the end, he manumitted only one slave, his personal slave, George.

Idealism still characterized the early years of the American Revolution, but the beginning of the war clarified the needs of blacks and whites in both states and crystalized the limits of freedom. African Americans in Massachusetts harnessed a military and ideological change within the white community to press for freedom. Most whites saw abolition as a way to add soldiers to their forces and to live up to their ideals of freedom, because black men joined the military and black women and men continued the intellectual argument against slavery. In contrast, South Carolina's blacks had little space in which, or time with which, to press white South Carolinians for freedom. Because white men in South Carolina depended on slave labor, they defined freedom in terms of property ownership and not rights. When Britain invaded Charleston in 1776, slaves found an opportunity, and white slave owners discovered a terrible threat to their economy and their freedom. This revulsion to abolition quashed all talk of emancipation, even among the most elite, such as Henry Laurens. When Massachusetts' national leaders became aware of South Carolina's disgust of abolition, they worked to bring the nation together by stopping their own legislature from ending slavery. Nonetheless, tensions rose as ordinary whites in Massachusetts embraced more universal ideas of freedom and as the second invasion of Charleston, in 1779, again threatened white slave property. This threat struck the Waccamaw Peninsula during spring and summer 1779.

CHAPTER THREE

The *Tyrannicide* Affair Begins, 1779–1782

The said Negroes are desirous of being returned to their former masters. . . . [I]t is agreeable that their desire be gratified . . . but the said Negroes should by no means be considered by this court as transferrable property.

—Massachusetts General Court

EVENTS IN SPRING 1779 in South Carolina would propel the Massachusetts General Court into a situation in which the complex and powerful combination of war and slavery converged. Beginning in April 1779, British privateers began trolling the shores of the Waccamaw Peninsula, hoping to create mayhem and find booty. In May of that year, one of these ships captured more than thirty slaves, who, after two months at sea, ultimately found themselves in Boston. No doubt exhausted by the perils of life on a privateer, they chose slavery over the possibility of freedom in Massachusetts. They requested that they return to the plantations of William Vereen, William Henry Lewis, Thomas Todd, and Anthony and Percival Pawley. This decision put Massachusetts officials in the position of having to confront the role of slavery in the war, in their state, and in their burgeoning nation. It appears that Massachusetts did offer freedom. It did not call the men, women, and children "slaves," and it referred to the slaves' owners as "former masters." Most important, it also declared that the black men and women were not transferable property. The Massachusetts General Court chose to reject the idea that they were property and recognized their humanity and the choices they made.

The Revolutionary War environment presented a multitude of new choices for slaves. Both the British and the Americans had turned the pre-war debates into military strategies by which to ally with the slaves. Some

Massachusetts slaves chose to bolster the ranks of the states' militias and the Continental army to become free. Still others pressed the state to end slavery altogether. The chaos of the war offered opportunities for slaves in South Carolina to gain some measure of freedom by slowing or stopping work and cutting plantation production.

Despite opportunities for greater freedom and control, these slaves learned, as would many others, that the tumult of war made them tools of other interests rather than people of free will. Forces much greater than themselves—such as British and American policies, military conflict, and individual choices by whites—would ultimately direct their fates. Little did the slaves know that they would end up in Boston Harbor. The travails of their trip from South Carolina to Boston exhausted the black men and women from Waccamaw so much that it made them miss their relatively stable life as slaves. Despite the choices they made, these slaves participated in remarkable events and witnessed how slavery changed over time and space.

The Capture

For most of the first five years of the war, the vast majority of slaves in South Carolina experienced the war as a distant and subtle force. The invasion of the privateers who swarmed ahead of the British army, disrupting the trade and production of South Carolina's plantations, probably only had an indirect effect on the slaves involved in the *Tyrannicide* affair, who were living on rice and indigo plantations throughout the Waccamaw Peninsula and had maintained their regular cycles of planting and harvesting. The primary differences between peacetime and wartime life probably were that the harvests were more profitable and the slaves more impertinent. The relative normalcy of their lives would be disrupted in April 1779, when a privateer raided the Waccamaw Peninsula and brought the war to them. The circumstances of the capture are clouded in mystery. Documents do not reveal most details of the capture. We do not know the name of the privateer or the captain who originally captured the slaves. The plantations of these owners dotted the farthest reaches of the peninsula, making it clear that this privateer did not attempt one capture but several. Most intriguing, we do not know whether the slaves themselves ran away to the ship, as thousands of slaves in the South had done, or whether the crew of the privateer forcibly captured the thirty-four men, women, and children. But luckily, much of the story is clear, and the events these ordinary slaves took part in give us extraordinary insight.

The 1779 Invasion of Charleston

To understand the story of the privateer and the Waccamaw slaves, it is vital to go back in time to the late 1778 British invasion of the low country that ended a period of relative quiet there. When the British began that assault on the low country, the coastal regions of South Carolina and Georgia, they took advantage again of the disparate power between the slaves and the elite. The British focused their efforts on conquering the city of North America's wealthiest men, Charleston. As the British forces drew near, privateers spread wider and approached the frontiers of South Carolina's rice country. The campaign had two phases and two conflicting goals. The British first hoped to invade South Carolina militarily with full support from the slave population and then work toward gaining control over the region's black and white populations. The goals of the second phase were both to reconcile with whites and to dominate them. Slaves and racial ideology became a central aspect of the British tactics. The British put blacks in positions of military and cultural power to disturb the white population. After they took over Charleston, they hoped to regain control over the black population, by reviving the traditional social order, as a way to reward white men for their loyalty. However, slaves took full advantage of this empowerment and resisted their enslavement in a multitude of ways, further frustrating the slave owners.

The British understood the low country well enough to know that the plantation owners sought complete control over the slave population. With this knowledge, the British military marched toward the low country in late 1778, accompanied by black troops. This concerted attack on Georgia and South Carolina ended a thirty-month period of relative quiet. The British captured the city of Savannah in December 1778, giving them control of the Savannah River basin. The following year began with battles on South Carolina's border. This offensive culminated in the successful British invasion of Charleston in 1780.

The British hoped to regain South Carolina's elite as subjects by being conciliatory toward them, but at the same time they sought to draw the slaves to their side. After Dunmore's famous proclamation, the British issued another, the Philipsburg Proclamation, which was delivered by Henry Clinton on June 30, 1779. Those slaves "taken in Arms," Clinton stated, would be requisitioned for "Public Service." Clinton promised refuge to "any Negroe the property of a Rebel" who escaped to the British army. Unlike Dunmore's proclamation, this proclamation did not promise freedom but instead offered the runaways work in "any occupation which he shall think proper." The proclamation did not penalize loyal slave owners; Loyalists could keep their slaves. The British used it to encourage slaves to run away, which they hoped would disrupt life in the American South. Most in the British military did not intend to free thousands of slaves, nor did many British officers believe that black freedom was a worthy cause. They merely sought to use the slave population to their advantage by undermining slave-holding societies and gaining additional labor.[1]

The Philipsburg Proclamation successfully drew at least five hundred black refugees to the British side before the invading force landed in Charleston. These men and women supplied both skilled labor, such as tailoring and nursing, as well as unskilled labor, foraging and building fortifications for the British. In October 1779, the British extended their endeavor by creating a black battalion to serve in Savannah. The battalion became "a permanent part of the city's garrison."[2] Loyalists reported that some of their slaves fought for the British. Thomas Boone claimed that one of his slaves was executed as a spy and another was drowned while serving on a war vessel. A third of the black Loyalists who ended up living in Nova Scotia at the end of the war stated that they donned the red coat, and three claimed the status of noncommissioned officer. Many slaves joined the cause when the British landed in Charleston, including Boston King, who would become a prominent black Loyalist leader. More common, however, were slave refugees, known as Black Dragoons, who did not receive official sanction from the British but followed the regular Redcoats and plundered plantations. Patriot captain James Hall reported on June 25, 1779, that "large droves of Negroes" accompanied the British. Slavery, then, became a central focus of the British strategy to dominate their former colonists.[3]

The British approached the invasion of Charleston with a complex mission: to dominate South Carolinians while also drawing them back in as loyal subjects. After they controlled Charleston, the British came face to face with the implications of their decision to use slaves strategically. Rather than continuing to take advantage of the rebellious black majority and to punish the South Carolinians for treasonous activity, they sought to reunite South

Carolina with the empire, which made a scorched-earth tactic impossible. During the two years of the campaign, the invaders tried to walk a fine line between fighting a war and regaining the loyalty of a lost colony.

Although the British wanted to bring white Charlestonians back into the fold, they still wanted to dominate them and used racial power dynamics to do so. The British allowed the Black Dragoons to patrol the roads of South Carolina. These runaways did not distinguish between loyal and rebel plantations. Loyalist William Bull's property, for instance, was attacked by a "great swarm of Negroes" who followed the Redcoats.[4] Likewise, Eliza Wilkinson lost much of her plantation's goods to a group of British soldiers and "several Armed Negroes." Wilkinson thought the presence of the black men was a final humiliation in a "day of terror." She did not differentiate further between the "Britons" and the blacks but called all the invaders names reserved for the most despicable people, often heard in reference to slaves: "inhuman monster," "mean, pitiful wretch," and "villain." She described the British as having descended into a state of savagery. Other South Carolinians described more organized groups, "ye British negro Captains and his Troop," who patrolled roads, harassed whites, and stole belongings until the British evacuated in 1783.[5] After the war ended, these dragoons may have gathered in groups of more than a hundred and settled in the swamps of the Savannah River. Although the British did not organize or formally sanction the dragoons, the disruption they created worked to British advantage by intensifying the sense that white South Carolinians had lost control.[6]

The British also expressed their domination through humiliation. They attempted to invert social relations in 1782 by holding "an Ethiopian Ball" in Charleston. To mock South Carolina's plantation society, British officers escorted female slaves, dressed in silk finery and powdered wigs to the dance. The officers' actions piqued Daniel Stevens, a soldier under Nathanael Greene who observed the ball. He disdained the audacity of the men calling "themselves Gentlemen" walking with these "pompous" women in front of their own mistresses. He also disliked the fact that "three Negro wenches" hosted the lush ball. The £80 dinner that was "wasted on" black women seemed particularly vexing to Stevens, especially because South Carolina had undergone a few years of bad crops due to the war. The ball flaunted the power, status, and wealth that the British had stolen from the South Carolinians during the war.[7]

Although the British sought to humiliate low-country slaveholders by inverting the social order with displays of black equality, they nevertheless wanted to reconcile with white Charlestonians. In an attempt to normalize life in Charleston in 1780, the British occupiers created a civilian board of police. The board, made up of loyal civilians and royal officials, sought to create order in the city by hearing legal cases, addressing security breaches, and setting policy. Under the guise of this board, the British supported the property of slave owners. For example, they stopped a Spanish ship that was illegally taking runaway slaves out of South Carolina.[8]

Policy decisions by the board reflected the challenge of juggling both domination and reconciliation. The British issued an ambiguous statement on how to handle refugee slaves. They wanted loyal subjects to believe that the royal government was not encouraging slaves to flee but was instead trying to recover those that ran away. Thus, the board announced a policy to persuade Loyalist slaves "to return voluntarily" to service. This policy simultaneously supported and betrayed both Loyalist owners and loyal slaves. Certainly, owners did not feel confident in a policy that depended on a voluntary return to the plantation. Slaves, similarly, had no desire to return to involuntary lives, voluntarily or otherwise. The runaways must have felt betrayed by the government that had seemed to offer freedom for joining its side. To make returning more palatable, the British took steps "to prevent the Negroes being punished by his Master for any Offence . . . committed by the slave in leaving his Service to join the King's Army." Slaves knew better than to trust such a promise, and owners must have resented the board for instructing them on how to discipline their slaves.[9]

The board intended its policy to serve several purposes. First, it would restore the labor of slaves to the plantations so that they would "cultivate the crop." Crops were important not only to the slave owners but also to the British, who depended on local food resources. Second, now that the British sought to restore order in Charleston, the board decided that it was unwise to continue to arm slaves. The British feared that the blacks would "contract bad Habits, and such as might be dangerous to the Community." The policy would also unburden the army of a large number of runaways who depended on British resources to live. Last, the board hoped to encourage the low-country elite to pledge their allegiance to the king because the policy supported only the return of Loyalist property.[10]

Despite the British effort to normalize South Carolinian life, its southern campaign provided slaves with the opportunity to challenge their enslavement. During the active periods of war, slaves on low-country plantations were able to shape their lives more effectively than at any other time.

When the British invaded Charleston, almost all forms of authority had disappeared. Owners had left their plantations out of concern for their own safety as Redcoats neared or to attend to wartime duties. Reportedly, there were no white owners remaining on James Island, in Charleston Harbor, when the British landed there, and the slaves had been left to fend for themselves. South Carolina merchant and slave owner Josiah Smith wrote to his friend George Appleby that although the slaves had planted a substantial crop in the spring, by December work on the plantation had ground to a halt. His overseer had joined the British, and smallpox had ravaged much of the slave population. Without a "white Person . . . left on the Plantation to see after the Negroes," work could not move forward. An overseer would have to be hired and the smallpox brought under control.[11] Likewise, Eliza Pinckney and Margaret Colleton recorded meager to nonexistent crops. The slaves, no longer being coerced, refused to work. Not only did order on the plantation decline, but the South Carolina and British governments stopped enforcing the law against slaves. William Bull noted that "the code of laws . . . could not be carried into execution."[12]

With a vacuum in authority, slaves did as they pleased within some broad limitations. William Bull observed that slaves "absent[ed] themselves often from the service of their masters."[13] Eliza Pinckney found that after the British took over Charleston slaves served as "their own masters." Her slaves "pa[id] no attention to . . . orders . . . and lived off the best produce of the plantation."[14] Henry Laurens's Mount Tacitus plantation lacked a white overseer; its only authority figure was Montezuma, a black driver. Some of the slaves left for other plantations and their families, but most stayed on the plantation without growing any "great crops" for the market.[15] Montezuma's leadership may account for the fact that only some of the slaves fled Mount Tacitus. Henry Lewis Gervais updated Henry Laurens after his imprisonment in the London Tower on the state of his plantation and credited Montezuma with maintaining his property. Gervais himself was much less lucky. The British stripped his plantation of goods and slaves, leaving nothing but the bare land.[16] More than likely, slaves who stayed worked on crops to feed themselves without any regard to the plantation's profit.

A significant number of slaves chose to run away, and those who did had a thorny path. Even the favored slaves that became the official three thousand British refugees, the black Loyalists, faced enormous challenges. Boston King provides an excellent example of how precarious life could be. King was born in Charleston around 1760. Slave traders had brought his father from Africa a few years before his birth. Boston King's owner beat and tortured him "severely" and in "an unmerciful manner." His parents lived twelve miles away, and King had permission to use his owner's horse to visit them. He had not planned to run away, but circumstances pressed him to flee. Another slave stole his horse, and fearing another severe beating, King threw himself on the mercy of the British. He quickly contracted smallpox and was put in a quarantine camp, where the British abandoned him and other slaves who had been struck by the disease, leaving them for dead. He escaped again. He was again captured and escaped, ending up in New York with other black Loyalists, where he married Violet, a refugee slave from North Carolina, but he was soon separated from her when a pilot boat he was sailing was captured again. He again rescued himself in time to leave with other black Loyalists for Nova Scotia with his family. There he became an important leader of the black Loyalists.[17]

Privateers Attack the Waccamaw

Privateers spread the invasion of Charleston to other areas of South Carolina, although these offensives lacked the sophistication of the British attack on Charleston. These privateers aimed merely to raid the low-country waterways for profit. Most of the privateers originated out of British-occupied Florida, and newspapers reported several privateer attacks. These plunderers crawled along the waterways looking for booty, and the stories of what they captured spread as far as Massachusetts, Pennsylvania, and New Jersey. These newspaper stories reflect a fraction of the attacks. The papers tended to cover situations in which the Americans successfully repelled a privateer. About nine British privateers cruised from Georgia to Virginia. They traveled up rivers and along coastlines.[18]

Privateers were ships that had received legal authorization from the state, known as letters of marque, to attack enemy ships during wartime, and both sides commissioned them. The owner of the privateer and the sailors had a right to the prize money on the capture. The letters of marque decreed the territory in which the privateer could attack enemy ships. These ships supported their nation militarily because they could disrupt or protect trade or military actions. Because the United States had a very small navy, privateers were important tools by which American states protected their trade. Despite the size of the British Navy, the English government also relied on privateers to disrupt commerce. Privateers that took part in the American

Revolution did not come only from America and Britain. Other nations such as Spain and France authorized privateers to patrol American waters.

Privateers would play an important role in the story of the *Tyrannicide* affair. A privateer took the Waccamaw slaves from their plantations. Later, privateers escorted the ships on which the slaves were held to Boston. These ships were engaging in a naval war that included not only Britain and the United States but also France and Spain before those countries officially entered the war.

In late spring and early summer 1779, the newspapers reported several attacks in South Carolina. In June 1779, two privateers traveled up the Santee River, taking at least ten slaves. In early June 1779, one raiding privateer just south of the Waccamaw Peninsula was met by a Georgetown militia infantry unit that sank the boat, killing a few of the crew. The South Carolina militia captured a St. Augustine privateer attempting to steal vessels docked at Georgetown's harbor in May 1779. Certainly, the slaves on the Waccamaw plantations heard of the havoc that the British had begun to wreak in their region along with the promises of freedom they were making.[19]

In early 1779, the slaves on the Waccamaw Peninsula were still enjoying the thirty-month peace that had favored South Carolina. We have no documentation that provides details, but these slaves' engagement with the war probably never went beyond an insolent look or a brief refusal to work. Despite the war around them, their day-to-day life was very likely the same as it had been for a couple of generations. On the rice plantations they maintained the canals and fields and during the winter and during the spring prepared the fields, plowing, breaking clods, leveling the ground, and trenching. In April, the slaves planted, and then in late April and early May, they flooded and drained the fields. Those who were not doing the skilled work of flooding the fields were planting sustenance crops on higher ground. Over the rest of the summer they tended to the subsistence crops and rice by controlling water and weeds. July and August were quieter months during which they protected and maintained the fields until harvest in September. After harvest, slaves would thresh, winnow, and hull the rice to prepare it for the mill and market.[20]

On indigo plantations, there were two harvests per year. Like on rice plantations, the slaves labored at maintenance during the winter. After preparing the land by manuring, slaves sowed the seeds in rows after the first significant rain in March or April. Fields were sown at staggered periods to keep the pace of work manageable and constant. Each field required careful inspection to ward off pests and weeds. In July, August, and, if it was warm, September, the slaves cut the plant, waiting until "the lower-most leaves gr[e]w yellow and beg[a]n to fall, and the blooms commence[d] opening."[21]

The Waccamaw Peninsula did not see any formal military action until 1781. Nonetheless, rumors of freedom must have milled through the conversations in 1776 of the slaves who would find themselves unwitting participants in the *Tyrannicide* affair—men, women, and children, such as Kittey, Smart, Fowler, Affa, and Jack from the plantations of Percival and Anthony Pawley, William Vereen, Thomas Todd, and William Henry Lewis—as word about the war and the king's offers of freedom spread throughout the slave population. However, after the South Carolinians repelled the British from a palmetto tree fort on Sullivan's Island, opportunities for freedom dwindled. The British rekindled these hopes in late 1778 when they began a campaign against the low country.

Slaves were important targets of the British privateers. Because of the Philipsburg and Dunmore proclamations, slaves did not resist capture as much as they might have otherwise. Moreover, the British privateers provided a military benefit when they compelled the captured slaves to work on the ships, which disrupted life for the Americans. More important, slaves could be sold in the West Indies for a profit. The West Indies grew accustomed to these illicit sales, creating black markets of war plunder and gaining slaves at a discount.[22]

The initial attack in 1779 provided opportunities for many slaves to run away, including the slaves of the *Tyrannicide* affair. A privateer, the name of which we do not know, traveled to the Waccamaw in May 1779. It appears that at least thirty-four slaves ended up on the vessel. Because, as noted, no definitive account of the capture exists, we are unsure whether the slaves chose to escape to the British or were captured. If many of them had run away, it would not be shocking. In the nineteenth century, David Ramsay estimated that two-thirds of South Carolina slaves ran away at one time or another during the war, although he might have exaggerated because most slave owners overestimated the impact of the war on themselves, while George Abbot Hall, a merchant in Charleston during the Revolutionary War, estimated that more than twenty thousand South Carolina slaves ran away during the war. Of course, many of these people would end up back at their plantations.[23]

With so many privateers cruising on the coasts and rivers, opportunities for the slaves on the Waccamaw to run away or to be stolen were legion. More than likely, the thirty-four slaves, who came from at least four plantations, probably reacted variously to the invasion. Some may have chosen to flee toward the ships. Privateer crews might have talked others into coming willingly with a promise of a new life. However, it is also possible that the privateer crews forcibly brought some of these men, women, and children aboard.

The owners collectively had seven properties spread around the peninsula. Among the Pawley family, Anthony and Percival owned three properties, two along the river and one in the upland that butts against the coast. The Pawley family properties were southernmost, closest to Georgetown. William Vereen and William Henry Lewis had plantations near each other, about ten miles from the North Carolina border, on the seaside. Henry Lewis owned another property very close to the North Carolina border on the riverside and Thomas Todd owned property on the upper reaches of the Waccamaw.[24]

The newspapers and geography provide clues that suggest the privateers likely captured the slaves on the seacoast as opposed to the river. All of the planters' families, except the Todds, had property along the barrier islands. Moreover, Paul Trapier, who was a friend of the Pawley family, wrote to Henry Laurens that the Pawleys had lost slaves on their "settlements on the seacoast of Wacamaw."[25] A privateer was caught attempting a similar seacoast raid nearby only a couple of weeks later. The *Pennsylvania Packet* reported that a privateer invaded south of Georgetown from the ocean side, seeking provisions. Ships could not dock on the east side of the peninsula, however. Planters used roads, not rivers, to transport their crops to Georgetown, the nearest city. Therefore, the operation to capture the slaves would have been complicated. The captain would have had to anchor the vessel and send a small crew by boat to the beach. The captures or runaways would have had to board the rowboat, return to the privateer, and then board it. The privateer would have had to stop several times because the Pawley and Vereen plantations were more than a dozen miles apart, and the rowboats could hold only a few passengers.[26]

Ship traffic was also very common on the river. Marauding privateers often made use of the river as well. The plantations had docks designed for easy access to vessels. South Carolinians seemed to believe that the rivers were the common route by which their slaves were apprehended. The *South Carolina Gazette* reported that "the enemy's privateers" were swarming the

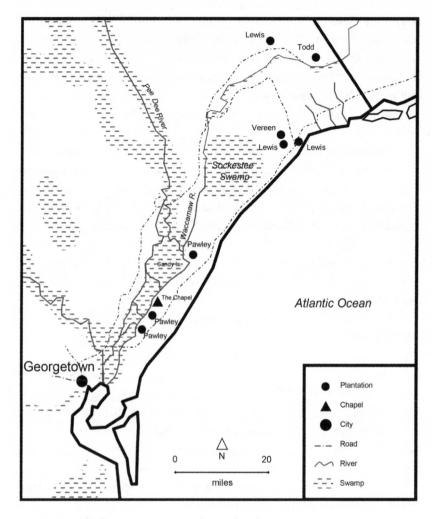

Waccamaw with plantations, 1778. Map by Emily White, 2013.

state's "inlets, and rivers to steal negroes, &c which it seems, they now do almost daily." However, some of the slaves in this particular case did not have easy access to the river. Still, escape to a vessel on the river would have demonstrated how determined at least some of the slaves were to run away.[27]

A privateer could travel only partway up the river, up to the Sockestee swamps, where the river narrowed. The Pawley family had a rice plantation near Winyah Bay, only about eight miles north of Georgetown, and up the river another ten miles, near the Socestee swamps, it had another rice plantation; therefore, a privateer could have reached its slaves. Lewis's, Todd's, and Vereen's plantations were well beyond the second Pawley plantation at the upper reaches of the river and along the seacoast, so their slaves would have had to travel to the ship if the attack had been by river.[28]

The Pawley family slaves worked right on the Waccamaw, giving them easy access to a passing vessel. The slave quarters probably overlooked the rice fields, giving them a relatively unhindered view of the river. However, more than likely, the overseer lived very close and had the same clear view. If the slaves had chosen to run away when the privateer arrived, the crew could have found fourteen men and three women, including Bob, Anthony, Jack, Affa, and Peggy, tiptoeing from their quarters to embark on this new phase of their lives. Although it is conceivable that the Pawley slaves ran away on the river, Trapier's letter suggests that they were stolen on the other side of the peninsula.[29]

For the rest of the slaves, it was much more challenging. The Todd plantation, for example, sat on the upper reaches of the Waccamaw. The river probably was too shallow for an oceangoing privateer. We could imagine that the single slave from the Todd plantation who ended up on the *Tyrannicide* traveled downriver seeking freedom. It is also possible that he had been hired out to one of the Pawley plantations or another bigger plantation down the river during the busy season and then left or was taken.

If the slaves of William Vereen and Henry Lewis ran away, they risked an overland journey to the vessel. Because Vereen and Lewis were brothers-in-law, communication between the slaves on the plantations was likely possible. These plantations, however, were not on the river. The slaves lived along the swash, the area where the waves still crashed against the beach. This sandy land grew indigo, not rice. The labor in May was not as intensive on the indigo plantations as it was in the rice fields. Perhaps this relative inactivity made it easier for the large group from the Vereen and Lewis plantations to disappear for a longer period.[30] The group of runaways included two boys named Smart and Richard, in addition to two other boys and a girl.[31] Seven men and seven women led these children. Perhaps, in this case, families within the group made the decision to leave together, even though the escape would be difficult with children. Generally, children rarely ran away. Parents typically did not want to risk the dangerous trip with their offspring, and children made the trip more dangerous because a child's fear or impulsive decisions could expose the whole group.

The Todd and Vereen slaves had three routes to the river, none easy. The slaves could have taken the most established but riskiest route south along the coast. It would have been difficult to get lost on this twenty-mile route, but the slaves would have risked being caught. It's ironic that an occasional white might have been just as afraid of encountering black slaves as the slaves were of encountering whites. In 1773, naturalist William Bertram vividly described the possibility of being confronted by a "predatory band of Negroes." He reported that rogue slaves frequently violently attacked travelers on the coastal road. In any event, when the coastal road was quiet, the runaways would then have had to move inland on a busy road to the Pawley plantation. The route safest from detection would have taken them through the Socastee swamp. This route would have been most direct, but it also would have been treacherous and very wet because the peninsula flooded during the late spring. At best, they would have traveled over soft, "black, soapy, rich earth, or stiff mud" and then would have had to ford the small rivers, deep swamps, and little streams that webbed the land. They also could have taken a short and risky trip on a well-traveled road to the Todd plantation and then boated downstream to the Pawley plantation or until they encountered the privateer.[32]

However they made their way to the river, the trip would have been treacherous. If they were running away, escaping from the ocean side of the peninsula would have been much easier for most of these slaves. If they had decided to run away either from the coast or the river, dangers lurked for all the runaways. Colonial South Carolinians had already established slave patrols to hunt down runaways. The militia was trained to aid in slave capture and organized all slave-owning residents, male and female, into nightly slave patrols, which continued during the war. The effect of the war on the patrols probably made the escape of the Waccamaw slaves both easier and more dangerous. It might have been easier to run away because the work of war and state building distracted slave owners, their overseers, and other white residents. However, escape was likely to be more difficult because the early connections between British invasion and disruption of the slave population in the late 1770s made it clear to South Carolinian plantation owners that they needed to watch carefully over their slave populations. Moreover, the Georgetown district was not yet participating in the traditional military campaigns that were so time consuming for the white population, so owners and overseers were able to stay alert for local threats. For instance, when South Carolina decided to boost its fleet, it pointed to the need to stop the privateers. Most certainly, local slave owners such as those in the Georgetown district would have taken similar kinds of precautions to stem the loss of their valuable property. Already the newspapers had reported local militias stopping raids of provisions and slaves on both the coast and rivers of South Carolina and the Georgetown district.[33]

When the slaves saw the crew of the privateer either docking on the river or rowing up to the beach, they had a choice. Did they place their hopes in the hands of these rough-edged seamen, who might bring freedom as they had heard? Or did they run away from the threatening privateers who were trying to take them from the world they knew? We do not know how much force privateers used to get slaves on their ships, but putting unwilling men, women, and children from the seacoast on the smaller rowboat probably required tying them up. It is not hard to imagine that the privateers tried to convince the slaves of a better life to entice them more easily to the ship. Trying to persuade them to leave of their own accord would perhaps have been easier and less dangerous than removing them by force, but if the privateer showed up unexpectedly, these families might have instinctively seen the intruders as dangerous rather than liberating. In addition, these Waccamaw slaves must have understood that if their break for freedom failed, they would be subject to serious punishment. The danger lay not only in a new, mysterious life ahead but also in the repercussions of a failed attempt. No matter whether they chose to go or were forced, the events of the next few months would be so challenging that they would ask to go back to the hard labor of the plantation.

By the nature of their status, slaves did not possess the ability to make important decisions in their lives. Therefore, a decision to run away could have provided an exhilarating feeling of self-determination. Still, if the slaves did decide to flee of their own accord, when they boarded the British privateer, they would have known that a new master controlled their fates. They would be freed from their plantations, but they would be taking a terrible chance.

Naval Battles in the Atlantic

The British privateer left the Waccamaw River and headed into Winyah Bay and out into the Atlantic Ocean with its new booty. Since the name of the ship and the captain are unknown, understanding the intentions of the ship's captain is difficult. Military tradition promised the captors ownership over the slaves as prizes of war, meaning that it was up to the captain to use the men, women, and children as he saw fit—to sell, hire, or use as slaves. We know that other captains had a variety of plans for captured slaves. Some slaves were promised freedom, but most were not, especially as the war went on and the number of black refugees swelled. In most cases, the slaves were required to work on the ship. If the slaves became a burden, they might be put in disease-ridden camps. Hundreds of runaways died of disease under British care. A few luckier men and women were eventually taken to England or Canada to become part of the black Loyalists. The most enterprising and deceptive captains would transport the slaves to the Caribbean islands and sell them. That the captain did not send this large group to a camp does make it distinctly possible that that was his intention.[34]

The Waccamaw slaves, however, did not get to find out their first captain's intentions; instead, they became embroiled in naval war as skirmishes erupted between privateers in the Atlantic Ocean. When two privateers engaged, the privateers tried to avoid causing too much material or human damage to the opposing ship because they profited from the goods and prisoners captured. Still, the ships would ram and shoot their cannons at each other. The ship with greater firepower, an advantageous position, or better luck would eventually prove its dominance. When the losing captain survived, he was dismissed from his ship. The new captain usually appointed new leadership from the crew to continue sailing the captured ship. Despite the efforts at civility, battles were frequent and sometimes deadly.

Sailing the Atlantic was dangerous and difficult. Starvation was a constant fear for sailors. Sailors depended on fishing and precise measurements of food and supplies, which was reflected in the importance accorded to a ship's weight. After a terrible squall, a ship could be thrown off course for days. If it took too long to arrive at their destination, the crew risked starvation. Merchant Charles Connor found himself stalled in the Caribbean for more than a week on a run between Charleston and Guadeloupe in late 1779; storms, he explained, also increased chances of starvation because turbulent seas made it nearly impossible to fish for "dolphins," the most desirable catch.[35] Fears of starvation had the further effect of making mutinies more likely. Connor spent one sleepless night awaiting a rebellion on his ship. Certainly, the thirty-four slaves from the Waccamaw that the unknown privateer had brought on board must have strained the stores and made the sailors worry. Even as the presence of the slaves offered hope of great wealth, if a storm crashed down on them, these additional black passengers could have meant the sailors' demise.[36]

Danger became real for the Waccamaw slaves very quickly. As the British privateer sailed away from South Carolina, its captain sighted the Spanish ship *Victoria*, captained by Don Francisco Ignatio Urezberoeta, and chose to attack it. Clearly intended to gain more booty and suggesting that the greedy British captain planned to sail to the West Indies and unload his cargo of thirty-four Waccamaw slaves for a hefty profit, the attack was a mistake. At the time, the Spanish were friendly to the American cause, owing to the long-standing antagonism between Spain and Britain. Freshly provisioned and ready for battle, Urezberoeta returned the attack and defeated the British privateer.[37]

Captain Urezberoeta brought the slaves and other goods aboard and released the British ship. On May 3, as the *Victoria* headed north and east in the Atlantic, it encountered two British letters of marque sailing from Liverpool to New York, and again the Waccamaw slaves came under attack. This time, Captain Urezberoeta lost to Captain Lewis Bowen of the *Byron*, who ordered the *Victoria* to sail to British-occupied New York. This time, the slaves did not change ships. The three ships sailed northwest toward New York.[38]

As they sailed on the morning of June 16, these three ships were attacked. Two Massachusetts brigs, the *Hazard* and the *Tyrannicide*, attacked the two British privateers and Spanish ship. The *Hazard* and *Tyrannicide* had received an order in May from the Board of War to sail southward and intercept ships traveling to and from New York. Specifically, the board ordered them to "Burn Sink and Destroy" enemy ships to protect trade and the "natural rights of man." Furthermore, the board instructed Captain John Foster Williams of the *Hazard* and Captain John Cathcart, then of the

U.S. Hazard and British Active, 1778. Courtesy of the Mariner's Museum, Newport News, Va.

Tyrannicide, to take all prisoners back to Massachusetts to trade them for American prisoners of war.[39]

Captain Cathcart ordered his sailors first to send out two broadside shots. Guns on privateers rarely had any long-distance range; thus, these shots were meant only to engage the enemy ships. He then had the *Tyrannicide* sail up close to one of the ships and shoot at it six or seven times. The *Tyrannicide* hit the enemy ship, and the British privateers surrendered. No one was seriously hurt on either ship, although the captains reported that several people on board one of the enemy ships were ill. The *Hazard* and *Tyrannicide* made their way to Boston Harbor with their captured ships and slaves. Still aboard the *Victoria*, the Waccamaw slaves saw land for the first time in more than a month.[40]

Waccamaw Slaves in Boston

When the Waccamaw slaves arrived in Boston, they came to a state where slavery was dying. Historians discuss theoretically the differences between slavery in different states and over time; these thirty-four men and women witnessed it. They entered a community where a combination of the white ideology of freedom and the activism of the black community had led to the dismantling of the institution. This confluence of factors was important: the white ideology of freedom meant that they would be offered the opportunity to be free, while the activism of the black community meant they would have a community to help protect their freedom as they witnessed slavery crumbling around them.

Massachusetts' Decision

On June 16, 1779, Kittey, Anthony, Richard, thirty-one other slaves, and a free black man named Old James from the Georgetown district, South Carolina, sailed into Boston aboard the *Victoria*. The Spanish captain of the *Victoria*, Don Francisco Ignatio Urezberoeta, steered the brig behind the two privateers waving Massachusetts flags. After months on the tumultuous sea, the *Victoria*, *Hazard*, and *Tyrannicide* began to pull in closer to the shore as they navigated the harbor. Looking past the other two vessels, the slaves would have seen uninhabited islands pass on either side of them. As they sailed through the bend of the harbor, the spires of Boston would have come into view ahead. On their left, they would have seen more dwellings and farms dotting the coast. As they approached Dorchester, where the land reached out into the harbor, they would have come on an island topped with a formidable fort. Captains Cathcart and Williams led the ships to the fortified island known as Castle Island. It was here that the slaves touched land again for the first time in weeks. News of this landing would reach the Massachusetts General Court, the legislative body of the state, which would have to decide how to handle the stolen property.[41]

Upon landing, Massachusetts officials on the island took stock of the captured men, women, and children. Fearing disease and unsure about the status of this human property, they sequestered the South Carolinians on the military base until Massachusetts political officials could decide their fate. They had landed nine hundred miles away from home, only to be detained by strange men.

This island was a miserable place to stop. Despite its relative closeness to Dorchester, soldiers served for weeks at a time at this dank outpost and were rarely able to go to the mainland. Colonel John Gray was stationed at Castle Island for two and a half months and documented what life for the soldiers was like there. Gray constantly complained that the commanders in Dorchester did not deploy boats to the island. He frequently needed the boats to transport the men under his command who became ill with dysentery. The filth of the place repulsed Gray; none of the barracks, he exclaimed, were "fit to live in." They had insufficient provisions for the soldiers as well. Some were "without Clothes some without Firelocks and almost all without ammunition." Even if Castle Island appeared wholly unpleasant, the Waccamaw slaves would soon discover that Boston, Massachusetts, was a very different place from whence they came.[42]

At first, this new situation, paired with the tumultuous life at sea, at least temporarily quashed any resistance by the slaves to their enslavement and perhaps even convinced them that South Carolina was the safest place to live. The stability of plantation life must have seemed preferable to battles on the seas or sleeping in the stifling heat of a strange fort or on an undulating ship. More than likely, they had spent their time at sea working for new masters, speaking British or New England dialects of English or a new language entirely, Spanish. Their time at Castle Island reminded them again that others saw them as laborers. Immediately, they were put to work for yet another set of masters.[43]

Given their wretched conditions, the slaves readily relinquished their owners' names to Massachusetts officials. When Affa, Roderick, Jack, and the others told officials who their owners were, the officials categorized the slaves by owner and by gender and age. In this accounting, most slaves aboard the ship belonged to William Vereen. The elderly free black man, Old James, whom the Massachusetts officials respected (but about whom nothing is known), informed them that the slaves were taken from the Georgetown area. Within only a couple of days, Massachusetts officials had a census of the slaves and their owners. Until the health of the slaves could be verified, the board of war wanted to keep the slaves quarantined from the mainland. They notified the officers on the island to keep "persons or any Cartel" on the island and informed the legislature of the captured slaves. In addition, the board instructed Lieutenant Paul Revere to keep the men, women, and children fed and clothed.[44]

The house created a committee to consider the matter. The committee had a few options. It could count the slaves as booty and give them to the captains as a prize for the captures. However, Massachusetts had already decided that slaves were not regular contraband and recognized them as people. Massachusetts would not return the Waccamaw slaves as contraband. In fact, in the subsequent trials when Don Francisco Ignatio Urezberoeta attempted to recover his booty from this adventure, these slaves were never mentioned as possibly being part of his losses. Later on that year, in November 1779, the *Victoria* and its goods, including casks of wine and salt, were auctioned off. Urezberoeta got half and the captains of the *Hazard* and *Tyrannicide* got the rest.[45]

Prior to the capture of the *Victoria*, Massachusetts had already freed three captured slaves. In November 1777, a twenty-five-year-old black woman named Cuba came to Boston aboard a Connecticut sloop with a revolutionary name: the *Oliver Cromwell*. The *Cromwell* had taken her from a British packet departing from Jamaica in an act of war. The officers of the *Oliver Cromwell* planned to sell Cuba back to Jamaica. The officers seemed aware that the tenuous state of slavery in Massachusetts left their prize in jeopardy, so they confined Cuba to the ship, where she was "scarcely permitted to see or speak to any Person."[46]

Despite their efforts to isolate her, Cuba learned that the new United States was a "Land of Liberty." Because she had landed in Massachusetts where slavery was eroding, she hoped to gain her freedom. She petitioned the Massachusetts Council for her freedom. She stated that she was "rejoyced" to hope that she could live in "Comfort and freedom." Whoever helped her with the petition knew that in 1776 the court had decided to free "Negroes taken on the high Seas." She received her freedom.[47]

Cuba was not the first captured slave who landed on Massachusetts' shore, and she would benefit from an event that had occurred in September 1776. A Massachusetts ship captured the *Hannibal*, a British sloop, also traveling from Jamaica. The Massachusetts sailors took two black men prisoner. When the men appeared in a list of the *Hannibal*'s cargo to be auctioned off, the maritime court condemned the sale on the grounds that slavery was repugnant and urged the House of Representatives to address their fate. The House quickly established a committee to consider the case. That same day, the committee resolved to prevent the sale. The resolution condemned slavery, although at that time Massachusetts citizens held thousands of men and women in bondage. The court drew from natural and divine law to make its claims, stating that "the selling and enslaving [of] the human species is a direct violation of the natural rights alike vested in all men by their Creator." The resolution forbade anyone to sell the two captives and declared that the state would treat them instead as prisoners of war.[48]

Cuba petitioned the legislature when she was told about this emancipation. Her act seems extraordinary for a new arrival in Boston. Obviously, she somehow tapped into the strong network of legal information that circulated among the black population. The petition not only expressed her desire to be free but also the reaction of the crew to her action. Lieutenant Chapman stated that "he did not Believe God ever made a Negro and that in Spite of all Courts and Person's whatsoever, he would have her sold as a slave." After describing the dubious beliefs and inhumane actions of the crew, the petition referred to the 1776 resolution of the two black men and requested the state to consider her a prisoner of war, not a prize. The General Court granted Cuba's request.[49]

The South Carolina slaves were different. They did not come from British territory but from an American state. In addition, the slaves requested to return to South Carolina. Massachusetts could have forced them into freedom but decided to recognize their right to choose. Moreover, this decision by the slaves probably suited the Massachusetts officials' ideas of slavery as a character flaw. Before the war, Sam Adams described freedom as something a virtuous person must "defend."[50] In the Patriot mind, the choice of these slaves to return was therefore the best decision; if they were unwilling to protect their own freedom, they did not deserve it. Within two days, the House of Representatives had decided to make an exception to the 1776 policy to free slaves captured on the high seas. They took a third option. The state relinquished its rights to the property and ordered the board of war to notify the South Carolina delegates in the Continental Congress that Massachusetts had their slave property. Noting the poor condition of the enslaved men and women, the legislature also ordered the slaves to be fed and clothed "to promote their health." Moreover, it ordered "able-bodied men" to work on fortifications and women to work as cooks and cleaners, again as a way to improve their condition. Last, it told the Board of War to keep a careful record of the expenditures made in supporting these slaves.[51]

The resolution to return these men and women to slavery reflects the shift toward antislavery thought. The General Court had been reviewing the responses to the state constitution, which included several complaints that slavery did not belong in the Commonwealth of Massachusetts. Precedent regarding contraband slaves suggested that the state preferred to free this property than to return it or profit from it. The resolution itself rejected the idea that the court was returning the slaves because they were property of the South Carolina owners. Instead, the reasoning relied on the slaves' decision. In fact, the resolution renounced the very idea of property ownership of the slaves. It stated that the "Negroes should by no means be considered by this court as transferrable property." It overtly rejected the idea that Massachusetts owned the slaves, thereby keeping the state from sullying itself by owning human property.[52]

One might also suppose that the decision of the slaves to return to South Carolina preserved national unity. If John Adams was correct that South Carolina was deeply concerned about any abolitionist talk, the direct and full emancipation of thirty-four slaves could have damaged the fragile alliances of the Continental Congress. But Adams's efforts to keep slavery from ending in Massachusetts for South Carolina's sake did not work. Despite his efforts and those of John Hancock, representatives from Congress such as Henry Laurens, a South Carolina delegate and president of the Continental Congress, believed slavery had been outlawed in Massachusetts. The General Court contacted Laurens to relay the information about the South Carolina slaves to their owners. When Henry Laurens informed the Pawleys and the other slave owners about the fugitive slaves, he noted that "slavery [was] entirely abolished" in Massachusetts. Laurens's claim was premature, but obviously slavery had so deteriorated in Massachusetts that an outsider could reasonably conclude it had crumbled. His statement that slavery had been abolished followed an explanation that Massachusetts did not see the slaves as property. This incident might have strengthened his perception that slavery had come to an end in the state. Yet South Carolina remained in Congress. Nonetheless, if Massachusetts had emancipated the slaves outright, it might have challenged the American alliance more deeply.[53]

Despite misgivings about calling the slaves property while Massachusetts officials awaited a response from the owners, the state would use their labor. The state informed Colonel Revere that the South Carolina slaves could work as servants after they were checked for disease and as long as the temporary master returned them when the state ordered. John Hancock took three of the people into his Beacon Hill home on June 24, 1779. He hired two women as servants, perhaps to take care of his new son, John. He also hired the free black man, James, who was the most desirable, because he would not be taken away. On June 30, 1779, Joshua Brackett chose a boy from among the South Carolina slaves, and about a week later, Henry Gardiner borrowed three more "boys." Nathaniel Appleton, who wrote the antislavery tract "Considerations on Slavery," requested a servant himself on June 22: "Your Petitioner being destitute of a servant and understanding that a number of Negroes lately captivated, are on Castle Island . . . [r]equest[s] the employment of one of them." He was granted one young servant of his choice, probably a woman. One other woman was hired along the way to another interested party because Revere lent out a total of ten slaves. An October roster of the slaves commissioned by the General Court would be missing four men, two boys, and four women.[54]

The slaves hired out in Boston probably could interact with each other and compare notes about how different life was there than in South Carolina, although if any of the ten young people hired out had been to Charleston, Boston would not have been too strange. Charleston and Boston were approximately the same size. The buildings might have been superficially different, but they would have seen a deeper difference in the people populating the streets. Charleston had noisy markets crowded with black female slaves selling their products and slaves with dark complexions scurrying through the streets doing their duties. The Boston streets would have had a much smaller number of black slaves. Boston's black population was about 10 percent whereas Charleston's ranged near 50 percent. As the hired slaves walked the streets, they were not far from the other borrowed slaves. The servants of Joshua Brackett and John Hancock, for instance, both lived on the south side of Beacon Hill. Conceivably, they had freedom to visit one another and share news periodically.

The remaining slaves lived in the fort and received provisions and work from Paul Revere. Directions to provision the slaves well were not carried out. John Hancock visited the slaves to observe their condition. Perhaps the women living under his care were worried about family and friends on the island and urged him to visit. He reported that the remaining men, women, and children seemed healthy (he described most as "stout"). However, he complained that "the scituation of these Negroes is pitiable with respect to Cloathing." Given the desire of Massachusetts to keep relations between South Carolina and Massachusetts strong, it wanted to make sure the slaves returned in strong condition, even if it disagreed with South Carolina about slavery.[55]

Claims on the Slaves

In South Carolina, the slave owners would be pleasantly surprised. They probably had assumed they had lost their slaves. Trapier's letter to Laurens that described the event stated that "the crew of an English privateer . . . robbed of many of their valuable negroes." They would not have expected to get their slaves back. Then they got a letter several weeks later from their Congressional representative, Henry Laurens.[56]

After the Massachusetts officials contacted Henry Laurens regarding the slaves' whereabouts, Laurens notified the governor of South Carolina, who notified the owners. Laurens explained the slaves' situation and how to recover them. Despite the fact that the Massachusetts resolution he attached to the letter clearly stated that the blacks were to return to their owners, a statement Laurens made in his letter revealed that he remained unsure of the slaves' true status. Laurens gave directions for the "recovery of so much as shall remain" and explained that the Board of War did not call the "Negroes" property. It is in this context that Laurens made the statement that slavery was "entirely abolished in Massachusetts."[57] Even though Laurens was an antislavery thinker, his reaction to Massachusetts' deteriorating institution already reveals defensiveness on the part of South Carolinians over slavery and concern that Massachusetts had determined the legal status of their slaves.

Despite doubts about the likelihood of success, Laurens arranged for help from Massachusetts to recover the slaves. He called on Massachusetts merchant John Codman to aid the South Carolinians in their effort to claim their slaves. Codman had appeared in the Continental Congress just a month earlier when he petitioned Congress to help him claim a prize from another privateer, *Our Lady of Mount Carmel*. Codman's merchant house, Codman, Codman, and Smith, would therefore represent, claim, and presumably ship the men, women, and children back to South Carolina. He assured the governor that the owners should expect "Justice and accuracy" in Massachusetts.[58]

The process proceeded smoothly. Three of the owners, Todd, Lewis, and Vereen, used Codman, Codman, and Smith as their agents to petition the House of Representatives to claim their slaves (it is unclear why Codman, Codman, and Smith did not claim all the slaves). The merchants completed the requisite paperwork and reimbursements and presumably sent the slaves back on one of their ships that traded with the French and Spanish West Indies. Although the house did not appear to trade in slaves, it did routinely sail southward to bring back food, wine, and salt.[59]

The brothers Percival and Anthony Pawley did not engage the merchant house. We do not know exactly why they didn't; we know only that Laurens may have doubted that the Pawleys had the resources to pay the merchant house. In October, their friend Paul Trapier wrote to Laurens on behalf of both Pawleys and William Henry Lewis to vouch for their credit. He assured Laurens that they were "very honest worthy men, and in general possessed of considerable property." Still, the Pawleys ended up hiring Massachusetts lawyer John Winthrop to claim their ten slaves. Winthrop had been a merchant who traded in South Carolina and so perhaps had some direct connection to the Pawley family. The House of Representatives gave Winthrop permission to "take charge of certain Negroes." The brothers, however, took four years to pick up their property. Percival Jr.'s wife, Constant, had died in September 1780, and perhaps the chaos of the war and the loss of Percival's wife made the arrangements to return so many slaves onerous, and this is why it took them so long to retrieve the slaves. The slaves stayed under the guardianship of Winthrop in Massachusetts. Under this guardianship, they enjoyed a good degree of freedom and would become deeply connected to the Boston black community. This delay, for reasons that the historical record has withheld from us, created momentous problems for the Pawleys.[60]

By the end of 1779, the fates of twenty of the *Tyrannicide* slaves were sealed. They returned to labor on their masters' property in South Carolina. We cannot know how their owners treated the slaves when they returned to the plantations. Some might have been beaten and others sold, but it's possible that they suffered no repercussions. Paul Trapier's letter to Laurens depicts the event as stealing, and the slaves publicly chose to return. The owners were likely glad to have their slaves return in an era when many did not. Most surely, the slaves were full of stories. Their families and fellow slaves must have sat around them as they told stories of capture, war, and imprisonment. Some could have described the streets of Boston and explained that slavery seemed to be evaporating in this distant city. They must have known that their masters in Massachusetts and South Carolina fought for the same side, even if slaves played very different roles in the two states.

As for their long-term fate, documents do not divulge much. Only three of the twenty appear in subsequent records. We do know that William Vereen willed Smart, Roderick, and Lucy to his sons Charles and Jeremiah in 1811, so they lived more than thirty more years as the property of Vereen and his children.[61]

Waccamaw Slaves Living in Boston

The fourteen others, however, remained in Massachusetts until their masters, Anthony and Percival Pawley, came to retrieve them. During this time, these men and women integrated with the black community of Boston. We have few specific details that illuminate their lives in Boston. We do have some clues, however, that tell us that they tried to live full lives.

These men and women sought to gain full legitimate lives that slavery denied them. Several of the Pawley slaves married, a right denied by law in South Carolina. Massachusetts recognized marriage among slaves as a full and legitimate union.[62] In a move that showed that these slaves might have begun to feel that this change was more permanent, Affa married Prince Hall, a resident of Boston. Boston was home to several black men named Prince Hall in 1790, one of whom was a major community leader. However, that Prince Hall, who founded the Black Masons, had married in 1782, so Affa probably married another Hall. Others, such as Anthony and Peggy and Robert and Hannah, found partners within the Pawley slave community.

Despite the supervision by Winthrop, Robert and Hannah escaped Boston. In a bold move that demonstrated their desire to stay, they left Boston and moved to Medford, a town outside of Boston. This escape was successful. Neither the Pawleys nor their agents ever saw these two again. Four other slaves disappeared or died as well.[63]

Some also gained a stronger sense of self-determination by changing their name, although a few took on the last name of their former masters. Marrying into the black community gave Affa a last name, Hall. When John and George were later imprisoned, the court recorded their last name as Polly. Jack took on the last name Phillips. We can surmise that they chose these names because, in the same document, Quosh, Robert, Anthony, and Peggy did not provide a last name.[64]

When they lived in the Boston area during this period, they saw first-hand how slavery changed over time and space. The households in Massachusetts were small, unlike the rice and indigo plantations of South Carolina. Work tended to be more domestic or skilled than the planting they'd done in the South. And they spent a great deal of time with whites, working beside them and directly for them at all hours of the day, whereas on the plantations there were few whites overseeing them and they spent their evenings together as a black community, separate from the white world. Nonetheless, when they did not live in their owners' homes, most blacks lived around the Beacon Hill district. In the off hours, the Boston black community took part in activities that strengthened their bonds. Through this community, the Pawley slaves would discover that politically active black leaders and black men and women who were accomplished in reading, oratory, and writing were not separate from white culture but nearly part of it.

In Medford, Robert and Hannah might have heard stories of slave life at the Medford plantation, Ten Hills Farm, and found that to be most similar to their experiences. Ten Hills Farm was a military base when they arrived but had at one time housed the only known slave quarters in New England. Although Massachusetts slave owners ordinarily owned only a handful of slaves each, Ten Hills Farm was different, an effort to reproduce a large-scale plantation in Massachusetts. On the same property where Puritan governor John Winthrop had once lived, Isaac Royall ran the six-hundred-acre plantation. The Royall family, native to Maine and Boston, gained its wealth from the sugar plantations of Antigua. His sugar plantations and hundreds of slaves provided the capital to purchase Ten Hills from the merchant John Usher.[65]

Ten Hills Farm, with its thirty to sixty slaves, operated on a totally different scale from any other Boston-area farm. On the six hundred acres, it grew corn. The stables and coach house required laborers to maintain livestock and transportation, and the large home required a significant amount of domestic labor. Royall's dozen female slaves indicated that unlike many of the neighboring slave owners, the white mistress of the household only had to manage the domestic labors. In a smaller, regular Massachusetts household, the white mistress had to stand beside the slaves making candles, sewing clothing, cooking meals, raising children, cleaning the house, and taking care of the other tasks necessary to run a well-appointed home in the eighteenth century.[66]

Ten Hills Farm operated as a synthesis of northern and southern slave life. Just as slaves in South Carolina could maintain large families with the advantage of leadership from elder generations, at least two families on Ten Hills Farm remained largely intact for three generations. Black Betty and Trace lived to see their grandchildren. The family honored these elders by naming their children after them. The Royalls, who saw themselves as benevolent owners, respected the family bonds of those directly related to these respected slaves. They held long tenures at Ten Hills Farm, surrounded by their family. Other slaves, with a tenuous or no relationship to these families, risked sale to new households. The Royalls owned a very large number of slaves for less than five years. Archaeological evidence also suggests that as with slaves on southern plantations, the Royall slaves maintained African cosmology. Archaeologist Alexandra Chan discovered several examples of "magical items."[67]

Despite the self-professed benevolence of the Royall family, clearly life was still hard on its slaves. Although a larger plantation allowed for more complex family structures in one family line, Royall did split families, selling and buying slaves frequently. At least one slave committed suicide to escape his life's stresses. Archaeological evidence shows that the Royall family gave slaves no opportunity for hunting or surplus gardening, as South Carolina's slaves had.[68]

Isaac Royall was a Loyalist. He left Boston weeks before the battle at Lexington in 1774. He took some of his slaves with him on his surreptitious escape to Halifax. He left several of his slaves, and the Revolutionary forces confiscated his house and used it as a military base. It is presumed that the slaves continued to labor on the property. When Royall died in 1781, he bequeathed most of his land to Harvard to begin a law school. The only slave mentioned explicitly was Belinda, who Royall stipulated could choose to be free or to remain his daughter's slave.[69]

The Pawley slaves might have heard about the elderly slave, Belinda, and her effort to gain restitution for her enslavement. In 1783, Belinda petitioned the General Court to draw money from her master's estate to help support her. Like some of the early petitions from the Boston black community, her petition requests monetary compensation for unpaid labor. However, it constitutes the first successful effort to gain such support. Her eloquent petition romanticized her life in Africa. It described how she lived free in Africa among "the mountains Covered with spicy forests, the valleys loaded with the richest fruits" that "yielded her the most compleat felicity." The petition then describes men "whose faces were like the moon" capturing and enslaving her "for the benefit of an Isaac Royall." The petition complained that freedom did not bring happiness, only the freedom to starve, because she was now an old woman with an ill daughter. She felt that she deserved something in return. America had "denied the employment of one morsel of that [Royall's] immense wealth" that her labor helped build. The General Court agreed and gave her a stipend of £15 per year. Perhaps because Royall was able to recover his estate, the state's treasury assumed the stipend in 1787; there is no record of any other former slave receiving a stipend.[70]

If the Waccamaw slaves had met Belinda, they might have become acquainted with the growing educated black community of the Boston area. Belinda's petition was perhaps too eloquently written to be the product of an illiterate woman—she did not write her name on the petition but marked it with an X. The petition bears the earmarks of two prominent writers from the area. Certainly, Prince Hall was highly experienced in writing petitions and clearly saw it as a tool for black empowerment. He also had espoused a romantic view of Africa that vividly emerges in this document. He had described Africa as "a populous and pleasant country" in his 1777 petition to abolish slavery, named his son Prince Africanus, and founded the African Mason Lodge. He was local, too. He lived in Medford, the same town as Belinda. The language and construction of the petition, however, resonates also with the poetry of Phillis Wheatley, speaking in a poetic fashion of an African cosmology that the two women might have shared. The petition evoked an African point of view. Belinda described "a tender Parent [who] was paying her devotions to the great Orisa who made all things." Also as in Wheatley's poetry, Belinda's African past is one of innocence. She referred to the middle passage as a "floating World" with "bows and arrows" that "were like thunder and lightening," adopting the perspective of an innocent people who did not have a concept of technologies such as ships or guns. No matter the author, the language of this petition revealed how the black community had begun to develop both a sense of activism and an understanding of how to use their African identity as a birthright.[71]

The slaves from South Carolina might have recognized this effort to express an African identity within an oppressive Western culture. South Carolinian slaves, whose interactions with whites was much less intense, possessed that African identity. These traditions emerged in their dialects, such as Gullah, and in their religious practices, family structures, and music. For Massachusetts' blacks, it emerged more deliberately and subtly within cultural forms that whites recognized. In their writings, the Massachusetts black community remembered their African past. Belinda's written petition reminds its Anglo readers that black slaves had origins very different from the English settler's and tells its black readers that they had a homeland where they or their ancestors once lived lives free of slavery. Likewise, during the Revolution, organizations such as Prince Hall's Masonic lodge defined themselves by their African past by using the word "African" in the name of the group.

In addition, in Massachusetts the Pawley slaves might have witnessed community events such as Black Election Days or funerals that evoked African traditions. For example, on Black Election Days, when the black community gathered to elect their own informal black leadership, black Bostonians paraded ostentatiously through the town, putting on what whites thought of as a gaudy show. The leaders who sought election could gain an upper hand if they could claim African royalty, although the partisanship that existed during the voting phase of the day evaporated when the leader was chosen. Rather than be loyal to a particular candidate, win or lose, the slaves in Massachusetts maintained West African traditions in which a leader gained full support from the entire community.[72]

After Massachusetts passed its constitution, some blacks demanded full voting participation. Paul Cuffe led a group of black men in Dartmouth, Massachusetts, in a crusade for the right to vote. The petition they wrote mirrored some conventions of the earlier ones; it asserted black manhood, highlighted the hypocrisy of Massachusetts' ideals, and noted the pitiful circumstances they were subsequently forced to endure. The petition first described the manliness of property ownership that was improved only "through much hard labor and industry." It then recalled the Patriots' own cries against taxation without representation and noted that black men were now in the same position, "having no vote or influence in the election of those that tax us." It also made clear that the taxes had destroyed their manhood by pressing them "to a state of beggary." Taxation without representation did not just keep them from a right; it tore down their dignity.[73] In April 1781, the black men of Dartmouth refused to pay taxes and demanded that the town decide in the next town meeting to extend explicitly "the same privileges . . . as the white people have." The black petitioners appealed to the county government as well to gain full citizenship privileges. They refused to pay their taxes for three years.[74]

The last aspect of the Boston black community that would have been very important to the Pawley slaves was their legal acumen. Due to the relative openness of the legal system to local blacks, they had legal experience and used the courts for their needs. This compares interestingly to colonial South Carolina, where owners used the metaphor of the king as a higher authority to establish legitimacy on the plantation. Each owner had his own kingdom, where his law was the highest. The law of the colony only seemed to bolster the owner's power. Slaves could not testify on behalf of their enslaved comrades, only against them. They had their own criminal justice system, wholly separate from that of whites. In contrast, the slaves in Massachusetts had access to the same legal system as whites. They were tried as criminals by the same laws (although there were a few exceptions). Increasingly throughout the eighteenth century, they began to see the court as a place that protected their interests above those of the owner.[75]

Slaves and free blacks felt free to use the courts for their own purposes. In nine cases, African Americans brought civil cases other than freedom suits before the Supreme Judicial Court. (This does not include the undocumented cases that probably came before the local justices of the peace.) They sued whites, were sued by whites, and sued other blacks. These cases demonstrate the ability of members of the black community to take on important legal personalities. They were not excluded from the law; the law recognized them as persons—a far cry from the experiences of South Carolinian blacks, free or enslaved. In 1768, a free black man with the last name Nickels (his first name is not recorded) sued three white men, Elisha and Seth Dunbar and John Kingman, in his capacity as executor of the estate of a free black woman, Phoebe Sackee. Nickels did not feel the need to bring in a white person to manage her estate. Nickels had enough confidence to sue these three white men for amounts owed to her estate. Cases such as these demonstrate a strong knowledge of the law and comfort with legal practices among the black population.[76]

In 1783, this familiarity with the legal system would benefit the South Carolina slaves, when they went before Boston's court system. They would not accept their return to South Carolina easily. They did not accept it when Pawley's agent, Samuel Hasford, came to take them back. It is not hard to imagine that as Hasford and the jailer tried to round up the Pawley slaves, blacks around them offered informal legal counsel. Although it is possible that the magistrate would have questioned the imprisonment on his own, he would have been spurred on by the Pawley slaves' questioning their capture. Because the slaves demanded full legal privileges, the magistrate might have felt compelled to reconsider Hasford's right to ask him to put the South Carolina slaves in a Massachusetts jail.

British Evacuate South Carolina, 1782

As the Pawley slaves settled in to their lives in and around Boston, learning the ways of a new system of servitude, South Carolina began to transition out of its twenty-month occupation, and South Carolinian masters became aware of the magnitude of their loss of slave property. Thousands ran away, many to the British. Peace negotiations had to settle the fates of thousands of men and women who ended up behind British lines during the war. South Carolinians had to negotiate the other losses because the Continental army and British occupiers had commandeered supplies from South Carolinian households.

After the British withdrew from South Carolina in December 1782, the Pawleys, along with other South Carolinian owners, began to reconstruct their old lives. It was not easy. The war had been hard on the Pawley family. Between 1780 and 1782, the Continental army requisitioned rice, pork, several horses, and more than a dozen slaves from Percival Pawley. The Pawleys put in a claim to the army for the requisitions, but the army paid nothing for the use of the slaves and horses. Percival received little more than £10 until 1785.[77] Anthony provided several bushels of rice and no slaves and received £46 from the army.[78] Certainly, the five battles that swept through Georgetown in 1781 created disorder on the Pawleys' plantations. They lost more than the fourteen slaves who made it to Massachusetts. Others ran away.[79]

The future of the slaves who ran away to the British depended on international diplomacy. The 1783 Treaty of Paris required the British not to carry "away any Negroes, or other property of American inhabitants." However, Guy Carleton, Henry Clinton's successor as British commander in chief, believed that any slaves who came to the army under the protection of the Philipsburg Proclamation should not be considered American property but rather "British Subjects." After strenuous objections from George Washington that the British were stealing American property, Carleton agreed to compensate owners.[80]

It was quite difficult for Carleton and his officers to turn this compromise into action. Even before the formal evacuation following the treaty agreement, the British began evacuating Charleston with the refugees. On October 3, 1782, Lieutenant General Alexander Leslie in South Carolina requested guidance on how to screen the "considerable" number of "sequestered negroes" to decide which belonged to American owners.[81]

This agreement still did not please South Carolinians, so local Loyalists and rebel leaders negotiated. Except for those slaves to whom the British overtly promised freedom or who were "particularly obnoxious on account of their attachment and services to the British Troops," they decided that the sequestered blacks would be returned to their owners. Moreover, England had to compensate the masters of those slaves taken. In accordance with the earlier Board of Police policy, owners were requested to refrain from punishing the returning slaves.[82] The only way of determining which slaves had a right to freedom was to interview the slaves themselves. The slaves had to testify to their allegiance to the British and their promises of freedom. This policy created near chaos as hundreds of blacks lined up to testify and leave with the British. In December 1782, Leslie requested provisions for "1000 men being Refugees and negroes from Charleston," but a total of more than five thousand slaves left.[83]

The fate of these thousands of blacks varied. Some went to St. Augustine, from which the English eventually fled, abandoning these black families to the Spanish. Many of those who made it to Nova Scotia followed in the footsteps of men such as David George, a South Carolinian black who became ordained, participated in a vibrant Black Loyalist community, and eventually moved to Sierra Leone.[84] Others went with their Loyalist masters to new plantations on the Caribbean islands, continuing their service. Still others served on behalf of the English as a black army. Governor Archibald Campbell of Jamaica thanked Carleton for the "three Battalions of Free blacks and people of color" sent to defend Jamaica.[85]

In the end, as many as twenty-five thousand slaves did not return to their masters' plantations in South Carolina. Some slaves achieved freedom through their loyalty to the British, but most did not. Others neither left with the British nor returned to their masters but integrated with the blossoming free black community of Charleston. Still others died in the war. Altogether, South Carolina had lost as much as a third of its slave property.[86]

It was in these circumstances that the Pawley brothers waved good-bye to Percival's son-in-law, Samuel Hasford, late in summer 1783. Hasford was a lawyer, and he expected to go to Massachusetts and bring back the fourteen slaves the Pawley brothers had left unclaimed. It is unclear how much trouble he expected to have in recovering the men and women. Although Vereen's, Todd's, and Lewis's slaves came back easily, the Pawleys had kept in touch with their Massachusetts lawyer, John Winthrop, and had to know that the slaves had begun to live very different lives in a very different place.

CHAPTER FOUR

Diverging Slave Law in the New Nation, 1783–1787

It was the opinion of the court that there was no legal ground for their detention in prison and that we consequently are obliged to liberate them.

—Chief Justice William Cushing, 1783

ALTHOUGH CHIEF JUSTICE CUSHING explained in his letter to Governor Benjamin Guerard that in stating the Waccamaw slaves could not be held legally and that he had to liberate them, he meant that they were liberated from prison, not servitude. South Carolinians undoubtedly read his statement as an affirmation that Massachusetts had emancipated their slaves from slavery, not prison. Even if they read the letter correctly, the slaves' emancipation from prison would have infuriated the South Carolinians further because it reminded them that slavery was weaker in this new nation. For his part, Cushing was explaining a basic legal right, habeas corpus, a right that was enshrined in the core document of English common law, the Magna Carta. However, habeas corpus was not a right that slaves received in most slave societies. This kernel of difference represented a distinctive concept of slaves' place in society. It would represent the beginning of an agitated relationship between the northern and the southern states over slavery.

Although Cushing drew from ancient law to substantiate his decision, it was Massachusetts that had undergone substantial changes, not South Carolina. Slavery in the new world could not grant basic rights to the enslaved. Rights denoted a position in society and provided openings for slaves to challenge their status. A strong slave system needed secure legal protections to keep enslaved human beings in their place, especially when the rights of the free expanded. Massachusetts' slave system had eroded throughout the

Revolutionary period and died by the end of the war. The legal history of slavery in the colony, a legal system that recognized that slaves had a basic civil status, gave the Revolutionary-era slaves power to change the system. This civil status could not have emerged in South Carolina's system. The legal system in South Carolina sustained the property rights of the white citizens of the state. This divergent law meant that two states with legal slavery—two states that appeared on the surface to hold an important institution in common—would drift deeply apart when the rights of citizens expanded.

The Pawley slaves began to witness a fundamental transformation in American society. Slavery was legally ending around them. Throughout the Revolutionary era, the law empowered slaves and free blacks in Massachusetts to use the courts to protect themselves, an option that slaves in South Carolina did not have. The freedom suits of the 1760s that had freed some individual slaves would evolve and accomplish ends that were more radical. Freedom suits would end slavery officially, and the *Tyrannicide* slaves would have their day in court. Little did they know that their court appearance would create tensions between South Carolina and Massachusetts in the nascent United States.

The slaves of the *Tyrannicide* affair forced the states to recognize their divergence at a key moment in 1783, the year the American Revolution ended. At that time, several other slaves were challenging Massachusetts' dedication to ending slavery in the state. They were lucky to have the legal system to help them, but the end of the Revolution created a change in the use of the courts that would give slaves' cases much more weight. However, just as quickly as Massachusetts had opened its doors to recognize more rights for blacks, it would quickly close them. South Carolina, similarly, would find itself with a great number of free blacks at the end of the war.[1] Although the elites had not sanctioned that expansion, it happened. In a similar fashion to Massachusetts, South Carolina snapped back to regain control over the slave population.

Abolition of Slavery in Massachusetts

South Carolina and Massachusetts had similar legal procedures for manumitting a slave before the 1780s. If an owner wished to free his or her slave, the owner had to register the slave with the colony. South Carolina, where the distinction between free and unfree had greater weight, kept these records systematically. Three hundred seventy-nine blacks recorded their emancipations in South Carolina by way of registration.[2] A 1703 Massachusetts law went further and required masters to post an expensive bond to their town whenever they freed a slave. Massachusetts' legislators required this bond to curb manumissions because most whites were uncomfortable with any rise in the free black population. In particular, they feared that freed blacks would become unemployed and thus become a burden to towns because freed blacks remained members of their ex-master's town. This was a major concern after the Revolution ended, because even though abolition came not from individual emancipations but through the freedom suit, the free blacks appeared to many as an economic burden. These cases pressed the court to define Massachusetts as a state that favored freedom over slavery for all its inhabitants.[3]

Individual Emancipation

Massachusetts law protected the towns. It charged that the town must "be given" security in the amount of at least £50. The law avoided specifying whether the owner or the slave was responsible for the bond to the town, but it did provide reassurance that emancipation of slaves would not lead to a huge burden on the town's pauper systems. There appeared to be real grounds for this fear. In 1742, when we have no data on the number of free blacks in Massachusetts, 7 percent of the blacks in Boston were free blacks in the almshouses. The law went further to state that those slaves freed without security were not considered free, but a charge of their former masters and a source of labor for the selectmen. This fee, which exceeded the price of a new slave, seemed to curb emancipations.[4]

Town selectmen and treasurer's records are not littered with evidence that £50 bonds were regularly issued to bolster the budgets of the overseers of the poor, but there is documentation suggesting that at least some owners complied with this law when emancipating their slaves. Samuel Upton paid security for his emancipated slave Thomas to the town of Salem. The town likely insisted because Thomas was already thirty-two and, therefore, at the decline of his productive years.[5] On August 5, 1771, Sank James offered security in the form of a claim on his real estate equal to the value of £60 for Abby Balhah to the town of Charlestown.[6] David Harris of Nantucket freed his slave, Prince, in 1773 but did not feel obliged to pay his security for Prince until 1774.[7]

Other owners tried to avoid paying the bond but nevertheless took responsibility for their ex-slaves' status. A clear example of an effort to comply with the spirit but not the letter of the law came in 1779, three quarters of a century after the law was introduced. Noted merchant Isaac Smith agreed to indenture and then manumit his slave Scipio Dalton after two years. He began the emancipation document with a clear reference to the law: "And whereas by a law of the late province now State of Massachusetts Bay made in the Second year of the Reign of Queen Ann intitled 'An Act relating to Molatto or Negro Slaves' . . ." Clearly, he was aware of the law and sought to comply with its provisions. The agreement did not result in a deposit to the overseers of the poor. Instead, Smith indemnified the town from responsibility. He and his heirs took on any costs. The document also included a contract with Dalton to pay Smith back.[8]

Despite the law, most other manumissions did not mention security at all. Less than a decade after Harris freed Prince, Nantucketers Hezekiah and Mary Starbuck freed the slaves that they had inherited from a relative without paying any consideration to the town.[9] Ebenezer Gardner freed his slave, Pompey, in 1750 in Nantucket with no mention of security.[10] In the same year, William Swain emancipated Boston and Maria and their infant child, Boston, immediately without supplying a bond to his town. He stipulated that the rest of their seven children would be freed once they reached the age of twenty-eight. Rather than insure the town, these ex-slaves remained bound to pay Swain forty shillings a year for the rest of their lives. No mention was made of the town.[11]

Most towns do not have records showing that these £50 bonds were purchased. There are no town records in Dorchester, Falmouth, New Bedford, Bolton, Rehoboth, Sudbury, or Cambridge of accepting a bond in return for an emancipated slave.[12] Some of these towns did have appreciable slave populations and very likely had a few emancipations. Cambridge had almost a hundred slaves and one of the highest percentage of free blacks in their community.[13] All of the communities had slaves. The numbers in 1765 ranged between a handful of slaves to a few dozen. Emancipations, however, are undocumented in the town records.[14]

Freedom Suits: One Road to Abolition

In Massachusetts, the court offered a route to freedom, which was hardly an option for South Carolina's slaves. These cases, of which there were only a few, speak to the tension between the desires of the owner and slave, not an agreement, as the bonds represented. Before 1780, the rise in freedom suits reflected the desire of the slaves to be free more than the desire of the state or owners to free slaves. The plaintiffs in those cases claimed they had been illegitimately enslaved. They did not challenge the rightness of slavery; these cases in fact make it clear that in Massachusetts, some blacks were legitimately slaves and others were not. In 1780, however, with the passage of the Massachusetts State Constitution, the freedom suit became a vehicle through which slaves delegitimized slavery rather than challenging their own enslavement.

The Patriot elite began to embrace the universal idea of freedom embodied in the state constitution's acknowledgment that "all men are born free and equal, and have certain natural, essential, and unalienable rights" after 1780. The leadership of Massachusetts claimed the mantle of freedom for slaves as well as for themselves after the immediacy of war with Britain evaporated. Ironically, the Loyalist exodus from Massachusetts marked an opportunity for Americans to embrace the antislavery banner more confidently. No longer was antislavery a Loyalist position. Many rebels who felt sympathy for antislavery ideas began to express them. In 1780, the Patriot leader Theodore Sedgwick, for instance, took on the case of Mum Bett, a slave who sought freedom based on Revolutionary-era principles. Although Sedgwick was a moderate antislavery advocate, refusing to aid runaway slaves and favoring indentured servitude for former slaves, he nevertheless believed that slavery was inconsistent with the ideals and constitution of the new state and argued on behalf of Bett's freedom based on the 1780 state constitution. No longer was a criticism of slavery an attack on the state; rather, it became part of its new mission.[15] After the case, Bett became something of a legend in western Massachusetts folklore.[16] As a result, information has survived about her historic legal struggle.

Mum Bett, a slave in Sheffield, Massachusetts, became determined to be free after her mistress, Hannah Ashley, swung a "heated kitchen shovel" at Mum Bett's younger sister, Lizzie. Mum Bett shielded her younger sister's body with her arm, leaving her crippled in the use of one of her arms and inspiring a deep desire for freedom. She was remembered as saying that she would be willing to die if she could just "stand one minute on God's *airth* a free woman." John Ashley, her owner, was a local judge. This exposure made her realize that the law could be appealed to for protection. When a young girl who was being abused by her father came to the Ashley house seeking refuge, Bett assured her that "she has a right to see a judge; that's lawful." It would take Bett several years to find a way out of her bondage. In 1781, after hearing a reading of the Declaration of Independence, she left her master's house and consulted lawyer Theodore Sedgwick. According to Sedgwick's daughter, she asked, "I heard that paper read yesterday that says 'all men are born equal' and that every man has a right to freedom' . . . wont the law give me my freedom?" With his help, Mum Bett sued John Ashley for her freedom.[17]

Bett and Sedgwick, joined by another Ashley slave, Brom, hoped to take advantage of the newly ratified state constitution and show that slavery was not a legal institution under the new state government. The new constitution and these freedom suits provided the new state with an opportunity to reshape its policies. For these reasons, historians have seen this case as a turning point in the legality of slavery in the state.[18] Although the Massachusetts Constitution did contain the vague statement that all men were free and equal from birth, it did not mention slavery.[19]

Sedgwick decided to use the case of Brom and Bett to test the meaning of the statement claiming that all men were born free and equal in the Massachusetts Constitution. We know about the case from a narrative by his daughter, Catharine, not from his notes. Therefore, details of Sedgwick's arguments are not available to us. Unlike the slaves in earlier successful cases, Brom and Bett had no technical point on which to rest their case; they were not promised manumission, did not have free mothers, and were not free blacks who had been abducted. But since we know that Sedgwick had planned to argue on the basis of the "free and equal" clause in the Massachusetts Constitution, then absent contrary evidence, we can assume that this is how he proceeded. The court record indicates that "according to the Usage of this Commonwealth," the slaves were not "repleviable," which must have proved convincing to the jury, who freed both Brom and Bett.[20] After gaining her freedom, Mum Bett changed her name to Elizabeth Freeman.[21]

The *Brom and Bett v. Ashley* case not only gave Brom and Bett their freedom but legal sanction to the abolition of slavery throughout Massachusetts. The decision of the lower court of Berkshire County affirmed that the intention of the constitution was to end slavery. The precedent of *Brom and Bett v. Ashley* proved significant. The new Massachusetts state government sought to achieve legitimacy as a state founded on the natural rights of liberty and equality. The government could prove its sincere attachment to those rights by granting relief to those who were most bound by oppression, enslaved men and women. The case of *Brom and Bett v. Ashley* would

Mum Bett, or Elizabeth Freeman, brought suit against her owner, John Ashley, on the basis of Revolutionary-era ideas. Courtesy of the Massachusetts Historical Society.

not have the power of a decision from the highest court, but such a case was already under way.

The lawyers for Quock Walker in 1781 argued that the new state constitution stated that all men were born free and equal, and therefore no one could be enslaved. Bett won in the inferior court of pleas at the same time that Walker's complicated case, which took two years to be decided, was weaving in and out of the Supreme Judicial Court. The cases of Bett and Walker are particularly significant because the enslaved themselves played such an important and direct role in them and thereby in abolishing slavery in their state.[22] African American enslaved men and women abolished slavery by attacking it personally, politically, and legally.

In 1783, in *Commonwealth of Massachusetts v. Jennison*, the supreme court of Massachusetts pronounced Quock Walker—and all other slaves in Massachusetts—free. In one stroke, the court transformed Massachusetts from the first colony to legalize slavery into the first state to deny all of its citizenry the right to hold human property.[23] The final decision did not emerge until after Massachusetts courts had made four others over the course of the preceding two years. In 1781, Quock Walker sued Nathaniel Jennison of Barre for assault and battery. Although Quock considered himself a free man, Jennison thought Walker his runaway slave. Jennison found him working for John and Seth Caldwell, and when he refused to accompany Jennison back to his home, Jennison and two other men beat him. After this brutal beating, Jennison imprisoned Walker in a barn.

Within a month, Quock Walker sued Jennison on a plea of trespass. The Worcester County Inferior Court of Common Pleas ordered Jennison to appear. People illegally enslaved usually used trespass to sue for freedom. Trespass, the unlawful injury of another's person or property, determined status because a master could legally injure a slave but not a free person. Therefore, if the jury found the defendant had injured the plaintiff, it *ipso facto* decided that he or she was free. From Jennison's perspective, injury was not possible because he could not injure his own property; Jennison had a right to beat or restrain Walker as he willed. Walker and his lawyers responded that Walker was a free man and had, therefore, suffered injury. Before Jennison owned him, Walker had made an agreement with James Caldwell, his original owner, to free him at the age of twenty-five. Jennison acquired Walker through marriage to one of Caldwell's daughters. After the daughter died and Walker came of age, Jennison refused to uphold

Caldwell's agreement. The jury found that Jennison had injured Walker, and, thus Walker was free.[24]

Jennison, in turn, sued the Caldwells. He sought compensation for the profits the Caldwells gained from the labor of Walker, his supposed slave, and for urging Walker to run away. He asked for £1000. In this case, he produced a bill of sale to prove his ownership. In a seemingly contradictory decision, the same court, but a new jury, found on behalf of Jennison.[25] The court found that the Caldwells had infringed on Jennison's right to his slave by employing him and for seducing Walker to run away and awarded Jennison £25 damages. Both cases were appealed.

One month before the Battle of Yorktown, the Supreme Judicial Court itself moved one step closer to accepting freedom. Walker's free status was further confirmed first when the supreme judicial court dismissed Jennison's appeal against Walker; Jennison conceded his case because he didn't appear. Walker's status was then reinforced even more in the appeal of *Jennison v. Caldwell*, at which Levi Lincoln, Caldwell's lawyer, presented an argument that took the first step toward freeing all slaves. The court indisputably freed Walker and accepted, at least partially, a moral argument against slavery itself.

Lincoln's argument supported freeing not only Walker but all slaves in Massachusetts. Lincoln provided a particularly stirring and unusual defense for this case. After establishing Walker's freedom with the facts surrounding his agreement with James Caldwell, he turned from the traditional legal argument to an ideological attack, similar to one Jonathan Sewall had attempted more than a decade earlier. He argued to the jury that slavery was contrary to natural law and God's law. His appeal to human rights did not fall on deaf ears; the presiding justice, Nathaniel Sargeant, might have been sympathetic in advance, having authored a proposal to end the slave trade in 1777.[26] The court overturned the inferior court decision and declared that the Caldwells had a right to employ Quock because he was a free man.[27]

Walker had become free, like many other individual blacks in Massachusetts, through a freedom suit. However, although the decision pronounced him free, Walker's freedom had no immediate impact on the status of other Massachusetts slaves. Although his lawyer appealed to human rights, Walker's case rested ultimately on the fact that Jennison did not own him, not on the illegality of slavery itself. By 1783, at least thirty men and women had sued their masters for freedom on similar grounds.[28] Before

Cushing became chief justice, the highest court was unsympathetic to enslaved people demanding freedom based on natural rights. The court demanded a specific point of law to decide in favor of the plaintiff. Lincoln's
dual defense incorporating natural law and Walker's faulty contract gave
the court new ideological reasoning but also, more immediately, a concrete,
legal reason to free Quock Walker.

Yet the case was not over. The state indicted Jennison on charges of
criminal assault and took him to court in May 1783. Although the case was
ostensibly no longer about Walker's freedom, the arguments on both sides
focused on his status. Attorney General Robert Treat Paine argued that
Walker was freed by agreement with the Caldwells. Jennison's lawyer, John
Sprague, offered evidence that Walker was indeed Jennison's slave and that
Jennison had a right to beat his own property.

The case was remarkable because in his charge to the jury, Chief Justice
Cushing pushed aside the traditional adherence to points of law and looked
to the state constitution of 1780. Echoing the natural rights language that
Lincoln had used in the appeal of *Caldwell*, he declared that the concept of
natural rights had obligated the framers to "declare *that all men are born free
and equal*" and that "*every subject is entitled to liberty.*"[29] In his legal instruction, he deemed slavery "as effectively abolished as it can be."[30] He ordered
the jury not "to consider whether the promises of freedom to Quaco . . .
amounted to manumission or not."[31] After issuing his oral charge, Cushing
wrote out his instructions in his legal notebook. He ended the entry with a
statement that explained the significance clearly: "The preceding Case was
the one in which by the foregoing Charge, Slavery in Massachusetts was
forever abolished."[32]

Despite this seemingly unequivocal assertion, slavery did not end in-
stantaneously in Massachusetts. Newspapers carried no stories about the
case. The abolition of slavery by judicial decree did not result in a mass
emancipation. Instead, it made it impossible for masters to maintain their
ownership when a case was brought to court. As legal historian A. Leon
Higginbotham puts it, the court had "signaled that it would no longer protect the legality of slavery."[33] Nevertheless, the burden lay on the enslaved
men and women to assert their freedom to their masters. Dramatic evidence that slaves did gain their freedom is found in the 1790 census, which
reported no enslaved inhabitants.[34]

Outside of Justice Cushing's courtroom, *Jennison*'s significance was not
widely appreciated. Cushing's brother Charles served as clerk of the court

Chief Justice William Cushing's notebook established that the jury had to recognize Quock Walker's freedom because slavery had ended in Massachusetts. Courtesy of the Massachusetts Historical Society.

at the time and probably attended the trial. Fifteen years later, he did not remember that *Jennison* ended slavery. In 1798, he stated that the "question [of slavery] has never come directly before our Supreme court." He remembered the *Jennison* case but declared that nothing distinguished "this case from any other common assault & Battery."[35] Obviously, he had no knowledge of his brother's case notes that stated clearly the significance of the case. By classifying *Jennison* as a common assault and battery case, he showed his generation's ignorance of slave law. No one could rate any assault and battery or trespass case that an enslaved person brought to court as common. Such cases not only addressed the matter of injury to another but the freedom of an enslaved person, but time had passed and, without court reports, he could not have expected the decision to be expressed anywhere but in his brother's notes. In effect, the case had little influence outside of the courtroom and, thus, was purely legal. The court would not defend masters' rights to slave property.

The case's near obscurity for decades, even in legal circles, raised questions even about its legal importance. Precedent was a weaker concept in early America than it is today because precedent depended on strong court reporting, and at the time, there was no systematic reporting of cases, especially of decisions. The use of cases depended on local memory. Therefore, when Cushing's brother forgot the case, its importance was put into question. Moreover, this case was not cited in any official court report until 1867, even though some cases during this period may have benefited from it as a precedent.[36] In *Winchendon v. Hatfield* (1808), an action regarding residency of an ex-slave, Chief Justice Parsons referred to *Jennison* without naming it. He cited, without a name, "the first action involving the right of the master, which came before the Supreme Judicial Court." But his description does not refer to *Walker v. Jennison* or even *Jennison v. Caldwell* (the original cases that established only Walker's freedom) because, he continues, "after the establishment of the Constitution, the judges declared, that, by virtue of the first article of the declaration of rights, slavery in this state was no more."[37] He never named *Commonwealth v. Jennison*, but the description of the case clearly points to it. The fuzzy judicial memory of the case remained fifteen years later—a clear symptom of the absence of a court report. Historians have wondered why, if *Jennison* had ended slavery, justices did not cite the case as establishing slavery's end in *Greenwood v. Curtis, Parsons v. Trask et al.*, and *Betty et al. v. Horton*.[38] However, they unfairly expect the justices to recall a case that had outgrown their legal memory.

The importance of the case is attested, in part, by the fact that it was forgotten. The case held so much power that freedom suits ended. Slaves stopped having to sue their owners for freedom. Between 1765 and 1783, suits were brought almost annually. After *Jennison*, no more slaves sued their masters. Mum Bett's case was pulled from appeal because of the *Jennison* case. Beginning in the late 1780s, Massachusetts worked to forget that it was a multiracial state with a history of slavery. It seems that the *Jennison* case was part of that forgetting.[39] The fact that no new freedom suits were brought for more than twenty years bears witness to the degree to which slaveholders understood that the courts would not uphold their property rights in owning slaves. There was no need to enter a case with a slave who sued; the slave owner knew that he would lose. Freedom suits would occasionally reemerge in the early nineteenth century as Boston became more radical and tested the boundaries of the law regularly with fugitive and traveling slaves. In the 1790 census, for instance, no one claimed to own slaves, but the census takers might have pressured masters to stretch the truth;

anecdotal evidence shows that a scattering of people did live as slaves in the 1790s.[40]

Justice Horace Gray resuscitated the case in 1867. After slavery had ended throughout the nation, Gray used the case in an overview of slavery's legal history in Massachusetts in *Jackson v. Phillips et al.* (1867). He pointed to *Caldwell v. Jennison* and *Commonwealth v. Jennison* as ending slavery in the state. If early nineteenth-century justices could not accurately cite the case, how could a late nineteenth-century justice? Actually, the resurrection of *Jennison* in 1867 makes perfect sense because a year earlier, George Moore, an abolitionist and key scholar of slavery in Massachusetts, had analyzed the case at length. A historian, Moore had gone through the archives and done research that justices and lawyers did not do. Moore's *Notes on the History of Slavery in Massachusetts* became the de facto court report eighty years later and served to remind the legal community of the case's existence and importance.

In issuing his instructions to the jury in *Jennison v. Caldwell*, Cushing thrust himself in an antislavery storm that was brewing in Massachusetts during the Revolutionary period. Popular opinion, etched by economic, political, and ideological changes, and the initiative of enslaved blacks such as Walker compelled Cushing to formalize a trend that had already begun. In many ways, the Massachusetts legislature forced Cushing to come to terms with his ambiguous sentiments because the legislature refused to make a decision over slavery. Because Adams and others were worried about offending South Carolina, they consistently rejected antislavery legislation, and in *Commonwealth v. Jennison*, Cushing opened the gates to the subsequent outlawing of slavery in the state. Slavery was ending, collapsing in on itself, and because of Cushing's decision, enslaved people no longer had to use the court to attain freedom. Although masters within Massachusetts understood that in the wake of *Commonwealth v. Jennison* they would be wasting their money if they hired a lawyer to enforce slavery and so did not bother, those from out of state did not face the same obstacle.[41]

Recapturing the Pawley Slaves

The Pawley slaves would bring this out-of-state distinction to the court. After four years, during which their slaves were loosely supervised by John Winthrop, the Pawleys finally decided to recover their property in August

1783, only four months after the terminus of the Walker cases. Those four years of relative freedom would suddenly be questioned. Despite rumors on the streets that all slaves were free with a court decree to match, the fugitive Pawley men and women were not.

John Winthrop recognized that on May 5, 1783, the winds had changed in Boston and advised the Pawleys that they would have to take strong measures if they wanted to get their slaves back. He urged them to ask the governor of South Carolina to write a letter requesting recovery of the slaves. Perhaps the Pawleys did not have the connections or the money or just ignored Winthrop's advice. Instead, they just provisioned a ship and issued a power of attorney to Samuel Hasford.[42] At the same time, they petitioned the Continental army to recover some of what it had requisitioned.

In Massachusetts, Hasford probably met with Winthrop immediately on arriving in Boston to locate the slaves. In a petition to Massachusetts' governor, Hasford was not clear about the number of slaves the Pawleys owned in Massachusetts. He asked for "*about* ten said Negroes." Hasford's decision to underline "about" might have indicated that he felt there were more. Indeed, the Pawleys claimed fourteen in 1779. Perhaps Winthrop had already told him that a few had gone missing (or had died). Nonetheless, he began by getting a magistrate, Joseph Henderson, to apprehend the Pawley slaves; this was not easy. The magistrate informed Hasford that "by the Constitution of this Commonwealth that magistrates are *unimpowered* to apprehend and secure this kind of property." The reasons why he denied Hasford's request were probably multiple. First, Massachusetts citizens increasingly believed that slavery had ended. Indeed, in a later petition, Hasford himself describes how people assured him that all slaves had been freed. Second, along with a stronger consciousness that Massachusetts was a new free society, habeas corpus rights were meaningful. Third, Henderson probably resented having this stranger order him to perform this difficult task and was reluctant to oblige. Fourth, the slaves, perhaps having connections in the well-informed black community, could have resisted their enslavement and questioned the legality of their apprehension.[43]

This refusal frustrated Hasford, and in counsel with Winthrop, he decided to petition Governor Hancock to imprison the slaves. In the petition, he expressed his frustration with a system that inadequately protected slave ownership. In addition to complaining about the fact that the magistrates were "unimpowered" to apprehend the slaves, Hasford raised questions about the promises of "intire liberty of every inhabitant." Despite these promises, he would refuse to allow these particular slaves an opportunity to become free. He even refused the slaves the option to purchase their freedom.[44]

Hasford expressed dismay at the serious divergence in laws between Massachusetts and South Carolina. He believed that these liberal acts would undermine the laws of other states in the United States. He concluded by requesting that the state assist him in recovering the slaves. The idea that a magistrate could not imprison a slave at will dumbfounded Hasford. He sneered at the "liberal" laws of Massachusetts. He could not believe that it should "respect . . . the intire Liberty of every Inhabitant belonging to it." Now that the states had ratified the Articles of Confederation, the subversion of one state's property in favor of another's law seemed wrong. The differences between the two states pressed him to accuse Massachusetts of "subvert[ing] the Barriers of a society which forms part of the great federal Government of the United States." He began to see the implications of nationhood, divergent laws, and slavery immediately.[45]

Governor John Hancock took the petition. Hancock probably empathized with Hasford's dilemma. He was familiar with this case. He had hired some of these slaves, including the free black man, who probably still resided in the area. In addition, he had owned slaves himself, and about seven years earlier, he aborted an effort to end slavery based on Felix Holbrook's petition because he was concerned about the impact that such a decision might have on national unity. Now he had to face this exact situation again. The war was over; the country was trying to unify; Massachusetts had ended slavery; and South Carolina had fugitive slaves within the Massachusetts borders.

Hancock must have worked assertively to address the situation in a way that respected both positions. He sent the case to the highest court, requesting that it decide immediately. The day after Hasford's petition on August 26, the court ordered a writ of habeas corpus for Jack Phillips. This document makes it clear that some Pawley slaves had already been detained, and it ordered the Supreme Judicial Court to investigate the cause of his imprisonment. The Supreme Judicial Court clerk, Charles Cushing, delivered writs of habeas corpus for Jack Phillips, Affa Hall, George Polly, John Polly, Quosh, Robert, Anthony, and Peggy. They found only eight of the fourteen men and women the Pawleys originally claimed.[46]

The matter was sent first to the justice of the peace, Thomas Crafts, who examined the case for imprisonment on August 29, 1783. By the time Crafts reviewed the case, Hasford had found one more of the Pawley slaves, Kate. Crafts examined the history of the case, including the resolves from the Board of War and General Court to return the slaves. He judged that there was sufficient cause to warrant imprisonment. Crafts wrote to the jailer to whom he had committed them based on their own confessions that they ran away from the Pawleys. The slaves, however, refused to return, requiring the jail to keep them "untill the vessel should be ready to receive them." Crafts's decision was consonant with colonial practice but was questionable in the new state. The Pawley slaves clearly now felt at home (and probably free) in Massachusetts and would not acquiesce to reenslavement.[47]

Although they saw only a glimpse of it, the Pawley slaves must have realized that they did not want to spend very long in the miserable Boston jail. Before the nineteenth century, the jail was custodial, not punitive. It served as a holding cell for pretrial suspects and debtors. Despite the fact that these custodial imprisonments were not intended to be punitive, inmates frequently spent months or even more than a year in the dismal and unhealthy prison. During the Revolutionary era, the Patriot leadership used the jail to hold prisoners of war and Loyalists who seemed particularly dangerous to the Patriot cause. Conceivably, the jail held some of these Loyalists along with the eight slaves.

In August, the cells were stiflingly hot. The August heat would have turned the cells, which had little more than a small barred window for circulation, into furnaces. Publisher Peter Edes spent several months in the jail as a prisoner of the British during August and described the heat as "suffocating."[48] Loud swearing by the inmates shocked Edes; he was also fed irregularly, and the dearth of time he was allowed outside only added to the discomfort of the hot conditions inside. Archibald Campbell, a captured British officer who would become governor of Jamaica, described the Concord jail as "a dungeon of twelve or thirteen feet square, whose sides are black with the grease and litter of successive criminals." This litter included "a necessary-house," which seemed not "to have been emptied" for the tenure of several prisoners.[49]

These problems arose from the purpose of the jail. In the eighteenth century, no one checked on the keeper's care of the inmates, because the intention of the jail was not to rehabilitate but to hold. Therefore, the necessities for a humane imprisonment—heat, regular, nutritious food, fresh air, fresh water, light sources at night, and sanitation—were provided at the whim of the keeper, who gained nothing by treating his inmates well.

Deaths in prison were not uncommon, especially when a suspect was held for years in unhealthy conditions.[50]

The current inmates were lucky. They had to withstand only one or two days in the jail because someone did not agree with Crafts's decision. The postwar legal community took the validity of habeas corpus claims very seriously, but this interest was new. In the past, runaway slaves had been kept in jail, a use that maintained its custodial role. In ads about runaways, a few owners asked for their slaves to be held there until they could retrieve them, but with a shift in culture, some wanted to test the legality of such an imprisonment and appealed the case. The clerk of the Supreme Judicial Court, Charles Cushing, issued an order for the jail keeper to bring the Pawley slaves to the state's highest court the next day.[51]

On September 1, 1779, the court heard the case on the "cause of detainment." Hasford represented the Pawleys, and the slaves had an unnamed representative. The court brought Jack Philips before the court first. After a "full hearing" on the validity of the mittimus, or the court order to imprison the slaves, the court decided that the mittimus was "insufficient" to hold him. After his hearing, the court heard the cases of six others, arriving at the same judgment. The magistrate released the eight men and women immediately, and they were freed from prison.[52]

Curiously, two of the slaves for whom writs of habeas corpus had been issued, Kate and George, were not brought before the superior court because they had disappeared. The fact that they were a male and female pair makes one wonder whether they had married. Perhaps the jailer could not find them to imprison them. This lapse must have added to Hasford's impression that the Massachusetts system was broken. By the end of this trial, Hasford believed that the slaves had been emancipated, and he left Massachusetts frustrated.[53]

South Carolina Responds

This fundamental difference between the two states' laws led to the Pawley slaves' release from prison and "troubled and vexed" Hasford, who went back to South Carolina empty-handed. Hasford felt as though Massachusetts had denied the Pawleys' property rights. South Carolina would have to respond to the Pawleys' perception that Massachusetts had taken their property.[54] Winthrop advised him on what he should do next. First, he should advise the Pawleys to avoid interacting with the liberal commonwealth legal system and to instead appeal to South Carolina's governor.

Winthrop wrote to the Pawleys on September 3, 1783, about Hasford's "Trouble & Vexation," observing that he feared the repercussions as much as the South Carolinians did. He fully supported the South Carolinians' desire to recover their slaves because he was "afraid that all the Negroes from the Southern States will pour in upon us like a Torrent." A clear precedent establishing the legitimacy of out-of-state ownership was important to keep the newly slave-free Massachusetts from becoming a fugitive slave refuge.[55]

In the letter, he noted the mistakes the Pawleys had made in this matter. First, he stated that they should have just had the slaves sent back with Vereen's and Lewis's slaves. If this had been done, he would have helped them without charge, but now they owed him for four years of supervision and expenses. In addition, in 1779, the "negroes appeared quite willing to return." He criticized the Pawleys' decision to send their son-in-law, a lawyer, alone. They needed the power of the South Carolina government to regain their slaves. "I did not mean a simple Power of Attorney," he wrote them. He urged the governor to write Hancock.[56]

The Pawleys contacted Governor Benjamin Guerard immediately. At the beginning of the next month, October 1, the governor's Privy Council reviewed the case and advised the governor to write to Massachusetts immediately. It too saw this incident as "a gross violation of the sovereignty and independence of this State" and asked for Massachusetts to pay for the return of the slaves.[57]

Guerard summarized the council's position in a letter to Governor John Hancock and expressed his anger over the situation, accusing Massachusetts of causing "mischief" that was "contrary to the Articles of Confederation." Article IV of the Articles of Confederation stated that "the free inhabitants of each of these states . . . shall be entitled to all privileges and immunities of free citizens in the several states." It specifically protected slaves by restricting "the removal of property." In addition, this same article guaranteed that fugitives from justice would be returned to their home state. Guerard explained that he saw this act "as gross Attack on the Dignity, Independence & Sovereignty of this State" and claimed that Massachusetts was trying to "assume domination or Controul over" South Carolina. He promised that he would report Massachusetts' action to the Continental Congress. He then demanded restitution from Massachusetts and delivery of the Pawley slaves.[58]

Guerard revealed an awareness of regional difference from Massachusetts that had been growing since the time of the Seven Years War; the South was forming its own regional identity. During that war, for example, the South Carolina Council urged Governor James Glen to "secure His Majesty's Southern Colonies."[59] This early sense of division had little to do with slavery directly. Instead, southerners described differences in character and economy. Although the southern economy depended more on slavery than their northern counterparts did, both had slaves and did not see this as a core difference. They described New Englanders as "Frugal and Industrious." A South Carolina writer lamented in 1743 that his province could not "Encrease in People" because the North's ability to attract white settlers would advance "the Wealth and Strength" of the northern colony.[60]

Guerard laced his letter with expressions of regional chauvinism. He encapsulated his distrust of Massachusetts in one word: "Puritanism." By calling attention to the history of Massachusetts as a former Puritan colony, Guerard accused Hancock and the Massachusetts government of imposing their moral worldview on others. He tried to turn the tables by posing their action as reprehensible because it broke their contract under the Articles of Confederation. He expressed his disdain by stating that he was disappointed that "Gentlemen of my Profession" would commit such acts, adding an extended quote in Latin. The quote likened the Massachusetts officials to snakes and fools, revealing the extent to which Guerard felt betrayed.[61]

This betrayal pushed Guerard to threaten Massachusetts with disunion. He feared domination by the North. Just as Virginian Jeremy Boucher had worried that if they entered the war southerners risked the subjugation of "these Southern colonies to those of the North," Guerard too feared that Massachusetts' action was an attempt to "assume domination or Controul over" its southern cousins. In a final flourish, he described the "injustice, imprudence impolicy & cruelty of the case" that was "repugnant to the spirit of the federal union."[62]

Massachusetts wanted America to unify peaceably. In his response, Hancock tried to repair relations while maintaining Massachusetts' sovereignty. Hancock asked Justice Cushing to explain the court decision to the South Carolinians. Hancock forwarded Cushing's letter to Governor Guerard. Despite the insults hurled at Massachusetts, Cushing refrained from responding in kind, although he could not help responding to Guerard's jab about Puritans. He informed Guerard that he could not conceive of how his decision had "any Connection with, or relation to *puritanism*."[63]

Cushing noted his decision had a limited range that supported the Pawleys' right to the eight men and women. Although the original resolution by the house of representatives in 1779 might have suggested that Massachusetts did not recognize the *Tyrannicide* slaves as property, Guerard's letter did not refer to that point at all. Cushing decided that "no law of the State" warranted committing the slaves to prison in "such Case."[64] He did not believe that releasing them from prison meant the same as liberating them from service: "If a man has a right to the Service of another who deserts his service, undoubtedly he has a right to take him up and carry him home to Service again, which has always been the case here without any action from the Magistrate."[65] He clarified by stating that the court did not decide whether a person had a right to the service "of those Negroes." He was not denying the South Carolinians the service of their slaves. He could not understand how the liberation of these particular slaves could infringe on the Articles of Confederation or on the sovereignty of South Carolina. Although he did not say so explicitly, one can read between the lines: South Carolina's demand that Massachusetts imprison the slaves would be a violation of Massachusetts law and could be taken as an encroachment by South Carolina on the sovereignty of Massachusetts.

At the same time, Cushing made clear that these slaves had basic rights. When he explained that the court decided on "writs of habeas Corpus," he described them as "the right of every person." Because he lived in an environment that respected slaves' legal rights, specifically that of habeas corpus, he assumed that other states would as well.[66]

This conflict arose from the origins of slave law in Massachusetts. The Puritan, idealistic vision of slave law established an unusual place for slaves in Massachusetts citizenry. This tense moment singularly wrapped up the development of slavery law over the course of more than a century. The differences between Revolutionary-era South Carolina and Massachusetts were not limited to the political economy and historical development. Even though the colonies shared common English legal roots, slaves in Massachusetts and South Carolina had fundamentally different legal statuses. In the case of the Pawley slaves, the fact of this difference becomes abundantly clear during this late August interaction. In Massachusetts, especially after the Revolution, the law could recognize habeas corpus rights of slaves, while South Carolinians could not conceive of it. To scholars, South Carolina's refusal to grant slaves the right to habeas corpus is unsurprising because historians have largely taken for granted that the antebellum-era law of slavery was *the* law of slavery in the United States. Scholars who study the legal status of slaves in America have generally focused on how the common law in the antebellum South treated slaves as persons or property. However, these legal studies do not expose the longer and more complex history of slaves' legal status in America in the colonial and Revolutionary period, when slavery was accepted over the entire continent.

The inclusion of slaves in the concept of citizenry requires a brief reflection on the meaning of citizenship. A citizen, most simply, is a person who has legal standing. Some historians define slavery as social death, but Massachusetts shows that slaves as citizens could have a recognized space within the polity. Massachusetts' legal system offered its slaves a social life in which they had legal rights. Citizenship is also "a state of active political participation and community involvement." In this sense, too, black male and unmarried female slaves in Massachusetts had legal rights, albeit legal rights that were circumscribed. Specifically, they could sue and own property. They had limited political rights because they could petition, and they were afforded social status for slaves by the recognition of their marriages and their ability to become free members of society. As America entered the Revolutionary era, slaves took advantage of these rights. Then Cushing pressed these rights further, first by decreeing slavery dead in the state in the *Jennison* case and second by providing habeas corpus rights to slaves.[67]

Massachusetts' refusal to hold the Pawley slaves in prison departed from both standard practice and law in South Carolina and in Massachusetts. Justice Cushing was changing the law and expanding rights for slaves. South Carolina had a separate body of law for slaves that did not include habeas corpus rights. The South Carolina slave code required jails to hold suspected fugitive slaves until their masters could recover them. What Cushing had conveniently ignored was that this was also customary in Massachusetts. Boston ads about runaways reveal that it was ordinary practice for a slave to be imprisoned until he or she could be recovered. In November 1777, James McCobb advertised two servants, Cato and James, who had run away. He instructed their captors to "secure them in any Gaol." This was not an isolated case. In 1777, at least four other owners requested their slaves to be imprisoned.[68]

In his choice of words, Justice Cushing danced around the terms "property" and "slaves." Instead, he talked about an owner's "right to the service of another." He described the Pawley laborers as servants, a labor relationship rather than one of ownership, thereby implying that the slave and master had a contract of service.[69] Cushing tried to avoid saying anything that could establish a precedent that suggested Massachusetts still regarded slaves as property. Although he did not use the words "property" or "slave," he did call the slaves "Negroes," which often connoted enslavement; this strategy may have appeased his conscience without essentially challenging South Carolina's right to its servants. Despite all his rhetorical ambivalence, Cushing accepted that they were slaves, the property of the South Carolinians.

The decision also established that masters retained ownership over their slaves perpetually. The captives lived in Massachusetts for four years before the Pawley brothers made an earnest effort to recover these men and women. Cushing upheld the Pawleys' rights as owners and did not stipulate that the owners had to recover the slaves by any particular deadline. He could have followed the lead of Pennsylvania, which placed a time limit on slave owners, allowing them only six months to retrieve their slaves from the state, after which time the state would emancipate them.[70] In contrast, Cushing was not willing to impinge even slightly on the property rights of Americans from other states.

Although Cushing acknowledged that these men and women remained the servants of the South Carolinians, he refused to use Massachusetts resources to round them up. He required the South Carolinians to pay for the transportation and capture costs. Moreover, he did not even respond to the request for restitution or delivery by South Carolina. The Pawleys still did not have their slaves.

Cushing ignored South Carolina's claim that Massachusetts had undermined the Articles of Confederation, but it was no oversight. He did not read the situation as Guerard had. This was not a case of freeing someone's fugitive slaves. He was releasing people bound to serve their owners in South Carolina from prison. He argued that he did not free them and that they were not fugitives. They were captives of war. He believed that in evoking Article IV, which guaranteed "all privileges and immunities of free citizens in the several states," he was supporting the property rights of the Pawleys.[71] The right of ownership extended to a citizen's "right to acquire and possess property of every kind."[72] Cushing surely felt he was upholding the "privileges and immunities" of the Pawleys by acknowledging their rights to the men and women they claimed. The Articles of Confederation specifically stated that property rights were sacred. Free inhabitants were "subject to the same duties, impositions and restrictions as the inhabitants thereof respectively, *provided that such restrictions shall not extend so far as to prevent the removal of property imported into any state"* (italics added). The framers probably crafted this passage with slave property in mind, and it could easily have been interpreted as suggesting that a state could not remove property from a traveling slave owner, especially as states ended and restricted slavery. However, that the second provision of Article IV related to this case is far less certain. A person could only be extradited if he or she had committed a felony-level crime; South Carolina was not requesting that these men, women, and children be returned to their state so that they could stand trial but so that they could be returned to their owners. Involvement of the justice system was unnecessary. The owners could recover their slaves without the help of Massachusetts jails. South Carolina never approached the Continental Congress about this issue, but it would reemerge at the Constitutional Convention less than five years later.[73]

Restoring Society

South Carolina

After the war, South Carolina worked to restore its society. The war proved to be a traumatic awakening for whites in South Carolina. South Carolinians battled one another in a vicious manner. The personal, class, and geographical resentment of the prewar era resurged in bloody conflicts throughout the state. Likewise, slavery became an Achilles heel for the white elite. The British humiliated them by inverting their society and putting blacks in positions of power. They took advantage of the fears of slaves by luring them to the British side and using them to occupy Charleston. Slaves themselves reminded their owners that power over their human property was tenuous. The thousands of slaves who resisted, ran away, and threatened rebellion challenged the stability of their owners' wealth, social structure, and family's well-being. Their way of life depended on complete control of their slaves and the free black population.

By the end of the war, the black community in Charleston had changed dramatically. Before the war, the free black population in Charleston was tiny. Only twenty-five black men and women officially lived in the city as free people. During the war, thousands of blacks left their plantations, and many never returned. Some remained in South Carolina as free blacks. By 1790, the twenty-five free blacks in Charleston had exploded to more than nine hundred. Half the state's free black population lived in the main city, a fact that could not have escaped white Charlestonians' attention. This new population must have reminded the white elite in South Carolina of the legacy of the war.[74]

The manumission records at the secretary of state's office reflect this apprehension on the part of the South Carolinian elite. These records chart the state's brief flirtation with emancipation. In 1786, the number of manumissions spiked to an unprecedented high of twenty-one, but the numbers are misleading.[75] The rise was merely apparent, as a number of these cases represented blacks who were already free but whose freedom had not been documented. Jesse Donaldson, for instance, was born free, sold back into slavery, and freed again in 1780. This deed was not registered until 1786.[76] Rene Chastain died in 1784 and freed his personal servant, Betty, but the executors did not register the deed until 1786.[77] These slaves probably felt a need to make their manumissions official because by 1786 restrictive laws against free blacks were again being enforced. Deeds provided protection from reenslavement.

South Carolina government officials attempted to control both the free and enslaved black population in other ways, too. The records of the House of Representatives show that several slaves were executed for crimes in 1786. There had been a lull in slave executions, but South Carolina was bent on reinstating its authority over free and enslaved blacks after years of revolutionary foment. Beginning in 1783, the governor urged the House of Representatives to increase enforcement in Charleston because of disorderly slaves in the city, particularly on the Sabbath. In 1787, the House of Representatives sought quicker return of runaway slaves, ordered the state gazette to print legal notices pertaining to runaway slaves, and tried to prevent illegal trading with slaves. Even when the legislature ended the slave trade in the 1780s, it did it to quell fears over a growing and uncontrollable slave population.[78]

The House of Representatives actively reinstated all laws to ensure legitimate authority. A committee resolved in 1784 that "the great Change in our political Establishment from a Monarchial to a Republican Form of Government" and the "Multiplicity and Confusion of the Laws" demanded a new, "concise and Accurate System of Laws, founded in Principles of Liberty and Humanity."[79] Although in the 1770s the legislature had paid Hugh Rutledge £1000 for completing a compilation of the laws of the state, the volume was never printed. In 1790, John Fauchereaud Grimke finally gave South Carolina's legislature what it had been requesting for decades: *The Public*

Laws of South Carolina—an update of Rutledge's laborious work. The most important piece of legislation in this volume was the slave code, which was more or less the same slave code that had existed before the war.[80]

The Public Laws of South Carolina was the first step in codifying statute law in South Carolina, and at its center stood recognition of the colonial slave code. This publication offered an authorized version of the law of the land; it reminded the citizens of its points and instructed them in the proper way to control their slaves in the new republic. However, Grimke was also aware that these laws were potentially problematic because they were all colonial laws written under the king. This awareness led Grimke to qualify the *Public Laws*, describing them merely as a guideline for the young state. He wrote in his preface that the laws were subject to change; it remained to be seen what kind of fit the colonial laws would make in the new, independent republic.

By printing these laws, Grimke was attempting to transform the king's law into the law of the state of South Carolina. Although most South Carolinians had a strong understanding of the laws of colonial South Carolina because even though no compilation had ever been made available, key laws of the colonial government had been published piecemeal, Grimke's book was an official restatement of those laws. Although theoretically South Carolinians, both black and white, were no longer subjects of a king, their allegiance now belonging to a state and the slave owner no longer symbolically a proxy for the king, practically the law as practiced and written in the colonial era remained verbatim and gave the slave owner tremendous power over slaves. Even before Grimke's publication, the legislature had reinstated the Negro Act, not for a specified period, as it had earlier done, but perpetually. Grimke placed colonial law in a new context, declaring it the law of a republican state, but this new context made little difference. South Carolinians, white and black, had endured a restoration, not a revolution.[81] Slave owners still held the same authority.

The only substantial law the colonial government wrote was its slave code because slavery, especially black slavery, did not have a clear counterpart in English law. The peculiar institution had undergone many challenges since the beginning of the war. From within, the British threatened to emancipate the slaves. The enslaved men and women themselves challenged their enslavement by running away, conspiring, joining the British, and securing manumission at unprecedented rates. From without, many northern states began to abolish slavery, and some northerners began to push for general emancipation. Grimke and the South Carolina state government chose to define and affirm its slave law.

An attempt was made to reestablish prewar slavery in other ways. Although many South Carolinians had grown averse to the slave trade during the war, this distaste disappeared afterward. By 1784, Josiah Collins had brought in his first shipment of eighty slaves after outfitting and repairing his ships in Boston. Between 1783 and 1785, slave traders imported eleven thousand people into the Carolinas and Georgia. The state would choose to suspend the trade in 1787, but that would be due to the poor economy and concerns that the trade was eating up credit and cheapening the value of the slave. There was no moral indictment in the suspension.[82]

For slaves within Charleston, the Magazine Street Workhouse was a reminder that the white elites had regained control over the slave population. Slave patrols took loitering slaves to the workhouse. In this dismal building, a room designed to muffle screams became a torture chamber for delinquent slaves. Slave owners who needed help breaking their slaves could send them to the workhouse to be whipped for a fee.[83]

Surprisingly, two of the three freedom suits in South Carolina's history came to court during this period, and both cases ended successfully for the slaves. In *The Guardian of Sally (a negro) v. Beaty* (1792), the superior court decided that one slave could save up money and purchase another slave and free her. The master tried to nullify the manumission, but the court, which would ordinarily deny a slave any right to property and allow the master the right to choose whether to free his slave, felt moved by this "singular and extraordinary act of benevolence" and freed Sally.[84] *Snow v. Cullum* (1797) revolved around a badly worded will. The court decided to read the will for the intention of the deceased rather than by its wording and freed the slave in question. The courts in both cases carefully framed these in terms of honoring white property ownership and making a "singular" exception to the norms of the state.[85]

Despite the harsh slave regime, the free black population had grown. Within Charleston, the black community began to build its society. Because life was tenuous, the African American community built cultural lives more than political ones. Free blacks built businesses, churches, and mutual aid organizations. Just as blacks in Boston and Philadelphia began institution building in their communities, a group of black men in Charleston came together to form the Brown Fellowship Society in 1790. Symbolically, they chose to describe themselves as brown. The designation might ironically indicate both a resistance to whites' racial hierarchies and the creation of a hierarchy of skin color within Charleston's black community. This philanthropic and mutual aid society of "free brown men" raised money to protect women and orphans "in the hour of distresses, sickness and death." The preamble of its mission statement defended a communal social vision wherein people must "contribute all they can" to promote "the welfare and happiness of one another."[86]

Massachusetts

Although Massachusetts had made a radical decision to end slavery in 1783, the end of the war brought a more conservative bent. As political tensions exploded in western Massachusetts and the state coped with debt, the idealistic era eroded. Although slavery did not seem as though it fit in the new Commonwealth of Massachusetts, neither did black people. Massachusetts did not wish to encourage slaves to flee to Massachusetts or become a welfare state for former slaves.

We do not know how slaves transitioned to freedom or even how they realized that they were free. More than likely, the laboring culture changed: servants continued to work but now masters paid them. For youngsters, new relationships had to be established, and indenture became a common way to establish a child in productive labor. The archives record few indentures for former slaves, although there probably were many more. A boy, Dick Morey, indentured himself to David Stoddard Greenough in 1786. Greenough filled out a preprinted indenture form for the deal. Interestingly, Morey had been a slave just a year earlier, having been purchased by Greenough. Greenough promised to train Morey, who was seen as an apprentice, to be a farmer until 1801.[87]

Isaac Smith, who had shipped the *Tyrannicide* slaves back to South Carolina, indentured a young man, Scipio Dalton, around the same time, in December 1779. He, drawing from the regulations about freeing slaves, took financial responsibility for Dalton. The indenture ended in 1781 when Dalton took control of his own life. It appears he did well. He joined the First Baptist Church of Boston in 1804.[88]

Indentures could provide a way to bring out-of-state slaves into the state. One master was John Ashley, Elizabeth Freeman's prior owner. Ashley purchased a female slave named Mary in 1789 from New York. When he brought her into the state, he indentured her for ten years. The other master was Theodore Sedgwick, Freeman's lawyer, who, in 1802, contracted a young man named Cato Freeman, perhaps Freeman's son. The boy's indenture ended in 1808 after he had learned the trade of being a "good servant."[89]

The tenuous line between slavery and freedom sparked the black community to protect itself from reenslavement. The legislature did begin to show awareness that the growing free population might need protection from nefarious slave dealers. In 1784, it resolved to fine anyone who kidnapped a free person of color from Massachusetts. This resolution was not enforced. For example, in 1787, Sedgwick became involved with a dispute over a black man who asserted that "armed men seized" him. After three free men were sold in the West Indies, Prince Hall organized another black petition. In addition, a group of Quakers and ministers sent in two other petitions to require a stronger statute to protect freed blacks from being sold. The legislature tried to increase protections for the slaves, but legislation could not stop free people from being reenslaved. Finally, in 1788, the legislature completed the last important step to ending slavery in Massachusetts by ending the slave trade. The law levied fines for importing, transporting, buying, or selling inhabitants of Africa as slaves. Despite this law, merchants would continue the trade until 1801.[90]

Most laws, however, limited the strength of the new free black community. In the late 1780s, the legislature reinstated its anti-interracial marriage law, attempting to ensure what they saw as the racial integrity of the state. In 1787, the General Court tried to block the perceived immigration of runaway slaves and other out-of-state free blacks by outlawing any "African or Negro" from staying in Massachusetts for more than two months unless he or she were "a citizen of the state."[91] This law assumed that all black residents were citizens and no longer slaves. Nonetheless, Massachusetts had established that blacks' citizenship status was distinct from that of whites. In 1800, the state enforced the law against loiterers by listing their names in the newspaper and instructing them to leave the state within two months or suffer penalties.[92] In the 1790s, the state also strengthened its poor laws. In the same vein, towns complained to the General Court and the judicial courts about supporting free blacks. In 1808, the town of Winchendon sued the town of Hatfield for support of Eden London, a free black. In this case, the justices established that the town of the slave's former master became his or her town of settlement. Winchendon, therefore, had to support its member, Eden London.[93]

Despite the fact that black suffrage was not illegal, there is little evidence that black men could vote everywhere in the state. Towns could deny suffrage, albeit illegally, as the petition brought by Paul Cuffe and other blacks of Dartmouth to the House of Representatives in February 1780 and then again a year later for the right to vote makes clear. Constitutional rights did not always translate into local practice. In 1795, Jeremy Belknap, a prominent white Bostonian who surveyed the demise of slavery in Massachusetts, reported the popular misreading of the Constitution. Many white citizens of Massachusetts he met believed that black people could not vote or be elected. Despite this misconception, Belknap recalled seeing black people vote and at least one mulatto man elected as clerk of a rural town.[94]

Abolition notwithstanding, white Massachusetts citizens viewed their state as a white society, leading the activist black community to protect itself. This desire to whiten the state led it to expunge and marginalize unwanted blacks through legal actions such as warning out. Warning out was a way to let an individual know that he or she was not welcome in the community, but substantively, it was an act by a town to disclaim responsibility for the individual, a way to deny that person any right to the services of the city such as the poor house. This governmental action indicated a cultural hostility toward the black community. In fact, town leadership would occasionally round up "all the Indians, mulattoes & Negros that does not belong." Towns warned blacks out more than any other population; historians have argued that this was an effort to whiten their society. Clearly, the black community felt this hostility.[95]

To halt kidnapping, Prince Hall organized the black community to help it gain further respect. In the midst of Shays' Rebellion, he wrote to Governor Bowdoin, offering seven hundred black soldiers to fight the rebellious farmers. Hall rekindled the memory of the important role that black men played in the American Revolution a decade earlier. He reminded Bowdoin of their common cause as a "fraternity" and the endeavor of the state to build a new government built on law and encourage "peaceable subjects to the civil powers." These memories did not hold importance for most whites. Bowdoin did not respond to the offer; although he probably did not need the forces, he also could not afford to upset the lower-class white farmers even more than he already had in militarily suppressing the uprising by inviting black regiments to fight against them.[96]

Blacks had begun to identify Africa as their ancestral land during the American Revolution. Now, Hall and others became so frustrated with the daily discrimination that they sought to leave America, just as the black Loyalists had begun doing. He sent another petition to the General Court, signed by seventy-three black Masons, that complained that black people had received little respite from "disagreeable and disadvantageous circumstances." Even emancipation had not made them feel comfortable in Massachusetts. Hall requested funds to return to Africa. A feeling of identification with Africa meshed with a sense of alienation from Massachusetts' society and encouraged a yearning to return to their homeland. The petition suggests that in Massachusetts, they felt unequal and excluded from the political process. Africa seemed to be a place that promised a life with "equals." As whites in Massachusetts could build a new constitutional state, Hall and other blacks hoped that in Africa they too could build "a civil society, united by a political constitution" and "mutual intercourse and profitable commerce." Through their labor, they could pay back Massachusetts funds that Massachusetts society would not allow them to earn themselves. This proposal promised Hall a full sense of male citizenship, the ability to lead, earn wealth, create a government, and feel equal. Witnessing the momentous change and world-transforming events that whites had participated in for the past two decades had inspired Hall and the other Masons to fulfill their own destinies.[97]

The Fate of the Pawley Slaves

The Pawley slaves became free, as did all slaves in Massachusetts during the 1780s. However, the Pawley slaves' freedom was tentative and illegal. In 1783, legal slavery ended for Massachusetts slaves by the Cushing court. This legal emancipation began decades earlier when slaves pressed for their own legal freedom from their masters and the colonial courts. Therefore, by 1783, Massachusetts blacks had a long tradition of pressing for their freedom with a modicum of success. This experience was vastly different from the potential for legal emancipation of the enslaved men and women from South Carolina. The enslaved people in South Carolina fought their enslavement using both legal and illegal means, and because South Carolinian society thwarted almost all legal means, South Carolina slaves had to escape enslavement in illegal and arguably treasonous ways. As a hybrid of Massachusetts and South Carolina, the *Tyrannicide* slaves found themselves legally enslaved but de facto emancipated.

When the war ended, both states had to use that experience and changes that emerged to create new states. Massachusetts tried to create a free state. At the same time, it began a process to forget that it was a state with slavery at all, first by limiting the black population. They had little desire to encroach on the systems in other states that owned slaves but did want to protect their own sovereignty. South Carolina, traumatized by the war, clamped down on slaves and free blacks. They regained control inside their borders. They then tried to protect their interests in the national arena. The Pawley slaves were lost, but they could not lose any more.

Despite the lack of a legal time limit, the practical time limit to recover the Pawley slaves must have passed. Without imprisonment, the ten men and women were probably impossible to find, detain, and ship. Because the general population thought that slavery had ended, most people thought these blacks were free. Hasford believed that the Massachusetts court had freed the South Carolinian slaves. After what seems to have been a feeble attempt to recapture them physically, Hasford still pushed for diplomatic means to recover the Pawleys' property. The Pawleys wrote again to the governor. Massachusetts did not respond. South Carolina threatened to go to the Continental Congress but never did so. The black community must have shielded the South Carolina slaves long enough to, in effect, free them.

In 1790, the Massachusetts census, which listed no slaves, listed three of the Waccamaw slaves by name as heads of household. In the census, Jack Phillips lived with a white man and woman. George "Pauley" lived with three other blacks, including a man named Cato Small. Jack "Pauley" lived in Boston with seven other blacks. Affa was married to a Prince Hall. Boston's census lists two Prince Halls; conceivably, she was in one of those households. Their appearance is remarkable because most of the 761 Bostonian blacks remained anonymous in the census as servants within white households or were listed generically as "Negroes and Mulattoes."[98]

Fugitive Slaves in the Constitutional Convention

No person held to service or labour in one state, under the laws
thereof, escaping into another, shall, in consequence of any law or
regulation therein, be discharged from such service or labour, but
shall be delivered up on claim of the party to whom such service or
labour may be due.

—Article 4, Section 2, Clause 3, U.S. Constitution

THE LANGUAGE OF THE fugitive slave clause in the U.S. Constitution resonates with the language of Chief Justice Cushing in his letter to Governor Benjamin Guerard: "If a man has a right to the service of another" then "he has a right to take him up and carry him home." The fugitive slave clause refers to the slaves as laborers, not property. It did not emancipate the "laborer" from his or her service, nor did it directly require the refugee state to return the slave. Cushing likewise was not emancipating the *Tyrannicide* slaves or requiring Massachusetts to return the slaves to their owners in South Carolina, but he was more direct than the fugitive slave clause, clearly stating that the owner was responsible for recovery. Although the events of the *Tyrannicide* affair might not have directly influenced the writing of this essential clause of the U.S. Constitution, the clause reflects the insights and the experiences of Massachusetts and South Carolina with slavery before 1787.

The debates over slavery reflect the contingent possibility that the U.S. Constitution might not have passed at all. These slavery debates were usually not about slavery itself but about the balance of power. Slavery became a centerpiece because it was a point of uneven power in the nation. Scholars have attributed the relative silence of Massachusetts on the issue of slavery in the Constitutional Convention to Massachusetts' conservative, commer-

147

cially centered politics and desire for union. Although one cannot discount Massachusetts' conservatism and aspirations for a unified United States, the story of the Pawley slaves sheds a new light on why Massachusetts was so apparently acquiescent. Likewise, the *Tyrannicide* affair helps us understand South Carolina's strong stand on the preservation of the institution of slavery; its reaction did not stem just from ideology or growing self-interest but from its experience with Massachusetts in the early 1780s. Although it cannot be proven conclusively that the *Tyrannicide* affair directly influenced delegates to the convention, it appears likely. The case reverberated for more than a year in the highest levels of South Carolina's government. Several influential leaders in Massachusetts' state government reviewed the case, including Elbridge Gerry, who would attend the Constitutional Convention. In the constitutional debates, the delegates used language and ideas similar to those that emerged during the *Tyrannicide* affair. That Massachusetts and South Carolina had exchanged heated messages over slavery must have influenced the roles they would play at the convention. They would agree that in most matters, slavery was an issue for the states, but some concerns required national attention, the slave trade and fugitive slaves especially. With respect to these two issues, both states showed a level of maturity regarding the slavery provisions in the Constitution that the rest of the states' delegates had not yet achieved. In turn, South Carolina and Massachusetts would become the major players in the formulation of slavery provision in the fugitive slave clause.

In the late 1770s, every state in the new United States was a slave state. As time passed, individual states, including Massachusetts, Virginia, and Pennsylvania, debated the issue of slavery in their state constitutions but did not outlaw the institution outright. Although slavery was still legal in every state, concerns over its status did emerge in the writing of the Articles of Confederation in 1777. By the time of the Constitutional Convention, the northern states had begun to end slavery, creating a much tenser situation. In the 1780s, several state legislatures and judiciaries began to emancipate their slaves. Powerful states such as Pennsylvania and Massachusetts were now at least partially free states. In addition, the disturbances of the 1780s caused South Carolina whites to be more defensive about and protective of their slave property. This changed context created a division that James Madison understood would be difficult to bridge. In the midst of the debates over representation, he announced that "the states were divided into different interests not by their difference of size . . . but principally from the effects of their having or not having slaves."[1]

The 1780s were crucial in establishing priorities for the delegates. Economic turmoil at home pushed Massachusetts to search for stability. It sought protection for its economic and commercial interests in the Constitutional Convention. This included the slave trade. Massachusetts had earned a reputation as a refugee state for escaped slaves, a development Massachusetts officials hoped to quash. In addition, Shays' Rebellion in western Massachusetts was an incentive to create a stronger central government, establish stability, and develop wiser tax policies. However, Shays' Rebellion might have influenced southerners even more than the delegates from Massachusetts. The rebellion brought home to the southerners the need for a strong government to fight insurrections, whether they were instigated by a few backcountry farmers or a collection of armed slaves.

The protection of slavery was crucial to the South Carolinian delegates who represented their state during the hot summer of 1787. They arrived in Philadelphia determined to defend their institution. The events of the American Revolution and the 1780s instilled a strong belief that slavery was under attack internally by the slaves and externally by the new free states. As we have already seen, the American Revolution sparked real fears among South Carolinians that their world could be turned upside down. Although South Carolina disagreed with England on several constitutional matters, the catalyst for fighting the war was England's use of the slave population to capitalize on these fears by supporting resistant behavior on the part of the slaves and by putting them in symbolic positions of equal or superior power. Slaves took advantage of the many opportunities that the war and the British offered them.[2]

Throughout the 1780s, South Carolina worked to recapture control over its slave population. Before the war even ended and Britain withdrew, South Carolinians fought to keep fugitive slaves from leaving South Carolina with the English. After Britain left, the government cracked down on the free black population. Many long-time free blacks felt a need to register their freedom with the state to protect themselves. The lull in executions of slaves during the war ended. The state suspended the slave trade, but that was a protective measure. South Carolinians began to fear that returning to a black majority would be dangerous and thought that increasing the balance of the white population might create more stability. Most slave owners also believed that newly imported slaves were more restive. In addition, the postwar economy was lagging. Quelling the influx of slave property would improve the price of domestic slaves and encourage capital investments in land and crops.

Massachusetts had undergone a transformation concerning slavery during the Revolutionary era. It began the era as a slave state and ended it as a free one. The liberal slave law along with a libertarian ideology and an activist black community forced citizens to grapple with the economic and moral benefits and challenges of slavery. The black population took a multifaceted approach. Some individual slaves took advantage of the milieu to sue their owners for their personal freedom. These men and women tested Massachusetts leaders' ability to uphold the rule of law for all its inhabitants. Others, organized by men such as Prince Hall, petitioned the state government to abolish slavery. These petitions pressed officials to grapple with the hypocrisy of American slavery and the immorality of keeping humans from fulfilling their basic roles as men and women. Some African Americans fought on behalf of the Patriots, proving their dedication to the American cause with their lives. A few African American men and women, such as Phillis Wheatley and Lemuel Haynes, excelled at their vocations and proved that African Americans were not inherently inferior.

This active African American community touched the conscience of the Massachusetts Revolutionary-era generation, who also found abolition served their needs in the economy and war. Within the state, whites debated the rightness of slavery. Increasingly, they argued on behalf of ending the institution. Poor white men needed work that was bound up in slave labor, the war effort needed dependable soldiers, and the raison d'être of the war seemed incongruent with the reality of slavery. However, at the same time, the Patriot leadership, headed by John Adams, felt pressure from South Carolina. Adams worried that the stability of the new union would be threatened if Massachusetts made a strong statement against slavery. The leadership attempted to quell the abolitionist movement in the state, but the swell had grown strong enough that even though the General Court held off abolition in the state, the slaves found another route to make Massachusetts a free state: the judiciary.

When the case of the *Tyrannicide* slaves began in 1779, it reverberated through many levels of Massachusetts society. Because of a growing distaste for slavery, Massachusetts hesitantly returned the slaves to South Carolina. Because the Pawley brothers failed to reclaim their slaves in Boston for four years, those men and women ended up swimming in libertarian and activist currents and acted as if they were not enslaved. They married, disappeared, and resisted legally and, presumably, physically when the Pawleys tried to recover them. When the Pawley family attempted to imprison the remaining men and women, it encountered the confluence of interstate diplomacy and emancipatory thought. Many ordinary Massachusetts residents responded as if the slaves deserved civil rights, and some contended that they were free. This emancipatory attitude reached South Carolina and fanned its fears about unifying with states in which slavery was weakly guarded. To calm South Carolina officials, the governor and chief justice made an effort to clearly acknowledge the primacy of their property ownership. However, Cushing felt compelled to recognize Massachusetts' liberal laws that allowed slaves certain rights. In the minds of the South Carolinians, the Massachusetts officials had freed their slaves.

The largely internal debates about slavery in Massachusetts and South Carolina took on interstate dimensions with the *Tyrannicide* affair. Until this time, there had been little national debate about slavery. The Continental Congress began discussing it only after the war's end and as other states ended slavery or moved toward ending slavery. Massachusetts and South Carolina continued the dialogue begun in 1783 at the Constitutional Convention in Philadelphia, when the course of the Eastern states away from slavery created a crisis more significant than that of the issue of small and large states.[3]

As the *Tyrannicide* affair demonstrates, Massachusetts' decision to end slavery early in the 1780s reverberated throughout the United States. At the Constitutional Convention, the *Tyrannicide* affair and the Quock Walker case, sparked by black resistance to slavery, had an impact on the writing of the U.S. Constitution. Convention delegates from Massachusetts and South Carolina joined other representatives in an attempt to unify the nation under one constitution, and slavery and antislavery events in the early 1780s strongly influenced the Massachusetts and South Carolina delegates.

*   *   *

Slavery did not become a key issue until the nation sought to expand its frontiers in the northwest. In this discussion, Massachusetts delegates played an important role. In April 1785, a committee of the Continental Congress chaired by Massachusetts delegate Rufus King had offered a resolution to end "involuntary servitude" in the Western territories by 1800. The proposal included a much less benevolent measure, however: the first national fugitive slave clause, which "provided always that any person escaping into the same [the Northwest Territories] from whom labor or service is lawfully claimed in any one of the original states, such fugitive may be lawfully reclaimed and conveyed to the person claiming his, or her labor, or service as aforesaid."

King, like Cushing, was careful to appease southern interests. The clause proclaimed that southern slavery was safe, even eternal, in its introductory phrase, "provided always." King also (again like Cushing) refrained from using the words "slave" or "property," and he carefully described the labor relationship in terms of servitude rather than ownership.[4] Finally, in remaining resolutely passive and refusing to assign responsibility for the capture and delivery of fugitive slaves, the clause implied that the master or his agent, not the state to which the person fled, was required to reclaim the errant bondsman.[5]

The inclusion of an antislavery provision in Continental Congress law was not new. In 1784, Thomas Jefferson first proposed such a provision in his bill on the Western territories to allow the entrance of new western territories into the union. Jefferson envisioned this land as a paradise for yeoman farmers, and thus this ordinance included a stipulation that would outlaw slavery after 1800. The resolution stated that "after the year 1800 of the Christian era, there shall be neither slavery nor involuntary servitude in any of the said states, otherwise than in punishment of crimes, whereof the party shall have been convicted to have been personally guilty."[6] This provision failed when a contingent of southerners struck it down.[7]

Both Jefferson and Rufus King would fail in their attempts to pass a Western territory antislavery petition, but King's version would be resurrected in part because it included the fugitive slave clause. Just as Rufus King's proposal showed he had knowledge of Cushing's decision, South Carolinian delegates must have been aware of the *Tyrannicide* affair because this event came before the House of Representatives, the Privy Council, and the governor several times. Charles Pinckney, for example, who was a member of the Continental Congress at this time, had also been elected to the South Carolina House of Representatives in 1779. He would also attend the Constitutional Convention. Perhaps with what they viewed as Massachusetts' betrayal fresh on their minds, the South Carolinian delegates balked at Jefferson's proposal. They would not approve any antislavery provisions that did not protect their rights, and Jefferson's proposal did not include a fugitive slave clause. During the *Tyrannicide* affair, Massachusetts had showed South Carolinians how easily free states could withhold support for their property, and so the delegate from South Carolina would not accept any confederation law that would not promise such protection. These provisions failed ultimately because they tried to end slavery in the entire Western territory, including the southern region. Southern delegates, however, were more comfortable with the idea of abolishing slavery in free territories that were not their neighbors. When Congress moved to limit the ordinance just to the Northwest, Rufus King's antislavery article would be used verbatim.

Indeed, South Carolinian delegates at the Continental Congress in New York approved the Northwest Ordinance, to which an antislavery and fugitive slave clause was attached at the last minute in 1787. Meanwhile, other delegates negotiated slavery provisions at the Constitutional Convention in Philadelphia. King's replacement and regular correspondent, Nathan Dane, headed the committee, which consisted of a majority of southerners, including South Carolinian John Kean, to write the ordinance. This southern-dominant committee (in a Congress that was dominated by the South) suddenly added the clause in the final reading on July 13, the day after the three-fifths compromise at the convention. On this day, Rhode Island, New Hampshire, Connecticut, and Pennsylvania were not present, but all the southern states were represented, and the acting president was Virginian William Grayson. Historians have tried to understand how this particular Congress could have possibly accepted ending slavery in the Northwest when all other attempts failed against the southern voting bloc.[8] Historian Staughton Lynd has offered a political reason. More than likely, the southern delegates acquiesced on the Northwest Ordinance because the North had backed out of the Jay-Gardoqui treaty with Spain. The northern delegates hoped the U.S. Constitution would allow them to bring their plans for westward expansion to fruition and were satisfied with short-term successes in Congress. Because they had achieved many of their goals in Congress, they were amenable to accepting certain slave provisions in the Constitutional Convention.[9]

Although Lynd's argument is convincing despite its conspiratorial tone, he and other historians ignore the importance of the fugitive slave clause in the equation. When Madison's secretary, Edward Coles, remembered the connection between the Northwest Ordinance and the Constitution in the 1850s, he described the fugitive slave clause as a significant aspect of the compromise. Lynd discounts Cole's recollection, arguing that Coles "may well have exaggerated the importance of that aspect [fugitive slave clause] of the compromise of 1787."[10] He believed Coles's memory was shaped by the significance of fugitive slaves in the 1850s political world. Still, although fugitive slaves did indeed dominate the national dialogue in the 1850s, they were also important in the 1780s. As the *Tyrannicide* affair attests, the problem of fugitive slaves was not an antebellum dilemma but began with the founding of the country.

The Constitutional Convention included many well-known compromises: between small and large states, between federal and state power, and between free and slave states. In these debates between free and slave states, slavery was primarily invoked as a tool with which to manipulate the balance of power. The South hoped to gain power through its wealth and slave population without being burdened with a greater tax responsibility. The North, less dependent on slavery and moving toward market economies, did not want to be responsible for maintaining slavery and sought equal representation in the government and expanded opportunities for trade. The primary exception to the focus on achieving a balance of power between North and South that was satisfactory to all was the fugitive slave clause. It was about a common value, owning property, but this human property moved on its own volition, forcing the northern states to decide how deeply it believed in abolition. Because of the *Tyrannicide* affair, Massachusetts and South Carolina had developed a vocabulary that enabled them to understand the challenges of this problem. That maturity, which came from experience, also manifested itself in their roles in the other slavery debates.

Once established in confederal law, South Carolina worked to secure the fugitive slave clause within the Constitution weeks later. South Carolina's delegates sought to add to a provision on the extradition of criminals. The passage the South Carolina delegates wanted to insert charged that the refuge state's executive must take responsibility for returning an escaped slave just as he would for any other fleeing lawbreaker. South Carolina's frustrations in the wake of the Pawley cases had not dissipated. Indeed, the language South Carolina delegate Pierce Butler introduced mimicked Governor Guerard's earlier letter to Hancock demanding that Massachusetts "deliver up" the slaves that had been transported there, just as Cushing's passive language resonated in King's fugitive slave clause. There is no record of Massachusetts' delegates objecting to Butler's proposal, but delegates from Pennsylvania and Connecticut did. Some delegates were more overtly abolitionist, especially the delegates from Pennsylvania. James Wilson protested that the governor of the refuge state should not be obligated to spend public money. Roger Sherman, in his usual delicate manner, remarked that he would no more agree to the "public seizing and surrendering a slave or servant, than a horse." Other states were equally reluctant to take responsibility for returning slaves.[11]

The clause in its final form demonstrated some acquiescence on the part of the South to northern interests. Both North and South wanted to maintain property rights. In this spirit, northerners agreed that slave property should remain property, but the future free states were concerned that their state would have to pay to protect a form of property that they had abandoned. Butler had to withdraw his proposal and decided to rewrite it in a way that was more appealing to his uncompromising northern neighbors. Butler's changes resonated with the passive tone of the Northwest Ordinance. The new language passed without debate or dissent: "If any Person bound to service or labor in any of the United States shall escape into another State, He or She shall not be discharged from such service or labor in consequence of any regulations subsisting in the State to which they escape; but shall be delivered up to the person justly claiming their service or labor."[12] The language of the new clause retained the language of labor, not property, and combined the language of Justice Cushing and the demand of South Carolina's governor Guerard that South Carolina should get its slaves back. Therefore, the fugitive slave clause was not a gift "given to the South without any quid pro quo"; rather, it had a substantial history that historians have failed to acknowledge, a history in which both the experiences of states like South Carolina and Massachusetts and rhetorical compromises figured.[13]

Because the clause focuses on labor, it sent a conflicting message about the personhood of the enslaved. This clause is, in fact, one of the handful of places in the Constitution in which the word "person" is used, helping to define what a person is within the confines of the Constitution. The emphasis on labor and the fact that the fugitive slave clause is attached to the extradition of criminals ironically emphasizes the personhood of the slave. Within the language and context of the Constitution, fugitives are criminals, not lost property. However, the criminal act by the enslaved is a theft of property. The property in question, however, is the laborer's own body, so that the clause manifests a tension in the idea that an individual might be at once both a person and property. Rhetorically, however, despite the desire of Massachusetts to protect property ownership, antislavery ideas ran deeply enough within the northern delegates that the slaves had to be described as laborers, not property. Later, judges, lawyers, and scholars would read the clause primarily as intending to protect property, not a labor relationship.[14]

The clause bridged a conflict between responsibility and obligation. The entire section uses the verb "shall." This word implies obligation. It is unequivocal that the status of the slave *shall* remain enslaved. The refuge state may not release a slave from his or her enslavement. Nonetheless, the verb phrase is still in the passive voice, giving free states more leeway than in Butler's first version. Just like Cushing's *Tyrannicide* decision, the clause avoids the word "slave" and upholds a master's ownership, and its passivity—"shall be delivered up"—does not dictate that the refuge state must expend state monies to return the slave. On the other hand, the clause uses Guerard's phrase, "deliver up," connoting the possibility that the refuge state was to have a role in the recovery, however vague it may be, whereas the Northwest Ordinance referred to a "claim." Claiming left the responsibility to the owner.

The *Tyrannicide* affair not only sheds light on the subtle compromise of the clause but also reveals, when Congress's frequent revisions of the clause are taken into account, the importance of the differences in interpreting these small words. Just as the South Carolinians had insisted, this clause demands the return of the slaves via the modal "shall." At the same time, just as the court had decided in 1783 with respect to Massachusetts, the refuge state was not necessarily responsible for returning the slaves themselves.

The fugitive slave clause helped define the status of slavery in the Constitution and undergirded some significant aspects of the Constitution such as federalism and the way the relationship between the states was defined. The delegates put the fugitive slave clause into article 4, which governed the duties between the states, and more specifically within section 2, which began with the privileges and immunities clause and secured comity for its citizens. In other words, the legal status and protections that one state gave its citizens had to be respected by other states, and so free states had to protect the slave property of citizens of slave states. However, because the clause was inserted in this article, not in article 1, which granted congressional powers, the fugitive slave clause also suggested that the *Somersett* doctrine governed slavery. Slavery existed where positive law granted it, and it was therefore regulated by the states, not by the federal government. Of course, as some scholars and jurists have noted, Congress immediately acted to clarify the fugitive slave clause in 1790 with the first fugitive slave act without having any explicit grant of power to do so. Only through a more liberal reading of the commerce or elastic clauses did Congress have a right to pass these controversial acts.[15]

Comparing the relative lack of debate over the fugitive slave clause to the extended debate over the enumeration of slaves to be counted for purposes of representation in the U.S. House of Representatives reveals how little the issue of conflicting slave law was really a concern for most at the convention. The fugitive slave clause, which sought to address the problem of contradictory state laws regarding slavery under a single federal government, received little attention. The delegates did deliberate endlessly on the issue of the three-fifths compromise, but that debate centered more on political power than on opinions for or against the institution of slavery. The issue of representation did not hinge on the fact of the existence of slavery as much as it did on the political and economic advantages derived from slavery. Because this debate was not about the validity of slavery, the delegates' rhetoric seemed to contradict their opinions about slavery. Massachusetts and South Carolina provided contributions to this debate that were grounded in solid experience.

A key point of controversy at the convention was the problem of representation. Under the Articles of Confederation, sovereignty and representation were based on states, not on numbers of people. Each state had an equal vote regardless of whether it was wealthy or highly populated. Madison led the charge to establish proportional representation within the Constitution. South Carolina, as the wealthiest state in the nation, sought representation based on wealth, whereas populous states, such as Massachusetts, thought that population should determine representation. Most troublesome for the entire body of delegates were those people who straddled the divide of property and population, the slaves. Because the states with large populations of slaves were generally also those with smaller populations (with the exception of Virginia), the dichotomy between large states and small states broke down.[16] Instead, states split based on the size of their slave populations.

Northern states, which had small slave populations or were in the midst of dissolving slavery, sought to minimize slave representation. First, they tried to limit representation to freemen.[17] Three of South Carolina's delegates responded by claiming that slaves were property and called for representation based on wealth. Invoking the three-fifths ratio that the Continental Congress had earlier proposed as a solution to the representation problem, they recommended that three-fifths of nontaxpaying inhabitants count toward representation.[18]

The three-fifths solution grew out of a 1783 debate over taxation. Congress sought to amend the Articles of Confederation to distribute the tax burden to each state on the basis of wealth. The primary indicator of wealth became slaves. The rhetoric in these debates, however, mirrored each state's general opinion of slavery. Southerners described slaves as a burden, not a benefit. Clothing and feeding slaves, they argued, made their labor much less valuable than that of freemen. Predictably, northern delegates pushed for all slaves to be counted as part of the population. The amendment required a unanimous vote to be passed and thus failed when Rhode Island and New Hampshire refused to ratify it.[19]

South Carolina's position flipped when the three-fifths proposal moved from taxes, under which slaves would be a burden, to representation, under which slaves would give the state more political power. South Carolina delegate John Rutledge, who seconded the three-fifths compromise for taxes in 1783, recommended it as a solution to the representation problem in the 1787 Constitutional Convention. After days of debate over the three-fifths proportion, during which northerners refused to view slaves as anything more than property, South Carolina decided to push the convention even further and proposed that slaves count equally as whites. Pierce Butler, another South Carolina delegate, reversed the 1783 argument by southerners that slaves were burdensome. He argued that slaves should count equally to freemen, because their labor was just as valuable as a freeman's. This argument was not wholly selfish, since at this point it was generally agreed that the three-fifths compromise would apply to taxes and representation. Nevertheless, South Carolina sat nearly alone on the push to count slaves as a whole person for representation. Virginia refused to count slaves as equal to freemen on principle, and indeed only Georgia joined South Carolina in the vote.[20]

Several northern delegates' language reflected a crude use of slaves and slavery as justification to keep slaves from being represented. The delegates consistently conflated being black with being a slave. Hugh Williamson and William Davie both used the term "black" to refer to slaves.[21] Even northern states with increasing free black populations conflated the two. Those who favored abolition did not necessarily view blacks as equal. For those from Pennsylvania, that conflation mixed with their antislavery ideas. Gou-

verneur Morris refused representation of "their negroes," for example, because representation would encourage slave trade, resulting in an incentive
to bring in more slaves.[22] James Wilson believed that the "blending of the
blacks with the whites" would alarm Pennsylvanians.[23]

South Carolina and Massachusetts, in contrast, spoke precisely about
race and slavery. Massachusetts delegates clearly distinguished between
blacks and slaves. Rufus King, for example, mentioned "the blacks, who
were the property of the South." Their discussion responded directly to
South Carolina's agenda. They did not make vague references to slavery,
the slave trade, or the amalgamation of the races. Massachusetts delegates
directly attacked the notion of using property as a basis of representation.
Elbridge Gerry argued that if slaves were counted, horses and cattle ought
to be counted as well. He made this sarcastic comparison to challenge South
Carolina's concept of slaves as merely property and directly spoke to South
Carolina's justification for the representation of slaves.[24]

Like Cushing, Massachusetts delegates had recognized the need to
achieve a balance between protecting slave property and burdening the state
with the costs of imprisonment and capture. They did not pressure other
states to end slavery as they had and did not come to the convention to
end slavery throughout the United States. They seemed unwilling to impose
their different and new society on others. Nevertheless, their respect for
slavery's existence in the United States did not preclude them from defending their status as a free state. Rufus King set out his state's basic agenda
on July 10. Although he wanted to unite with "their Southern brethren," he
believed that the southern states sought to "subject" the North to a "gross
inequality."[25] On this day, at the same time that the Continental Congress
was negotiating whether to insert his own fugitive slave clause into the
Northwest Ordinance, he assured the South again of Massachusetts' intent
to protect the South, "giving them more security." Yet he stood for his own
state's sovereignty and was not willing to allow southern interests to force
his state to spend its resources to protect southern property.[26] This agenda
reflected the state's desire to create the Constitution with southern interests
in mind but not to the extent that they infringed on Massachusetts's new
status as a state without slavery.

South Carolina's delegates were equally lucid. They said "slaves" when
they meant slaves. Slaves were a form of property that took on human qualities for purposes of representation. The South Carolina delegates, in fact,
used the words "black" and "white" only when they proposed that blacks

and whites receive equal representation. Under these circumstances, blacks referred to the entire population of blacks, free or enslaved. They were careful to avoid using these terms when proposing the original three-fifths compromise on June 11. The proposed section instead referred to those "persons bound to servitude."[27]

Gaining ground on the three-fifths compromise was not enough for South Carolina, and Charles Coatsworth Pinckney made that clear on July 23. He requested that the Constitution stipulate that slaves could not be emancipated and that exports—the products of slaves—could not be taxed, thereby providing more "security to the Southern States." He threatened to vote against any report that did not further support slavery. This protest came after Massachusetts' Elbridge Gerry suggested forming a committee of detail to create a draft of the Constitution. The creation of the committee was delayed for three days. On July 26, the convention appointed the committee, naming five members, including southerners Randolph and Rutledge.[28]

The committee submitted its report on August 6. The new report did not include the fugitive slave clause, but it did include most of the protections guaranteed in the final version of the Constitution and more. Most glaringly, the new draft called for the three-fifths compromise for taxation only; slaves would count as whole people for representation. This obvious attempt to shift the direction of the Constitution in the South's favor was quickly corrected. Rufus King would not allow the South extra representation that the convention had already ruled out after having debated the issue for days. The draft, however, also included a clause protecting the slave trade, prohibiting taxes on exports and slaves, and ensuring that the federal government would help aid states in quelling domestic violence.[29]

The summer had brought hot weather and long debates that began to leave the delegates exhausted, allowing the southern delegates to insist on further, subtler changes to the Constitution to protect slavery. The southern delegates focused on molding the structure of the government to support the power they had gained. The decision to elect the president through the Electoral College extended the power of the three-fifths compromise. The number of Electoral College delegates was based on the number of congressional representatives a state sent to both the House of Representatives and the Senate. The South's advantage would extend to the election of the president. In the minds of southerners, this power would grow even stronger because most southerners assumed that they would one day dominate the Senate as the southwestern territories became slave states.[30]

The Constitution further protected slavery by requiring a supermajority to propose amendments to the document. This provision, secured by southerner James Madison, meant that the Constitution would remain conservative and that changes to the document would come only with the approval of the southern states. In other words, it gave the South a veto over any provisions that changed the existing Constitution.[31]

The Articles of Confederation included a privileges and immunities clause that was imported almost verbatim into the final Constitution. The privileges and immunities clause was the basis of comity between the states. Each state would respect the laws of the other when such laws came into conflict. South Carolinians believed that the articles had failed to protect their property during the *Tyrannicide* affair. From their point of view, the state of Massachusetts had freed fourteen of their slaves. They were wrong, but their perception led them to protest the inclusion of the clause. Charles Coatsworth Pinckney, who had the most extensive experience in the South Carolina government at the time of the *Tyrannicide* affair, called for an explicit "provision . . . in favor of property in slaves." His protest was ignored, and only South Carolina voted against the clause. Even Georgia, always faithful to South Carolina's efforts to protect slavery, remained divided.[32]

Nevertheless, South Carolina secured an additional safeguard for its property by protecting itself against its own property. Protection from slave insurrection did not originate in the committee of detail's draft of the Constitution. South Carolina delegate Charles Coatsworth Pinckney's alternative plan for government, submitted days after Randolph and Madison's Virginia plan, sought to shield his state from "domestic insurrection."[33] The committee of detail embraced this suggestion, authorizing Congress to quell any "domestic violence," but the experience of domestic violence had varied manifestations, and each state raised different concerns about rebellion when the delegates discussed the provision. In Massachusetts, armed conflict meant Daniel Shays. In North and South Carolina, the Regulators and Tories represented domestic violence. In addition to fearing white rebellions, Pinckney and other southerners feared slave rebellion. The experience with Massachusetts over the Pawley slaves could not have instilled confidence that South Carolina's sister states would come to its aid. In the mid-1780s, Georgia and South Carolina were able to quell insurgencies, slave maroons, and refugee fighters by themselves, but a large-scale slave rebellion struck fear in southerners' hearts. In article 4, South Carolina received assurance that "the United States . . . shall protect each of them [each state] against Invasion; and . . . against domestic violence," despite other states' varying views on slavery.[34]

Just as Massachusetts sided with South Carolina on the issue of protecting themselves from domestic rebellion, Massachusetts joined South Carolina in arguing that the slave trade should be safeguarded. The debate over the slave trade centered on its morality and that of slavery itself. Some scholars have argued that taking the moral high ground against the slave trade endowed certain states with political power, especially if ending the slave trade had economic benefits. The beneficiaries of the slave trade were not strictly divided by region. Rhode Island and Massachusetts ships carried most of the slaves who arrived at American ports. Still, even despite its economic benefits, many Revolutionary-era Americans developed distaste for the trade in Africans. The involuntary capture and shipment of Africans seemed directly contrary to the nation's new ideals of human rights. Moreover, as states such as Virginia experienced agricultural decline, they developed surpluses of slaves, not shortages. More slaves meant lower prices for the slaves Virginia sold further south (although James McHenry of Maryland thought the prohibition of the slave trade would give Virginia "a monopoly").[35] Nonetheless, although every single state, including South Carolina, had banned the slave trade at least temporarily in 1787, South Carolina wanted the option to reopen the trade at any time.

Massachusetts delegate Rufus King questioned the protection of the slave trade on August 8. King protested this provision from a practical, not an ideological standpoint. He offered three basic arguments. First, he disliked the limitation on the legislature to make laws that it saw fit. He believed that the government's role was to ensure safety and that protecting the slave trade contradicted that goal. It was widely held that imported slaves tended to be more rebellious; thus, the influx of foreign slaves would mean more insurrection. This led to his third point. He felt it unfair that the northern states then must pay to protect the South from its own slaves.[36]

Other northerners chimed in with their protests against the slave trade clause. Because the committee of detail's draft had ignored the three-fifths clause, the slave trade debate now became enmeshed in the representation question. Gouverneur Morris used these two issues to make clear again his ideological objection to slavery. He thought that slavery would land the country in poverty and that it was particularly odious that those states who participated in morally reprehensible activities should get extra representation and be rewarded for "importing fresh supplies of wretched Africans."[37]

South Carolina's John Rutledge responded to the other delegates' misgivings by arguing that any limitation on the South's commerce proved that the Union did not really desire to include the South. He further stated that he believed that the three-fifths clause did not encourage importation. He brushed off any moral complaints against slavery. Later, Charles Coatsworth Pinckney would historicize the idea that there was nothing morally wrong with slavery by recalling that "if slavery be wrong, it is justified by the example of all the world," citing both ancient and modern precedents.[38] Last, Rutledge responded to King's concern that the slave trade would increase slave rebellions by stating that he "would readily exempt the other States from the obligation to protect the Southern [states] against them."[39]

South Carolina won another provision in the debate over the slave trade. The debate monopolized two days of the convention, after which the committee came back with a compromise on the issue of the slave trade: the prohibition of any laws restricting the trade for twenty years, until 1808. South Carolina, of course, rejected the idea of a twenty-year time limit. Its complaint was ignored and after a brief debate about whether to include the word "slave" in the compromise, it passed, with a small concession on South Carolina's part. Imported slaves could be taxed up to $10 by the federal government.[40]

John Rutledge had one last trick up his sleeve. On September 10, in the last week of the convention, he requested an additional clause to article 5, which allowed amendments to the Constitution. He knew that even the upper South disagreed with the slave trade clause, which meant that only three-fourths of the states supported the clause, not enough to guarantee that the twenty-years provision would survive, and so he pressed the convention to add a clause that there should be no amendments to the slave trade article. He threatened, once again, his state's withdrawal from the union if this concession were not granted. The tired convention acquiesced, thus allowing the only exception to the ability of the states to introduce amendments to the Constitution.[41]

These debates over slavery underscored the extent to which the events of the 1780s informed these delegates' dialogues. Many scholars have inadequately addressed the reason the South gained so many concessions from the northern states. Some scholars point to the surrender of states such as

Massachusetts as proof that these states, or at least the delegates to the convention, were still essentially proslavery.[42] They argue that slavery ended there because it just did not serve local commercial interests well. Others have turned this around and shown how integral slavery in the South was to America's economic world, North and South.[43] What many scholars have missed is that most of these debates were not about the existence of slavery but about its magnitude. In these two debates, slavery became a basis of power, not an institution to be debated morally. Although some delegates most certainly used moral arguments, the sincerity of the moral outrage is questionable given that these same men twisted their language for various political purposes. Historians focus on representation and the slave trade clause because the lengthiest debate erupted during these discussions. However, the states were not debating the survival of slavery in the Union but the balance of power. For South Carolina, achieving a balance of power rested on the protection of slavery. For Massachusetts, slavery did not figure at all in the balance of power. The events of the 1780s make it clear that, for Massachusetts, stability and union were more important than the extension of freedom to black Americans. A stable union meant a strong environment for its commercial ambitions. Massachusetts' delegates sought to quell the paranoia of the southerners, particularly of the delegates from South Carolina. Despite the fact that their state was the first to completely end slavery, Massachusetts' delegates did not believe it was necessary that slavery be abolished in other states. They defended their own power while acquiescing to South Carolina's demands as little as possible. For the northern states, achieving a balance of power in the union meant minimizing the importance of slave wealth. Massachusetts and South Carolina delegates were not engaging in a moral battle during the debates but in a power struggle. The fugitive slave clause was different from the other slavery provisions. The delegates hardly debated the clause, yet it was the only provision that really forced the states to grapple with their diverging identities as free and slave states and, more significantly, the conflicting laws regarding slavery that were emerging. Moreover, it was the provision through which South Carolina and her southern partners lost the most protection. Massachusetts did not need to participate extensively in this debate because it had already discussed the matter. It had helped develop the Northwest Ordinance and the plan to introduce the clause behind the scenes and so did not enter the fray when it was brought to the floor. Moreover, the entire country had engaged in these debates over the western and northwestern territories. This most significant compromise had already been made before the convention voted on the fugitive slave clause in the Continental Congress.[44]

The ratification of this compromise-laden Constitution was not certain. Ratifying conventions in both Massachusetts and South Carolina discussed the slavery provisions. These debates revealed the strong regard that all the delegates (except Gerry, who refused to sign the document) now had for the Constitution. In the ratification debates, many citizens of both Massachusetts and South Carolina questioned the slavery provisions of the Constitution. Massachusetts' ratifying convention challenged both the three-fifths clause and the slave trade clause on the grounds that it was illogical and threatened unity rather than that it was immoral or gave one region more representational power than another. While discussing the three-fifths clause, the delegates deliberated on concepts of representation and the slaves' role in representation.

For the Massachusetts delegates, slavery was not about social status or political power and only obliquely about property. Primarily, slavery was an institution of labor. Slaves were laborers who did not impart great amounts of wealth or status. The delegates viewed slavery as a viable institution as long as the labor was affordable. Judge Francis Dana agreed with the proportion argument because he thought that slave labor was unreliable and about as valuable as three-fifths of a freeman. Others responded to Dana by recounting anecdotes and their own experiences in South Carolina, which they believed enabled them to judge the relative value of slave labor. Thomas Dawes of Boston reminded the other delegates that the nation viewed blacks and slaves in a multitude of ways. He embraced a federal system and urged that "every particular state" be "left to its own option" when it came to slavery. He stated that he was willing to abide by this kind of pluralism in America and suggested that black slaves were persons and property, Massachusetts' own vision of blacks as freemen notwithstanding. Moreover, the Constitution further supported this pluralism, he argued, by allowing the slave trade. He urged the other delegates to try to appreciate the difficulty of stripping slave owners of their property in a moment of unity. He reminded them that "it would not do to abolish slavery . . . in a moment, and so destroy what our southern brethren consider property." A common assumption by many in the North and Upper South that slavery "will die of a consumption" as it already had in the North made this argument easier to swallow.[45] The debate on the slave-trade provision concentrated on the vagueness of the language and remoteness of the twenty-year time limit.

The absence of the word "slave" in the document has kept many wondering ever since whether the framers had indeed intended the slavery provisions to uphold slavery.

Although the delegates to the Constitutional Convention in Massachusetts did not have strong moral views on slavery, some at the ratification debates did. As had happened throughout the Revolution, the clergy led the campaign in questioning the morality of slavery and the slave trade. James Neal, a Quaker minister, for example, objected morally to the continuation of the slave trade. He stated that as a reverend, he had to "bear witness against any thing that should favor the making merchandise of the bodies of men." He refused to speak an oath over a document that condoned the slave trade. He was further appalled that there was no provision to begin freeing the slaves in time. His emotional plea sparked other moral reactions. General Samuel Thompson exclaimed that George Washington had shamed himself because he "holds those in slavery who have as good a right to be free as he has."[46] Others, however, saw light at the end of the tunnel. They believed that the twenty-year time limit was a "door . . . to be opened for the annihilation of this odious, abhorrent practice."[47]

Ultimately, Massachusetts ratified the Constitution by a vote of 187 to 168. The issue of slavery did not appear in the convention's list of proposed amendments. General William Heath might have summed up the feeling of the Massachusetts delegates on this issue when he stated that "no gentleman, within these walls, detests every idea of slavery more than I do" and expressed his hope that "our brethren in the Southern States will view it as we do, and put a stop to it." He concluded, however, that "we have no right to compel them." Massachusetts' delegates believed they were joining a pluralistic union of separate states. They thought that they were not embracing the "other men's sins" through the union. In the end, most delegates believed that the compromises were acceptable. Certainly, these men did not foresee the problems of comity that would tear at the heart of this acquiescence. The ambiguous fugitive slave clause would force them to deal with these other men's sins. The slaves would arrive in free states, as they already had, and would force the citizens of Massachusetts to decide whether they would partake in the sins of their brothers.[48]

In South Carolina, Pinckney and Rutledge pressed on their ratifying delegates the great achievements of the Constitution as a protector of slavery. Only a few of South Carolina's delegates challenged the Constitution's slavery provisions. They believed that the House of Representatives was unfairly balanced against the South and were concerned about the fact that the slave trade would end after 1808. Rawlins Lowndes worried that if the "new Constitution should be adopted, the sun of the Southern States would set, never to rise again." He worried that the early majority of northern congressional representatives would overpower the South, especially because they were "jealous" of "our slaves." He believed that if the North had achieved the wealth that South Carolina had with its slave population, it would not have any designs to end slavery. He wanted no limitations on the slave trade in perpetuity and felt that the tax on slave imports was particularly burdensome. Although Massachusetts' delegates seemed comfortable with a pluralist nation, South Carolina was suspicious of being "governed by prejudices and ideas extremely different from ours." As foreseen in Governor Guerard's letter to Hancock in 1783, South Carolina was afraid of domination by the northern states.[49]

Pinckney and Rutledge responded to these criticisms by stressing the power that the Constitution gave the South. They had worked hard during the convention to ensure every protection for slavery that they could secure. They pointed out important safeguards such as the twenty-year uninterrupted continuation of the slave trade that was exempt from amendment. Certainly, they believed that they had protected slavery and made sure that the South Carolina ratification delegates knew that. Rutledge recounted the advantageous tax situation that the South found itself in owing to slaves counting as only three-fifths of a person and the prohibition on export taxes. He pointed out that taxes on slave imports were sharply limited, whereas other imports had no limit on their tariffs. Moreover, because Massachusetts and Rhode Island ships carried slaves for South Carolinian consumers, South Carolinians could demand that the carriers take on the burden of the taxes. He concluded by stating that "the Southern States should be the last to object" to the taxes.[50] Pinckney emphasized the number of concessions they had extracted from the North. It was to the South's advantage for slaves to be counted for representation, especially with the dissolution of slavery in the North. According to Pinckney, South Carolina's delegates had defended the slave trade against overwhelming opposition, including some from other southerners. In light of this opposition, he argued, they should be grateful that they had "secured an unlimited importation for twenty years." He reminded them of the fugitive slave clause and their increased representation because of the three-fifths clause. He concluded, "We have made the best terms for the security of this species of property it was in our power to make."[51]

South Carolina ratified the Constitution in a very close vote, seventy-six to seventy-five. In the end, the delegates believed that slavery was adequately protected. The dissenting voices came mostly from the western, more anti-federalist, portions of the state; their opposition did not stem principally from concern over the slavery provisions. Rather, they disliked the Charleston establishment and were wary of strong governments in Charleston or New York, reflecting the east-west divide that plagued many states. Despite the western protest, South Carolinians unified to pass the Constitution. Even Rawlins Lowndes of Charleston, who had stated that the lack of protection for slavery and the slave trade in the Constitution would destroy the South, voted "aye."[52]

With this vote, South Carolina became the eighth state out of the nine necessary to ratify the Constitution. Once the Constitution was in effect, South Carolina and Massachusetts continued to play similar roles in Congress and at home as they had before. Through the 1830s, Massachusetts continued to limit its free black population, not welcoming outsiders and ignoring the needs of its black citizens. Nationally, Massachusetts still adopted moderate stances in Congress, accepting differences between the states at the same time that it sought to protect its particular interests. South Carolinians remained suspicious of both their slaves and their sister states in the North, and over the following seventy or so years that suspicion would grow, until finally, on December 20, 1860, they would secede from the union they had so carefully crafted during the American Revolution.

Slavery, historians have established, sits at the center of early American society right alongside its opposite, freedom. The Constitution wove this paradox into the very fabric of American culture, law, and society. This base emerged not out of philosophical musings as much as out of the experiences of the founding generation. A nexus of experiences shaped how each state, and each delegate for that matter, approached constituting the United States. These diverse experiences meant that the creation of the United States as a nation and the creation of the Constitution that would guide it were contingent. As the ratification conventions in both Massachusetts and South Carolina suggest, the Constitution was not a foregone conclusion. The *Tyrannicide* affair provides a glimpse into the context of the paradox of freedom and slavery in the 1787 constitution. The writing of the fugitive slave clause, the antebellum battleground of the free and slave states, depended on an understanding of the antebellum problem of a dividing society. This story makes clear that this was not an antebellum problem but an issue from the moment of America's inception.

The Pawley slaves' experiences in war and then in their resistance to recapture compelled the two most divergent states, South Carolina and Massachusetts, to crystalize their stances on this paradox. This study's central narrative moment takes place on the Atlantic Ocean when the fate of a group of Africans twisted and turned as British, Spanish, and Americans fought over the ships that carried them. This book has emphasized how those with seemingly little power were able to take advantage of larger political changes in the Atlantic world and assume charge of their own lives and future.

However, the fluidity of national or state borders notwithstanding, the power of state and national governments remained critically important not just to those at the top of society but to those at the bottom as well. This power was wielded in large part through the legal institutions and culture of Massachusetts and South Carolina, which played decisive roles in the fates of black people in their own states.

The story of the Waccamaw slaves, their owners, and the men who wrestled with what to do with them in the 1780s is a fascinating opening into this complex story of the origins of slave law in America. The *Tyrannicide* case brought together the two states in the new nation with the most divergent viewpoints on slavery and freedom, but it shows that these differences were rooted not so much in economic orientation or racial ideology as in subtly different legal traditions. The case also helps highlight the complex role black slaves played in this turbulent period.

Buffeted by forces outside of their control, the Waccamaw slaves followed a path similar to so many of their contemporaries in both South Carolina and Massachusetts. Black and white Americans entered the 1770s hoping to commit tyrannicide, to end tyranny in their world. Some saw little they could do about that tyranny, whereas others took advantage of changing circumstances to reshape their future. Although most blacks did not test the legal boundaries in the new republic, the few who did had a profound impact.

Notes

INTRODUCTION. FORGING AN AMERICAN SLAVE LAW

1. The story of Captain Urezberoeta has been drawn from Board of War Letters, 1777–80, MAC, 153:229–30, Massachusetts Archives, Boston, Board of War Minutes, 1776–80, MAC, 151:292, Massachusetts Archives, Boston, and Board of War for *Massachusetts v. The Ship Victoria*, 1779, Records of the Court of Appeal in Cases of Capture, Revolutionary War Prize Cases, 1776–87, M162, Massachusetts, #59, NARA, Washington, D.C.

2. John Cathcart to Massachusetts Board of War, June 24, 1779, Board of War Letters, 1777–80, MAC, 153:229–30, Massachusetts Archives, Boston.

3. Eric Foner, *The Story of American Freedom* (New York: Norton, 1999), xvi.

4. Benjamin Guerard to John Hancock, October 6, 1783, Charleston, S.C., Records of the General Assembly, Governor's Messages 262, 7–9, SCDAH, Columbia. A summary of the event is included in the epigrammatic letter. See chapter 3 and chapter 4 for specific documents, including the letter, that substantiate the basic narrative of the story.

5. Jonathan Mayhew, *A Discourse Concerning Unlimited Submission and Non-Resistance to the Higher Powers: with Some Reflections on the Resistance Made to King Charles I* (Boston: Fowle and Gookin, 1750).

6. Gardner W. Allen, *Massachusetts Privateers of the Revolution* (Boston: Massachusetts Historical Society, 1927), 310.

7. This, of course, did not mean oppression ended. Racism and an effort to whiten Massachusetts after the war meant that African American lives continued to be challenging.

8. Joanne Melish's *Disowning Slavery: Gradual Emancipation and "Race" in New England, 1780–1860* (Ithaca, N.Y.: Cornell University Press, 1998) highlights the North's act of forgetting its slave past. Other studies emerged in the 1940s, but the field has blossomed in the past ten years. See Lorenzo J. Greene, *The Negro in Colonial New England* (1945; rpt., New York: Atheneum, 1968); Arthur Zilversmit, *The First Emancipation: The Abolition of Slavery in the North* (Chicago: University of Chicago Press, 1969); Edgar McManus, *Black Bondage in the North* (Syracuse, N.Y.: Syracuse University Press, 1973); John Wood Sweet, *Negotiating Race in the American North* (Philadelphia: University of Pennsylvania Press, 2006); Catherine Adams and Elizabeth Pleck, *Love of Freedom: Black Women in Colonial and Revolutionary New England* (New York: Oxford University Press, 2010); and Joel Lang and Jenifer Frank Anne Farrow, *Complicity* (New York: Ballantine Books, 2007).

9. Edmund Morgan, *American Slavery, American Freedom* (New York: Norton, 1975); David Brion Davis, *The Problem of Slavery in the Age of Revolution, 1770–1823* (Ithaca,

N.Y.: Cornell University Press, 1975). Scholarship that addresses slavery and African American experiences during the Revolution and Northern slavery includes Sylvia Frey, *Water from the Rock: Black Resistance in a Revolutionary Age* (Princeton, N.J.: Princeton University Press, 1991); Gary B. Nash, *Race and Revolution* (Madison, Wis.: Madison House, 1990); George Van Cleve, *A Slaveholders' Union: Slavery, Politics, and the Constitution in the Early American Republic* (Chicago: University of Chicago Press, 2010); William Dillon Piersen, *Black Yankees: The Development of an Afro-American Subculture in Eighteenth-Century New England* (Amherst: University of Massachusetts Press, 1988); Simon Schama, *Rough Crossings: Britain, the Slaves, and the American Revolution* (New York: Ecco, 2006); Douglas R. Egerton, *Death or Liberty: African Americans and Revolutionary America* (New York: Oxford University Press, 2009); and Robert Olwell, *Masters, Slaves, and Subjects: The Culture of Power in the South Carolina Low Country, 1740–1790* (Ithaca, N.Y.: Cornell University Press, 1998).

10. I use the term "Patriot" merely as a title to distinguish between the British and the American rebels. It was a term they used to describe themselves. It does not necessarily reflect a statement about the rightness of their cause. I use the term "Loyalist" to refer to Americans who fought on the side of the British.

11. Not only historians but also lawyers are interested in the fugitive slave clause. Westlaw reveals that 539 law review articles use the phrase "fugitive slave clause," although rarely do these articles look at the origins of the clause with any depth. The vast majority (415) of the articles refer to the clause only once or twice, and none mention it more than six times. Among those (122) that mention it between three and six times, there is a small handful that explore the clause's origin closely. Most reflect on the implementation and enforcement of the clause in the antebellum period. For example, many of the articles discuss major antebellum cases such as *Dred Scott v. Sanford* (33) and, especially, *Prigg v. Pennsylvania* (85). A number of these articles consider the question of implementation and enforcement as a means of reflecting on the meaning of the fugitive slave clause, looking at issues such as congressional power to write the fugitive slave acts, the nature of federalism and comity in the Constitution, extradition, and the Constitution's influence in protecting private property. Other articles examine the dismantling of the proslavery Constitution, focusing on the Thirteenth and Fourteenth Amendments (14), taking up contemporary problems such as immigration, abortion, and judicial interpretation. At least 10 articles respond to Richard Dworkin's theories of adjudication and how to manage immoral law, using the fugitive slave clause and the acts that followed as prime examples of immoral law. The debates of historians have also bled into the law reviews, especially the argument between Paul Finkelman and Don Fehrenbacher on the extent to which proslavery ideology informed the writing of the Constitution. Finkelman has regularly submitted articles to the law reviews, and other historians, such as James Oakes, have used them to debate Finkelman's provocative Garrisonian reading of the constitutional debates.

On slaves as property, see Kaimipono David Wenger, "Slavery as a Takings Clause Violation," *American University Law Review* 53.1 (2003): 191–259, and Robert Kaczorowski, "Congress's Power to Enforce Fourteenth Amendment Rights: Lessons from Federal Remedies the Framers Enacted," *Harvard Journal on Legislation* 42.1 (2005): 187–282. Recently, given the anniversary of *Dred Scott v. Sanford*, much has been written about the infamous fugitive slave case; see Daniel A. Farber, "A Fatal Loss of Balance: Dred Scott Revisited," *Pepperdine Law Review* 39.1 (2011): 13–48. On *Prigg v. Pennsylvania*, see Leslie Friedman Goldstein, "'A Triumph of Freedom' after All? *Prigg v. Pennsylvania*

Reexamined," *Law and History Review* 29.3 (2011): 763–96. On congressional power and the fugitive slave acts, see James A. Kraehenbuehl, "Lessons from the Past: How the Antebellum Fugitive Slave Debate Informs State Enforcement of Federal Immigration Law," *University of Chicago Law Review* 78.4 (2011): 1465–1502. On the morality of the Constitution, see Richard H. Fallon, "Legitimacy and the Constitution," *Harvard Law Review* 118.6 (2005): 1787–1853. On federalism and the privileges and immunities clause, see Robert G. Natelson, "The Original Meaning of the Privileges and Immunities Clause," *Georgia Law Review* 43.4 (2009): 1117–93.

12. See, for example, Paul Finkelman, *Slavery, Revolutionary America, and the New Nation* (New York: Garland, 1989); John P. Kaminski, *A Necessary Evil? Slavery and the Debate over the Constitution* (Madison, Wis.: Madison House, 1995); Staughton Lynd, *Class Conflict, Slavery, and the United States Constitution: Ten Essays* (Indianapolis, Ind.: Bobbs-Merrill, 1968). For a deeper consideration of the fugitive slave clause, see George Van Cleve's *Slaveholders' Union*.

CHAPTER ONE. SLAVERY, RHETORIC, AND REALITY BEFORE THE WAR, 1764–1774

1. John Adams, *Legal Papers*, vol. 2, *Cases 31–62*, ed. L. Kinvin Wroth and Hiller B. Zobel, *The Adams Papers*, ed. L. H. Butterfield (Cambridge, Mass.: Belknap Press of Harvard University Press, 1965), 54.

2. Jack P. Greene, "'Slavery or Independence': Some Reflections on the Relationship among Liberty, Black Bondage, and Equality in Revolutionary South Carolina," *South Carolina Historical Magazine* 80.3 (1979); Duncan J. MacLeod, *Slavery, Race, and the American Revolution* (New York: Cambridge University Press, 1974); Bernard Bailyn, *The Ideological Origins of the American Revolution* (Cambridge, Mass.: Belknap Press of Harvard University Press, 1967); Patricia Bradley, *Slavery, Propaganda, and the American Revolution* (Jackson: University Press of Mississippi, 1998); Peter A. Dorsey, *Common Bondage: Slavery as a Metaphor in Revolutionary America* (Knoxville: University of Tennessee Press, 2009).

3. Dorsey, *Common Bondage*, xii.

4. Margaret Newell, "Indian Slavery in Colonial New England," in *Indian Slavery in Colonial America*, ed. Alan Gallay (Lincoln: University of Nebraska Press, 2009), 43. Christopher Tomlins shows how transitory white indentured servitude was in colonial America. It was a short-lived state for those drawn into it and it was a short-lived phenomenon in the history of the colonies. The nature of society in the colonies and the need for labor meant that it became challenging to keep white indentured servants; moreover, the supply dwindled in the late seventeenth century. After then, indentured people in Massachusetts were predominantly white youths, for whom indenture was a stage of life, and Indians, who were driven into a life in and out of indenture by social, legal, and political forces (*Freedom Bound: Law, Labor, and Civic Identity in Colonizing English America, 1580–1865* [New York: Cambridge University Press, 2010], 54–56, 255–56).

5. Margaret Newell, "The Changing Nature of Indian Slavery," in *Reinterpreting New England Indians and the Colonial Experience*, ed. Colin G. Galloway and Neal Salisbury (Boston: Colonial Society of Massachusetts, 2003), 108–9; Newell, "Indian Slavery in Colonial New England," 37–38; Katherine Hermes, "Jurisdiction in the Colonial Northeast: Algonquian, English and French Governance," *American Journal of Legal History* 43.1 (1999): 52–73.

6. Compare this to Virginia, for example, which took forty years to develop laws instituting and regulating slavery.

7. Emanuel Downing to John Winthrop, 1645, MHS collections, ser. 4, 6:65, MHS, Boston.

8. George Moore, *Notes on the History of Slavery in Massachusetts* (New York: Appleton, 1866), 49. It is worth noting that this desire to keep blacks out of the Puritan mission did not extend to the second major Puritan experiment in America, Providence Island; see Karen Ordahl Kupperman, *Providence Island, 1630–1641: The Other Puritan Colony* (New York: Cambridge University Press, 1995), 177.

9. Newell, "The Changing Nature of Indian Slavery," 111–16; Joyce Chaplain, "Enslavement of Indians in Early America: Captivity without the Narrative," in *The Creation of the British Atlantic World*, ed. Elizabeth Mancke and Carole Shammas (Baltimore, Md.: Johns Hopkins University Press, 2005), 66.

10. Newell, "Indian Slavery in Colonial New England," 53; Daniel R. Mandel, *Behind the Frontier: Indians in the Eighteenth-Century Eastern Massachusetts* (Lincoln: University of Nebraska Press, 1996), 143; Chaplin, "Enslavement of Indians in Early America," 61.

11. U.S. Bureau of the Census, *Historical Statistics of the United States, Colonial Times to 1970*, 2 vols. (Washington, D.C.: U.S. Department of Commerce Bureau of the Census, 1976), 1:Z1-10; Moore, *Notes on the History of Slavery in Massachusetts*, 49–51.

12. Cotton Mather, *Rules for the Society of Negroes, 1693* (Boston: Bartholomew Green, 1714); Cotton Mather, *The Negro Christianized* (Boston: Bartholomew Green, 1706). Cotton Mather to Reverend Thomas Prince, June 16, 1723, *Diary of Cotton Mather*, 2 vols. (New York: Fredrick Ungar, 1957), 2:687.

13. Ellis Ames, Abner Goodell, and Melville Biglow, eds., *The Acts and Resolves, Public and Private of the Province of the Massachusetts Bay*, 21 vols. (Boston: Wright and Potter, 1869–1922), 3:318, 997; *Records of the Colony of New Plymouth in New England*, 12 vols., ed. Nathaniel Shurtleff and David Pulsifer (1855–61; rpt., New York: AMS Press, 1968), 1:21, 29, 47–48, 66, 113.

14. Ames, Goodell, Bigelow, *The Acts and Resolves, Public and Private of the Province of the Massachusetts Bay*, 3:318, 997; Gary Nash, *The Urban Crucible: Social Change, Political Consciousness, and the Origins of the American Revolution* (Cambridge, Mass.: Harvard University Press, 1979) 161–97.

15. William Dillon Piersen, *Black Yankees: The Development of an Afro-American Subculture in Eighteenth-Century New England* (Amherst: University of Massachusetts Press, 1988).

16. George Sheldon, *History of Deerfield, Massachusetts*, 2 vols. (Deerfield, Mass.: Pocumtuck Valley Memorial Association, 1896), 2:898.

17. Sharon Carboneti Davis, "Vermont's Adopted Sons and Daughters," *Vermont History* 31.2 (1963): 123; Sheldon, *History of Deerfield, Massachusetts*, 2:898; Gretchen Holbrook Gerzina, *Mr. and Mrs. Prince: How an Extraordinary Eighteenth Century Family Moved out of Slavery and into Legend* (New York: Amistad Press, 2008) 62.

18. Sheldon, *History of Deerfield, Massachusetts*, 1:359.

19. Sheldon, *History of Deerfield, Massachusetts*, 2:898; 1:540–49, 567; Josiah Gilbert Holland, *History of Western Massachusetts*, 2 vols. (Springfield, Mass.: Samuel Bowles, 1855), 2:860.

20. On the Prince family legal disputes, see *Records of the Governor and Council of the State of Vermont*, vol. 3 (Montpelier, Vt.: Steam Press of J. and J. M. Poland, 1875) 66–67,

"U.S. Circuit Court Docket, 1793–1797," *Records of the United States Circuit Court for the District of Vermont*, in Katz/Prince Collection, Schomberg Center for Research in Black Culture, reel 2; Abby Maria Hemenway, ed., *Vermont Historical Gazetteer*, 5 vols. (Brandon, Vt.: Mrs. Carrie E. H. Pope, 1867–91), 5.3.79. On the Williams College event, see John F. Ohles and Shirley M. Ohles, *Private Colleges and Universities*, vol. 2 (Westport, Conn.: Greenwood Press, 1982), 1407. Biographical information for the Prince family comes from Gerzina, *Mr. and Mrs. Prince*, 91–107; Sidney Kaplan, *The Black Presence in the Era of the American Revolution, 1770–1800* (Washington, D.C.: Smithsonian Museum Press, 1973), 214–15; Broad Brook Grange No. 151, *Official History of Guilford, Vermont, 1678–1961* (Brattleboro: Vermont Printing Company, 1961), 145; Sheldon, *History of Deerfield, Massachusetts*, 899–900; and David R. Proper, "Lucy Terry Prince: 'Singer of History,'" *Contributions in Black Studies* 9–10 (1990–92): 196.

21. Catharine M. Sedgwick, "Essay on Mumbet," Catharine M. Sedgwick I Papers, box 6, folder 6, 2–6 (roll 6, p. 354, on microfilm), MHS, Boston.

22. Lorenzo J. Greene, *The Negro in Colonial New England* (New York: Atheneum, 1968), 110–19.

23. William Piersen, *Black Yankees*, 19. This survey mostly included vital statistics collected from the Massachusetts towns of Arlington, Bedford, Brimfield, Burlington, Chelsea, Dartmouth, Dracut, East Bridgewater, Hamilton, Hopkinton, Lincoln, Manchester, Marblehead, Medford, Medway, and Norton. In these vital statistics records, 125 marriages up to 1850 are recorded. Sixty-four couples included enslaved men or women (Arlington, Mass., *Vital Records of Arlington, Massachusetts, to the Year 1850* [Boston: New England Historic Genealogical Society, 1904]; Bedford, Mass., *Vital Records of Bedford, Massachusetts, to the Year 1850* [Boston: New England Historic Genealogical Society, 1903]; Brimfield, Mass., *Vital Records of Brimfield, Massachusetts, to the Year 1850* [Boston: New England Historic Genealogical Society, 1931]; Burlington, Mass., and Thomas W. Baldwin, *Vital Records of Burlington, Massachusetts, to the Year 1850* [Boston: Wright and Potter, 1915]; Chelsea, Mass., and Thomas W. Baldwin, *Vital Records of Chelsea, Massachusetts, to the Year 1850* [Boston: Wright and Potter, 1916]; Dartmouth, Mass., *Vital Records of Dartmouth, Massachusetts, to the Year 1850* [Boston: New England Historic Genealogical Society, 1929]; Dracut, Mass., *Vital Records of Dracut, Massachusetts, to the Year 1850* [Boston: New England Historic Genealogical Society, 1907]; East Bridgewater, Mass., *Vital Records of East Bridgewater, Massachusetts, to the Year 1850* [Boston: New England Historic Genealogical Society, 1917]; Hamilton, Mass., *Vital Records of Hamilton, Massachusetts, to the End of the Year 1849* [Salem, Mass.: Essex institute, 1908]; Hopkinton, Mass., *Vital Records of Hopkinton, Massachusetts, to the Year 1850* [Boston: New England Historic Genealogical Society, 1911); Lincoln, Mass., *Vital Records of Lincoln, Massachusetts, to the Year 1850* [Boston: New England Historic Genealogical Society, 1908]; Manchester, Mass., *Vital Records of Manchester, Massachusetts, to the End of the Year 1849, Essex Institute, Salem, Mass. Vital Records of the Towns of Massachusetts* [Salem, Mass.: Essex Institute, 1903]; Marblehead, Mass. and Joseph Warren Chapman, *Vital Records of Marblehead, Massachusetts, to the End of the Year 1849* [Salem, Mass.: Essex Institute, 1903]; Medway, Mass., *Vital Records of Medway, Massachusetts, to the Year 1850* [Boston: New England Historic Genealogical Society, 1905]; Norton, Mass., *Vital Records of Norton, Massachusetts, to the Year 1850* [Boston: New England Historic Genealogical Society, 1906]).

24. Piersen, *Black Yankees*, 19; Greene, *The Negro in Colonial New England*, 217.

25. Newell, "Indian Slavery in Colonial New England," 49.

26. John Locke, "Fundamental Constitutions of South Carolina, March 1, 1669," http://avalon.law.yale.edu/17th_century/nc05.asp.

27. Efforts to enslave the Native population ended with the bloody Yamassee War in 1717 (South Carolina Historical Society, *Collections of the South Carolina Historical Society* [Charleston: South Carolina Historical Society, 1897], 5:15).

28. Alan Gallay, *The Indian Slave Trade: The Rise of the English Empire in the American South, 1670–1717* (New Haven, Conn.: Yale University Press, 2002), 4, 50; William Ramsay, *The Yamassee War* (Lincoln: University of Nebraska, 2008), 24–29, 34, 174, 178; Paul Kelton, *Epidemics and Enslavement: Biological Catastrophe in the Native Southeast* (Lincoln: University of Nebraska, 2007), xviii.

29. Peter Wood, *Black Majority: Negroes in Colonial South Carolina from 1670 through the Stono Rebellion* (New York: Norton, 1996), 19–22, 95; Denise Bossy, "Indian Slavery in Southeastern Indian and British Societies," in *Indian Slavery in Colonial America*, 216, 226; Ira Berlin, *Many Thousands Gone: The First Two Centuries of Slavery in North America* (Cambridge, Mass.: Belknap Press of Harvard University Press, 1998), 370; U.S. Bureau of the Census, *Historical Statistics of the United States, Colonial Times to 1970*, 2:1168.

30. Judith Carney, *Black Rice: The African Origins of Rice Cultivation in the Americas* (Cambridge, Mass.: Harvard University Press, 2002), 83–106; S. Max Edelson, *Plantation Enterprise in Colonial South Carolina* (Cambridge, Mass.: Harvard University Press, 2006), 63, 71–76.

31. Edelson, *Plantation Enterprise in Colonial South Carolina*, 89.

32. Edelson, *Plantation Enterprise in Colonial South Carolina*, 103–13; Carney, *Black Rice*, 78–106.

33. Thomas Cooper and David McCord, eds., *The Statutes at Large of South Carolina: Containing Acts, Records, and Documents of a Constitutional Character*, 12 vols. (Columbia, S.C.: A. S. Johnston, 1836–98), 1:341–42.

34. Cooper and McCord, *The Statutes at Large of South Carolina*, 7:397–416. Interestingly, the code introduced new types of racist language as well. In part 17, the code stated that justices had discretion to alter sentences of slaves except in cases of a slave committing homicide against a "whiter person."

35. J. H. Easterby, ed., *The Journal of the Commons House of Assembly, September 12, 1739–March 26, 1741* (Columbia, S.C.: Historical Commission of South Carolina, 1952), 325–26; Wood, *Black Majority*, 324; Cooper and McCord, *The Statutes at Large of South Carolina*, 7:397.

36. Tomlins, *Freedom Bound*, 446–52.

37. Cooper and McCord, *The Statutes at Large of South Carolina*, 7:353.

38. Cooper and McCord, *The Statutes at Large of South Carolina*, 7:353.

39. McCord, ed., *The Statutes at Large of South Carolina*, 7:397.

40. Josiah Quincy Jr., *Memoir of Josiah Quincy* (Boston: Cummings Hilliard Company, 1825), 115.

41. Eliza Lucas Pinckney to Mrs. Boddicott, July 1740, in *The Letterbook of Eliza Lucas Pinckney*, ed. Elise Pinckney and Marvin R. Zahniser (Columbia: University of South Carolina Press, 1997), 8; Max Edelson, *Plantation Enterprise in Colonial South Carolina*, 42–44; George Rogers, *The History of Georgetown County, South Carolina* (Columbia: University of South Carolina Press, 1970), 79, 53; Suzanne Cameron Linder, Marta Leslie Thacker, and Agnes Leland Baldwin, *Historical Atlas of the Rice Plantations of Georgetown County and the Santee River* (Columbia: South Carolina Department of Archives

and History for the Historic Ricefields Association, 2001), 119; Edelson, *Plantation Enterprise in Colonial South Carolina*, 111.

42. Edelson, *Plantation Enterprise in Colonial South Carolina*, 146, 151; Henry Laurens to Peter Broughton, October 1, 1765, in *The Papers of Henry Laurens*, 16 vols., ed. George C. Rogers Jr. et al. (Columbia: University of South Carolina Press, 1968–2002), 5:14; Leland Ferguson, *Uncommon Ground: Archaeology and Early African America 1650–1800* (Washington, D.C.: Smithsonian Institution Press, 1992), 73–82.

43. Ellen Hartigan-O'Connor, *The Ties That Buy: Women and Commerce in Revolutionary America* (Philadelphia: University of Pennsylvania Press, 2009), 129–51.

44. Court of General Sessions, journal, January 15, 1770, 43, SCDAH, Columbia; *South Carolina Gazette*, October 8, 1772; "Conclusion of the Stranger's Letter," *South Carolina Gazette*, September 24, 1772; Robert Olwell, "'Loose, Idle, and Disorderly' Slave Women in the Eighteenth-Century Charleston Marketplace," in *More Than Chattel: Black Women and Slavery in the Americas*, ed. David Barry Gaspar and Darlene Clark Hine (Bloomington: Indiana University Press, 1996), 97–110.

45. Ramsey, *The Yamassee War*, 34, 38–40; Ferguson, *Uncommon Ground*, 114–116.

46. Jeffrey Young has explained the influence of capitalism on the ideology of the lowcountry elite in *Domesticating Slavery: The Master Class in Georgia and South Carolina, 1670–1837* (Chapel Hill: University of North Carolina Press, 1999).

47. Henry Laurens to Elias Ball, April 1, 1765, in *The Papers of Henry Laurens*, 4:595–96; Henry Laurens to Richard Oswald, in *The Papers of Henry Laurens*, October 16, 1767, 5:370.

48. Henry Mouzon, *An Accurate Map of North and South Carolina with Their Indian Frontiers* (London: Sayer and Bennet, 1775).

49. Johann David Schoepf, *Travels in the Confederation*, trans. and ed. Alfred J. Morrison (New York: Burt Franklin, 1911), 152–54.

50. Schoepf, *Travels in the Confederation*, 152–54.

51. Linder, Thacker, and Baldwin, *Historical Atlas of the Rice Plantations of Georgetown County and the Santee River*, 107, 119; Edelson, *Plantation Enterprise in Colonial South Carolina*, 111.

52. For reasons that remain unclear, the Pawley family lost its prominence on the Waccamaw Peninsula soon after the Revolution, so details that would come out of collections such as personal papers are scarce. The daughters (and presumably many of the slaves) remained in the area, marrying into the prominent families of the Waccamaw neck. There are many more details of slave life (some of which come from slave narratives) on the plantation of the Pawleys' neighbors and relatives, the Allstons.

53. Will of Percivell Pawley, 1723, Pawley Family File, South Caroliniana Library, University of South Carolina, Columbia.

54. Edelson, *Plantation Enterprise of Colonial South Carolina*, 137, 177.

55. Robert Edgar Conrad, *In the Hands of Strangers: Readings on Foreign and Domestic Slave Trading and the Crisis of the Union* (State College: Penn State University Press, 2004), 34–38.

56. "Family Records from the Pawley Bible," Pawley Family File, South Caroliniana Library, University of South Carolina, Columbia.

57. Dorsey, *Common Bondage*, 30–32, 35–42.

58. Bernard Bailyn, *The Ordeal of Thomas Hutchinson* (Cambridge, Mass.: Belknap Press of Harvard University Press, 1974); Richard D. Brown and Jack Tager, *Massachusetts, a Concise History* (Amherst: University of Massachusetts Press, 2000), 64–75.

59. *Boston Gazette*, October 7, 1765.

60. *Boston Gazette*, September 9, 1771.

61. Douglas R. Egerton, *Death or Liberty: African Americans and Revolutionary America* (New York: Oxford University Press, 2009), 44; James Otis, *The Rights of the British Colonies Asserted and Proved* (Boston: Edes and Gill, 1764), 29.

62. Bradley, *Slavery, Propaganda, and the American Revolution*, 81–84; Joshua Coffin, *A Sketch of the History of Newbury, Newburyport, and West Newbury* (Boston: S. G. Drake, 1845), 339.

63. Nathaniel Appleton, *Considerations on Slavery* (Boston: Edes and Gill, 1767), 1, 12; John Allen, *The Watchman's Alarm to Lord N——H* (Salem, Mass. E. Russell, 1774).

64. "Virtue" is a specific eighteenth-century term in republican ideology. Virtue was the quality of a man who was independent and not corrupted by the power of others. Power could be political or economic. Thus laborers were not virtuous because they depended on their employer for their livelihood and therefore could be controlled by their employer. Slaves and women most certainly lacked virtue because of their "natural" status in society.

65. Qtd. in Bradley, *Slavery, Propaganda, and the American Revolution*, 13.

66. *Boston Gazette*, October 14, 1771.

67. *Boston Evening Post*, July 7, 1755, September 22, 1755; "Indictment of Mark and Phyllis," case no. 147038, SJC Record Books, Massachusetts Archives, Boston, Mass.; Bradley, *Slavery, Propaganda, and the American Revolution*, 1–24.

68. *Somersett v. Stewart* was decided in 1772 by Lord Mansfield (William Murray), who argued that slavery was different in each locality and "so odious, that nothing can be suffered to support it, but positive law." The case, as Mansfield made clear, did not end slavery in any of the British colonies, nor, as he showed in subsequent cases, did it end slavery in England; however, it did prevent owners from forcibly detaining slaves and deporting them for sale. Some alarmed colonists did read the case as emancipating slaves in the colonies. It would remain very significant as the foundation for making slave law a state's prerogative.

69. Bradley, *Slavery, Propaganda, and the American Revolution*, xxi, 68–70.

70. The documented freedom suits found in Massachusetts (documents allude to five additional unnamed cases), in order of date (not all sources are provided), include *Adam v. Saffin* (1703) (see Abner C. Goodell, Jr., "John Saffin and His Slave Adam," *Publications of the Colonial Society of Massachusetts, Transactions 1892–94*, vol. 1 [Boston: Colonial Society of Massachusetts, 1895], 87–112); *Pricilla v. Nathan Simmons* (1722) (see "Slavery in Essex County," *Historical Collections of the Essex Institute*, vol. 7 [Salem, Mass.: Essex Institute, 1865], 73); *James v. Burnell* (1735) (see Greene, *The Negro in Colonial New England*, 295–96; *Caesar (Mayhow) v. Goddard* (1737) (SJC case no. 44243); *Peter*, deposition [1745] (SJC case no. 60349); *Pompey v. Faneuil* (1753) (SJC case no. 69970); *Prince v. Bull* (1763) (SJC case no. 84076); *William Benson v. Joseph Collins* (1764) (SJC case no. 147284); *Slew v. Whipple* (1765) (SJC case no. 131426); *Oliver v. Sale* (1765) (see Robert M. Spector, "The Quock Walker Cases (1781–83): Slavery, Its Abolition, and Negro Citizenship in Early Massachusetts," *Journal of Negro History* 15.12 [1968]: 24); *Newport v. Billing* (1768) (SJC case no. 157509); *Margaret (Peg) v. William Muzzy* (1770) (SJC case no. 147830); *James v. Richard Lechmere* (1769) (SJC case no. 147752); *Swain v. Folger* (1769) (SJC case no. 102427); *Kate v. Moody Bridges* (1769) (see Charles L. Hill, "Slavery and Its Aftermath in Beverly, Massachusetts: Juno Larcom and Her Family," *Essex Institute Historical Collections* 116 [1980]: 120); *Jude v. Daniel Hale* (1769) (see Hill, "Slavery and

Its Aftermath in Beverly, Massachusetts," 120); *[Slave] v. Stockbridge* (1770) (see Thomas Pemberton to Jeremy Belknap, March 12, 1795, *Massachusetts Historical Society Collections*, 5th ser., 3 [1877]: 392); *Caesar v. Watson* (1771) (SJC case no. 142381); *Caesar v. Taylor* (1772) (SJC case no. 132190); *Caesar v. Greenleaf* (1773) (Essex County Court of Common Pleas Court Records, 1766–80, 5:8, Mormon reel no. 0877222); *Bristol v. John Osgood* (1773) (see Hill, "Slavery and Its Aftermath in Beverly, Massachusetts," 120); *[Slave] v. Caleb Dodge* (1774) (see Coffin, *A Sketch of the History of Newbury, Newburyport, and West Newbury*, 241); *Juno v. David Larcom* (1774) (Salem Court Records, as cited by Hill, in "Slavery and Its Aftermath," 120); *Cato v. Conant* (1777) (SJC case no. 92584); *Timon v. Peter Osgood Jr.* (1777) (see Hill, "Slavery and Its Aftermath in Beverly, Massachusetts," 120); *Prince v. Thomas Osgood* (1778) (see Hill, "Slavery and Its Aftermath in Beverly, Massachusetts," 120); *Brom and Bett v. John Ashley* (1781) (SJC case no. 159966); *Cloe Hale v. Nathaniel Hale* (1782) (see Hill, "Slavery and Its Aftermath in Beverly, Massachusetts," 120); *Walker v. Jennison* (1781) (SJC case no. 153101); and *Scipio Freeman v. Josiah Ober* (1783) (see Hill, in "Slavery and Its Aftermath in Beverly, Massachusetts," 120).

71. Catherine S. Menand, *A Research Guide to the Massachusetts Courts and Their Records* (Boston: Massachusetts Supreme Judicial Court, Archives and Records Preservation, 1987), 15.

72. Michael L. Nicholls, "'The Squint of Freedom': African-American Freedom Suits in Post-Revolutionary Virginia," *Slavery and Abolition* 20.2 (1999): 47–62; Eric Robert Papenfuse, "From Recompense to Revolution: *Mahoney V. Ashton* and the Transfiguration of Maryland Culture, 1791–1802," *Slavery and Abolition* 15.3 (1994): 38–62; Christopher Phillips, "The Roots of Quasi-Freedom: Manumission and Term Slavery in Early National Baltimore," *Southern Studies* 4.1 (1993), 53–58.

73. John Adams to Jeremy Belknap, March 21, 1795, Belknap Papers, MHS, Boston.

74. Adams, *Legal Papers*, vol. 2, *Cases 31–62*, 54.

75. The petition is reprinted in Gary Nash, *Race and Revolution* (New York: Rowman and Littlefield, 2001), 171–73.

76. Egerton, *Death or Liberty*, 58. I consider the nature and impact of this decision in chapter 2 in my discussion of the Declaration of Independence.

77. Lover of True Liberty, *The Appendix; or, Observations on the Expediency of the Petition of the Africans Living in Boston, &C* (Boston: E. Russell, 1773).

78. Kaplan, *The Black Presence in the Era of the American Revolution*, 12–14, 45–47; "Petition for Freedom (manuscript copy) to the Massachusetts Council and the House of Representatives," January [13], 1777, Jeremy Belknap Papers, MHS, Boston.

79. The essay is reprinted in Nash, *Race and Revolution*, 167–70. Other blacks, such as Phillis Wheatley, also began to write at this time. Since Wheatley's writing extended into the Revolution itself, she is covered in chapter 2.

80. Qtd. in Greene, "'Slavery or Independence,'" 195.

81. Qtd. in Greene, "'Slavery or Independence,'" 196–97.

82. *South Carolina Gazette*, March 16, 1769.

83. Rusticus, *Liberty: A Poem* (Charlestown, S.C.: T. Powell, 1770), 24. This poem is infused with allusions comparing the situation of Britain's "sons" to the enslavement of blacks. The poem uses both racial and servile imagery to illustrate the depths to which British oppression had pressed the Americans.

84. William Henry Drayton, "Presentment of Grand Jury, Charleston, April 23, 1776," Court of General Sessions, SCDAH, Columbia.

85. Qtd. in Greene, "'Slavery or Independence,'" 200.

86. Hugh Alison, *Spiritual Liberty: A Sermon, Delivered at James-Island, in South-Carolina, October, the 9th, 1769, in Consequence of the Late Resolutions* (Charlestown, S.C.: Printed for the author, 1769); Greene, "'Slavery or Independence,'" 200.

87. "This Day the House of Commons," *South Carolina Gazette*, December 8, 1769; Egerton Leigh, and Arthur Lee, *The Nature of Colony Constitutions; Two Pamphlets on the Wilkes Fund Controversy in South Carolina*, ed. Jack P. Greene (Columbia: University of South Carolina Press, 1970), 6–7.

88. Qtd. in Greene, "'Slavery or Independence,'" 200.

89. Qtd. in Greene, "'Slavery or Independence,'" 201.

90. Egerton Leigh, "A Man Unmasked," in *The Papers of Henry Laurens*, 7:2; Daniel J. McDonough, *Christopher Gadsden and Henry Laurens: The Parallel Lives of Two American Patriots* (Cranbury, N.J.: Susquehanna University Press, 2000), 19–24.

91. Henry Laurens, *A Letter from Henry Laurens to His Son John Laurens, August 14, 1776* (New York: printed privately for Columbia University Libraries, 1964), 20.

92. Jonathan Mercantini, "'Most Contemptible in the Union': South Carolina, Slavery and the Constitution," in *Ambiguous Anniversary: The Bicentennial of the International Slave Trade*, ed. David Gleeson and Simon Lewis (Columbia: University of South Carolina Press, 2012), 35–51.

93. Henry Laurens to Lewis Gervais, January 29, 1766, in *The Papers of Henry Laurens*, 5:53–54; David Duncan Wallace, *The Life of Henry Laurens* (New York: G. P. Putnam's Sons, 1915); Peter Wood, "'Taking Care of Business' in Revolutionary South Carolina: Republicanism and Slave Society," in *The Southern Experience in the American Revolution*, ed. Larry E. Tise and Jeffery J. Crow (Chapel Hill: University of North Carolina Press, 1978), 277–78.

94. Robert Olwell, "Becoming Free: Manumission and the Genesis of a Free Black Community in South Carolina, 1740–90," in *Against the Odds: Free Blacks in the Slave Societies of America*, ed. Jane Landers (Portland, Oreg.: Frank Cass, 1996), 5–6.

95. Miscellaneous Records, MM:130, 225, NN:264, SCDAH, Columbia.

96. Leander's story is based on his manumission record and bill of sale to Willeman (Miscellaneous Records, OO:385, 387, SCDAH, Columbia).

97. Miscellaneous Records, OO:385, 387, SCDAH, Columbia.

98. Memorial of Charles Skinner to Governor Montague, May 2, 1767, *South Carolina Historical Magazine* 30.2 (1929): 36–37. *Johnston and Henderson v. Dilliard* (1 Bay 233–235 [S.C. Superior Court 1791]), *The Guardian of Sally (a negro) v. Beaty* (1 Bay 260–263 [S.C. Superior Court 1792]), and *Snow v. Cullum* (1 Des. 541 [S.C. Superior Court 1797]) are the only three recorded freedom suits. In addition, the fate of a slave's freedom was determined in *Clarinda's Case*, even though this was not a traditional freedom suit, in 1767.

99. During the American Revolution, the court was more open to free blacks' testimony; see *John Mayrant v. John Williams* (1764). But in 1831, this right was denied to a free black; see *Groning v. Devann* (A. Leon Higginbotham, *In the Matter of Color: Race and the American Legal Process* [New York: Oxford University Press, 1978], 206).

100. Memorial of Charles Skinner to Governor Montague, May 2, 1767, in "Garth Correspondence," 36–37.

101. Chris Brown, *Moral Capital: Foundations of British Abolitionism* (Chapel Hill: University of North Carolina, 2006), 122.

102. The etching is reprinted in Amelia Rauser, "Death or Liberty: British Political

Prints and the Struggle for Symbols in the American Revolution," *Oxford Art Journal* 21.2 (1998): 168–69.

103. Bliss's antislavery feelings became clear later, in 1773, when he wrote the epitaph for a gravestone for a freed slave that recognized the hypocrisy of the Americans: "Tho he lived in a land of liberty/He lived a slave." Although Bliss opposed slavery, he argued this one case only (Clifford Shipton, *Sibley's Harvard Graduates* [Boston: Massachusetts Historical Society, 1962], 12:309). The marker for John Jacks is photographed and reprinted in Tom Malloy and Brenda Malloy, "Slavery in Colonial Massachusetts as Seen through Selected Gravestones," *Markers* 11 (1994): 122.

104. It is worth noting that positive law did exist, so this case won despite a poorly constructed argument. See *Newport v. Billing* (1768) (SJC case no. 157509) and *James v. Richard Lechmere* (1769) (SJC case no. 147752).

CHAPTER TWO. SLAVERY AND THE START OF THE REVOLUTION, 1775–1779

1. "William Pawley, 5769," Claims Against the Government, 1776, RW2800, SCDAH, Columbia; Robert Olwell, *Masters, Slaves, and Subjects: The Culture of Power in the South Carolina Low Country, 1740–1790* (Ithaca, N.Y.: Cornell University Press, 1998).

2. Bernard Bailyn, *The Ideological Origins of the American Revolution* (Cambridge: Belknap Press of Harvard University Press, 1967); Gary B. Nash, *Race and Revolution* (Madison, Wis.: Madison House, 1990); Douglas Egerton, *Death or Liberty: African Americans and Revolutionary America* (New York: Oxford University Press, 2004).

3. Abigail Adams to John Adams, September 22, 1774, Adams Family Correspondence, 1:162, MHS, Boston.

4. *Boston Gazette*, January 7, 1771.

5. Benjamin Quarles, *The Negro in the American Revolution* (Chapel Hill: Institute of Early American History and Culture, 1996), 52–55.

6. Quarles, *The Negro in the American Revolution*, 78–80.

7. Quarles, *The Negro in the American Revolution*, 73.

8. February 10, 1784, Court Records, 45:226 General Court Records, Massachusetts Archives, Boston; Quarles, *The Negro in the American Revolution*, 10–12. Black men serving in the militia was not new. Many black men fought in the colonial wars, especially in the French and Indian War.

9. Joyce Malcolm, *Peter's War: A New England Slave Boy and the American Revolution* (New Haven, Conn.: Yale University Press, 2009), 76, 97, 102, 125–29, 155, 192–93, 225.

10. So little is known about the Bucks that it is unclear whether the name represents an early form of the postbellum stereotype of black buck. The term "buck" to refer to a black man, however, appears not to have been in wide use until the 1840s, making it seem likely that the fact that the regiment was called the Bucks of Boston was largely coincidental (Sidney Kaplan, *The Black Presence in the Era of the American Revolution, 1770–1800* [Washington, D.C.: Smithsonian Museum Press, 1973], 55–59).

11. Jeffery Bolster, *Black Jacks: African American Seamen in the Age of Sail* (Cambridge, Mass.: Harvard University Press, 1998), 6; Quarles, *The Negro in the American Revolution*, 83–85.

12. "Book of Negroes," Canada's Digital Collections, www.blackloyalist.com/canadian digitalcollection/documents/official/book_of_negroes.htm; May 13, 1775, May 18, 1775,

and May 22, 1775, Journal of the Committee of Safety, MAC, 154:37, 48, 60, Revolution Royalists, 1775–79, reel 163, 13, Massachusetts Archives, Boston.

13. John R. Alden, ed., "John Stuart Accuses William Bull," *William and Mary Quarterly*, 3rd ser., 2.3 (1945): 318.

14. Qtd. in B. D. Bargar, "Charleston Loyalism in 1775: The Secret Reports of Alexander Innes," *South Carolina Historical Magazine* 63.3 (1962): 128.

15. Qtd. in Peter Wood, "'Impatient of Oppression': Black Freedom Struggles on the Eve of White Independence," *Southern Exposure* 12.6 (1984): 12.

16. William Campbell to Lord Dartmouth, August 31, 1775, 35:192, BPRO, London.

17. William Bull to Lord Dartmouth, December 19, 1774, 34:230–31, BPRO, London.

18. Thomas Hutchinson to the Council of Safety, July 5, 1775, in *The Papers of Henry Laurens*, 16 vols., ed. George C. Rogers Jr. et al. (Columbia, S.C.: University of South Carolina Press, 1968–2002), 10:206–8.

19. J. William Harris, *The Hanging of Thomas Jeremiah: A Free Black Man's Encounter with Liberty* (New Haven, Conn.: Yale University Press, 2009); Peter Wood, "'Taking Care of Business' in Revolutionary South Carolina: Republicanism and the Slave Society," in *The Southern Experience in the American Revolution*, ed. Jeffrey J. Crow and Larry E. Tise (Chapel Hill: University of North Carolina Press, 1978), 284; Testimony of Sambo as told by John Coram, in William Campbell to Lord Dartmouth, August 31, 1775, 35:215, BPRO, London; Olwell, *Masters, Slaves, and Subjects*, 229–30.

20. William Campbell to Lord Dartmouth, August 31, 1775, 35:211, BPRO, London.

21. William Campbell to Lord Dartmouth, August 31, 1775, 35:196, BPRO, London.

22. William Campbell to Lord Dartmouth, August 31, 1775, 35:200, BPRO, London.

23. Indeed, the evidence against Jeremiah appeared compromised. The slaves could have easily been coerced into testifying against him. The prosecutors depended solely on these slave testimonies in their case against Jeremiah. No supportive testimony for Jeremiah was allowed. Ordinarily, slaves and free black men or women were not allowed to testify, but the state could use the testimony of an African American if the person was testifying against another African American. That said, Jeremiah did have the resources and skills to accomplish the deeds attributed to him and might have detested the widespread enslavement of blacks in the colony. He might have been like many other free blacks who purchased others as a way of freeing them without raising the suspicion of the white community (William Campbell to Lord Dartmouth, August 31, 1775, 35:196, BPRO, London).

24. William Campbell to Lord Dartmouth, August 31, 1775, 35:208–9, BPRO, London.

25. Jonathan Mercantini, *Who Shall Rule at Home? The Evolution of South Carolina Political Culture, 1748–1776* (Columbia: University of South Carolina, 2007), 243; William Campbell to Lord Dartmouth, August 31, 1775, 35:212, BPRO, London.

26. William Campbell to Lord Dartmouth, August 31, 1775, 35:213, BPRO, London.

27. William Campbell to Lord Dartmouth, August 31, 1775, 35:199, BPRO, London.

28. Jacob Milligan, report on the state of South Carolina, September 15, 1775, 35:235, BPRO, London.

29. William Campbell to Lord Dartmouth, August 31, 1775, 35:191, 199–202, BPRO, London; William R. Ryan, "'Under the Color of Law': The Ordeal of Thomas Jeremiah, a Free Black Man, and the Struggle for Power in Revolutionary South Carolina," in *George Washington's South*, ed. Tamara Harvey and Greg O'Brien (Gainesville: University Press of Florida, 2004), 223–56; Sylvia R. Frey, *Water from the Rock: Black Resistance in a Revo-*

lutionary Age (Princeton, N.J.: Princeton University Press, 1991); Olwell, *Masters, Slaves, and Subjects*; Wood, "'Impatient of Oppression.'"

30. William Campbell to the general committee, September 30, 1775, in *The Papers of Henry Laurens*, 10:442; Olwell, *Masters, Slaves, and Subjects*, 237.

31. Olwell, *Masters, Slaves, and Subjects*, 237.

32. Many regard Sullivan's Island as the black Ellis Island because as much as half the black population in the United States alighted at Sullivan's Island.

33. Journal of the second Council of Safety, in *Collections of the South Carolina Historical Society*, vol. 3 (Charleston: South Carolina Historical Society, 1859), 63.

34. Journal of the second Council of Safety, 63, 75, 88.

35. Journal of the second Council of Safety, 89.

36. Journal of the second Council of Safety, 89.

37. Henry Laurens, *A Letter from Henry Laurens to His Son John Laurens, August 14, 1776* (New York: printed privately for Columbia University Libraries, 1964), 20.

38. "This was not, however, the first bloodshed in South Carolina, nor were these the first shots fired in the Lowcountry" (Olwell, *Masters, Slaves, and Subjects*, 241). The British and Americans had a brief yet bloodless encounter in November, and blood had been shed in the backcountry in early December.

39. Henry Laurens to Richard Richardson, September 19, 1775, in *The Papers of Henry Laurens*, 10:576.

40. Journal of the second Council of Safety, 102.

41. Sullivan's Island would be the site of the legendary first battle with the British only a couple of months later, when William Moultrie repelled a British assault by using the distinctive palmetto trees as a defense (journal of the second council of safety, 102).

42. Continental Congress, *Journals of the Continental Congress, January–June 1776* (Washington, D.C.: Government Printing Office, 1906), 257–58.

43. Mercantini, *Who Shall Rule at Home?*, 19; Pauline Maier, *American Scripture: Making the Declaration of Independence* (New York: Vintage, 1998), 70; 1776 Constitution of South Carolina, www.nhinet.org/ccs/docs/sc-1776.htm.

44. Maier, *American Scripture*, 59–60.

45. George Van Cleve, *A Slaveholders' Union: Slavery, Politics, and the Constitution in the Early American Republic* (Chicago: University of Chicago Press, 2010), 20–23. The petition is reprinted in Maier, *American Scripture*, 239.

46. Qtd. in Henry Steele Commager and Richard B. Morris, eds., *The Spirit of Seventy Six: The Story of the American Revolution as Told by Participants* (New York: De Capo, 1995), 312–13.

47. Commager and Morris, *The Spirit of Seventy Six*, 312–13.

48. John Adams to Jonathan Dickinson Sergeant, August 17, 1776, in *Founding Families: Digital Editions of the Papers of the Winthrops and the Adamses*, ed. C. James Taylor (Boston: Massachusetts Historical Society, 2007), http://64.61.44.187/publications/apde/portia.php?id=ADMS-06-04-02-0215; James Warren to John Adams, June 22, 1777, in *Founding Families*, http://64.61.44.187/publications/apde/portia.php?id=ADMS-06-05-02-0139; Harlow G. Unger, *John Hancock: Merchant King and American Patriot* (New York: Wiley, 2000), 185; Van Cleve, *A Slaveholders' Union*, 48; Egerton, *Death or Liberty*, 58, 75.

49. Oscar Handlin and Mary Handlin, eds., *The Popular Sources of Political Authority: Documents on the Massachusetts Constitution of 1780* (Cambridge, Mass.: Belknap Press of Harvard University Press, 1966), 9.

50. Handlin and Handlin, *The Popular Sources of Political Authority*, 8–54.

51. Kenneth Lockridge, *A New England Town: The First Hundred Years* (New York: Norton, 1970).

52. The *Essex Result* is reprinted in Handlin and Handlin, *The Popular Sources of Political Authority*, 324–65.

53. The extensive debate over and prolific disquisitions on the Constitution have sparked a small industry of scholarship. Among the key issues, particularly in the 1960s and 1970s, have been the balance between individual and corporate rights. See especially Willi Paul Adams, *The First American Constitutions: Republican Ideology and the Making of the State Constitutions in the Revolutionary Era* (Chapel Hill: Institute of Early American History and Culture, 1980), Handlin and Handlin, *The Popular Sources of Political Authority*, and Ronald M. Peters, *The Massachusetts Constitution of 1780: A Social Compact* (Amherst: University of Massachusetts Press, 1978).

54. Handlin and Handlin, *The Popular Sources of Political Authority*, 22, 217, 231, 302, 313, 340–41; A. Leon Higginbotham, *In the Matter of Color: Race and the American Legal Process* (New York: Oxford University Press, 1978), 89–90.

55. Handlin and Handlin, *The Popular Sources of Political Authority*, 302.

56. Handlin and Handlin, *The Popular Sources of Political Authority*, 23; Higginbotham, "In the Matter of Color," 90.

57. Van Cleve, *A Slaveholders' Union*; William O'Brien, "Did the Jennison Case Outlaw Slavery in Massachusetts?" *William and Mary Quarterly*, 3rd ser., 17.2 (1960): 219–41; Arthur Zilversmit, *The First Emancipation: The Abolition of Slavery in New England* (Chicago: University of Chicago Press, 1967); Edgar McManus, *Black Bondage in the North* (Syracuse, N.Y.: Syracuse University Press, 1973); Egerton, *Death or Liberty*; Higginbotham, "In the Matter of Color"; Lorenzo J. Greene, *The Negro in Colonial New England* (New York: Atheneum, 1968); George Moore, *Notes on the History of Slavery in Massachusetts* (New York: Appleton, 1866).

58. Chris Brown, *Moral Capital: Foundations of British Abolitionism* (Chapel Hill: University of North Carolina, 2006), 138–39; Richard Brown and Jack Tager, *Massachusetts: A Concise History* (Amherst: University of Massachusetts Press, 2000), 90–91.

59. Moore, *Notes on Slavery in Massachusetts*, 187–91.

60. Moore, *Notes on Slavery in Massachusetts*, 187–91.

61. William Hemphill, ed., *Extracts from the Journals of the Provincial Congresses of South Carolina* (Columbia: South Carolina Archives, 1960), 53, 154–56; David Duncan Wallace, *South Carolina, a Short History, 1520–1948* (Chapel Hill: University of North Carolina Press, 1951), 271; Max Edelman, *Plantation Enterprise in Colonial South Carolina* (Cambridge, Mass.: Harvard University Press, 2006), 12; Adams, *The First American Constitutions*, 21, 70–71.

62. South Carolina, *An Act for Establishing the Constitution of the State of South-Carolina, Passed the 19th Day of March, 1778* (Charles-Town, S.C.: Peter Timothy, 1778); Adams, *The First American Constitutions*, 71–72; Wallace, *South Carolina, a Short History, 1520–1948*, 277–82.

63. Hemphill, *Extracts from the Journals of the Provincial Congresses of South Carolina*, 53, 154–56; South Carolina, *An Act for Establishing the Constitution of the State of South-Carolina, Passed the 19th Day of March, 1778*; Adams, *The First American Constitutions*, 21.

64. Maurice Wallace, "'Are We Men?': Prince Hall, Martin Delany, and the Masculine Ideal in Black Freemasonry, 1775–1865," *American Literary History* 9.3 (1997): 397–99.

65. Ruth Bogin, "'Liberty Further Extended': A 1776 Antislavery Manuscript by Lemuel Haynes," *William and Mary Quarterly* 40.1 (1983): 85–90; Rita Roberts, "Patriotism and Political Criticism: The Evolution of Political Consciousness in the Mind of a Black Revolutionary Soldier," *Eighteenth Century Studies* 27.4 (1994): 571, 574.

66. Richard D. Brown, "'Not Only Extreme Poverty, but the Worst Kind of Orphanage': Lemuel Haynes and the Boundaries of Racial Tolerance on the Yankee Frontier, 1770–1820," *New England Quarterly* 61.4 (1988): 511–13.

67. John Saillant, *Black Puritan, Black Republican: The Life and Thought of Lemuel Haynes, 1753–1833* (Oxford: Oxford University Press, 2003), 155; John Saillant, "Lemuel Haynes's Black Republicanism and the American Republican Tradition, 1775–1820," *Journal of the Early Republic* 14.3 (1994): 293. Historians have debated whether the founding generation was more republican or liberal. Republican values tended to promote communal interest ahead of individual needs. Liberals focused a great deal on the need for individual freedom. Haynes fell into the republican category, which would come to be associated with the Federalist Party.

68. Bogin, "'Liberty Further Extended,'" 85–90; Roberts, "Patriotism and Political Criticism," 580–81.

69. Bogin, "'Liberty Further Extended,'" 92; Roberts, "Patriotism and Political Criticism," 580–81.

70. Saillant, *Black Puritan, Black Republican*, 81; Bogin, "'Liberty Further Extended,'" 91–92; Pauline Maier, introduction to *Declaration of Independence and the Constitution of the United States* (New York: Bantam Classic, 1998), 42; Roberts, "Patriotism and Political Criticism," 585.

71. Quarles, *The Negro in the American Revolution*, 45; Will Harris, "Phillis Wheatley, Diaspora Subjectivity, and the African American Canon," *MELUS* 33.3 (2008): 27–28.

72. *Connecticut Gazette*, March 11, 1774.

73. Quarles, *The Negro in the American Revolution*, 45; Harris, "Phillis Wheatley, Diaspora Subjectivity, and the African American Canon," 37.

74. Paula Bennett, "Phillis Wheatley's Vocation and the Paradox of the 'Afric Muse,'" *PMLA* 113.1 (1998): 66; Henry Louis Gates, *The Trials of Phillis Wheatley: America's First Black Poet and Encounters with the Founding Fathers* (New York: Basic Civitas Books, 2003), 37–40.

75. Olwell, *Masters, Slaves, and Subjects*, 230–31; Josiah Smith to George Appleby, 16 June 1775, Charleston, S.C., Josiah Smith Letterbook, #3018, folder 1, 405, Southern Historical Center, University of North Carolina, Chapel Hill.

76. Walter Edgar, *Partisans and Redcoats: The Southern Conflict That Turned the Tide of the American Revolution* (New York: HarperCollins, 2003), 37, 40; David Ramsay to William Henry Drayton, September 1, 1779, in "David Ramsay, 1749–1815: A Selection from his Writings," ed. Robert Brunhouse, *Transactions from the American Philosophical Society* 55.4 (1965): 64.

77. Arthur H. Shaffer, "Between Two Worlds: David Ramsay and the Politics of Slavery," *Journal of Southern History* 50.2 (1984): 181; Gregory D. Massey, "The Limits of Antislavery Thought in the Revolutionary Lower South: John Laurens and Henry Laurens," *Journal of Southern History* 63.3 (1997): 502–4. For a thorough examination of the growth of sentiment during the American Revolution, see Sarah Knott, *Sensibility and the American Revolution* (Chapel Hill: Omohundro Institute of Early American History and Culture, 2009).

78. Laurens, *Letter from Henry Laurens to His Son John Laurens, August 14, 1776*, 20, 21.

79. John Laurens to Henry Laurens, January 14, 1778, in *The Papers of Henry Laurens*, 12:305.

80. Robert M. Weir, *"The Last of American Freemen": Studies in the Political Culture of the Colonial and Revolutionary South* (Macon, Ga.: Mercer University Press, 1986), 89–104.

81. Qtd. in Massey, "The Limits of Antislavery Thought in the Revolutionary Lower South," 512.

82. David Ramsay to William Henry Drayton, September 1, 1779, in "David Ramsay, 1749–1815," 64; John Ford et al. *Journals of the Continental Congress, 1774–1789*, vol. 8 (Washington, D.C.: Library of Congress, 1909), 1386.

83. Ford, *Journals of the Continental Congress*, 29 March 1779, 1386–1388.

84. Massey, "The Limits of Antislavery Thought in the Revolutionary Lower South," 516.

85. Massey, "The Limits of Antislavery Thought in the Revolutionary Lower South," 516.

86. Massey, "The Limits of Antislavery Thought in the Revolutionary Lower South," 518–21.

87. Rutledge to delegates of South Carolina in Congress, May 24, 1780, in "'Letters of John Rutledge,' John Rutledge and Joseph W. Barnwell," *South Carolina Historical and Genealogical Magazine* 17.4 (1916): 135; William Bell Clark, William James Morgan, William S. Dudley, and Michael J. Crawford, eds., *Naval Documents of the American Revolution*, 11 vols. (Washington, D.C.: Naval History Division, Department of the Navy, 1964–2005), 321; Quarles, *The Negro in the American Revolution*, 7:75, 96–97, 104–105; John Rutledge to the general assembly, committee report, 1783, Records of the General Assembly, #44, SCDAH, Columbia.

88. Massey, "The Limits of Antislavery Thought in the Revolutionary Lower South," 523–24; A. S. Salley, ed., *Journal of the House of Representatives of South Carolina, January 8, 1782–February 26, 1782* (Columbia: Historical Commission of South Carolina, 1916), 56, 79, 101.

CHAPTER THREE. THE *TYRANNICIDE* AFFAIR BEGINS, 1779–1782

1. "Proclamation by His Excellency Sir Henry Clinton," Papers of Guy Carleton, June 1–August 1, 1779, 30/55/17, #2094, BRPO, London.

2. Robert Olwell, *Masters, Slaves, and Subjects: The Culture of Power in the South Carolina Low Country, 1740–1790* (Ithaca, N.Y.: Cornell University Press, 1998), 257.

3. Olwell, *Masters, Slaves, and Subjects*, 245, 256–57; Cassandra Pybus, *Epic Journeys of Freedom* (Boston: Beacon Press, 2006), 40–41; James Hall Jr. to Mr. Guerard, June 25, 1779, Benjamin Lincoln Papers, reel 4, 147, MHS, Boston.

4. Henry DeSaussure Bull, "Ashley Hall Plantation," *South Carolina Historical Magazine* 53.2 (1952): 63.

5. Qtd. in Olwell, *Masters, Slaves, and Subjects*, 259; "Extracts from the Journal of Lt. John Bell Tilden, Second Pennsylvania Line, 1781–1782," *Pennsylvania Magazine of History and Biography* 19.2 (1895), 225.

6. Olwell, *Masters, Slaves, and Subjects*, 259.

7. David Stevens to John Wendell, February 20, 1782, in "Boyd-Stephens Letters," *MHS Proceedings*, vol. 48 (Boston: Massachusetts Historical Society, 1915), 342–43.

8. Proceedings of the Board of Police, CO 5/521, BRPO, London.

9. Proceedings of the Board of Police, CO 5/520, 2, BRPO, London.

10. Proceedings of the Board of Police, Co 5/520, 2–6, BRPO, London.

11. Josiah Smith to George Appleby, December 2, 1780, and Josiah Smith to George Appleby, March 15, 1781, Josiah Smith Letterbook, #3018, folder 1, 405, 431, Southern Historical Center, University of North Carolina, Chapel Hill.

12. William Bull to George Germain, March 22, 1781, in K. G. Davies, ed., *Documents of the American Revolution, 1770–1783*, vol. 20 (London: Irish University Press), 94–95; Jerome J. Nadelhaft, *The Disorders of War: The Revolution in South Carolina* (Orono: University of Maine at Orono Press, 1981), 72–74; Olwell, *Masters, Slaves, and Subjects*, 261–63.

13. William Bull to George Germain, March 22, 1781, 94–95.

14. Qtd. in Olwell, *Masters, Slaves, and Subjects*, 262.

15. Qtd. in Olwell, *Masters, Slaves, and Subjects*, 263.

16. Henry Lewis Gervais to Henry Laurens, September 27, 1782, John Lewis Gervais papers, 1772–96, South Caroliniana Library, University of South Carolina, Columbia.

17. Boston King, "Memoirs of the Life of Boston King, a Black Preacher," in *Face Zion Forward: First Writers of the Black Atlantic, 1785–1798*, ed. Joanna Brooks and John Saillant (Boston: Northeastern University Press, 2002), 212–16.

18. *Pennsylvania Packet*, July 25, 1778, January 28, 1779, June 8, 1779, July 20, 1779; *Pennsylvania Evening Post*, April 26, 1779; *New Jersey Gazette*, May 5, 1779; *Massachusetts Spy; or, American Oracle of Liberty*, February 1, 1779.

19. *Pennsylvania Packet*, July 25, 1778, January 28, 1779, June 8, 1779, July 20, 1779; *Pennsylvania Evening Post*, April 26, 1779; *New Jersey Gazette*, May 5, 1779; *Massachusetts Spy; or, American Oracle of Liberty*, February 1, 1779.

20. Charles Joyner, *Down by the Riverside: A South Carolina Slave Community* (Urbana: University of Illinois Press, 1984), 46.

21. Johann David Schoepf, *Travels in the Confederation 1783–1784*, trans. and ed. Alfred J. Morrison (New York: Burt Franklin, 1911), 157–58, 160.

22. Robert H. Patton, *Patriot Pirates: The Privateer War for Freedom and Fortune in the American Revolution* (New York: Random House, 2008), 73.

23. Simon Schama, *Rough Crossings: Britain, the Slaves, and the American Revolution* (New York: HarperCollins, 2006), 100, 8; *South Carolina Gazette*, July 11, 1779; *Pennsylvania Packet*, June 20, 1779, 3; David Ramsay, *The History of South Carolina: From Its First Settlement in 1670, to the Year 1808*, vol. 1 (1858; rpt., Cleveland, Ohio: Reprint Company, 1959), 272; Benjamin Quarles, *The Negro in the American Revolution* (New York: Norton, 1961), 51; Sylvia Frey, *Water from the Rock: Black Resistance in a Revolutionary Age* (Princeton, N.J.: Princeton University Press, 1991), 142.

24. Henry Mouzon, *An Accurate Map of North and South Carolina with their Indian Frontiers* (London: Sayer and Bennett, 1775). The map can be seen at www.battleofcamden.org/mouzon.jpg.

25. Paul Trapier to Henry Laurens, October 7, 1779, Charles Francis Jenkins Collection, Historical Society of Pennsylvania, Philadelphia.

26. *Pennsylvania Packet*, June 8, 1779.

27. *South Carolina Gazette*, July 11, 1779.

28. Mouzon, *An Accurate Map of North and South Carolina with their Indian Frontiers*.

29. Massachusetts Board of War Elbridge Gerry, James Lovell, and Samuel Holtin, June 29, 1779, Board of War Letters 1776–80, MAC, 151:292–94, Massachusetts Archives, Boston; "Map of Roseberry," South Caroliniana Library, University of South Carolina, Columbia; Michael Trinkley, ed., *Archaeological and Historical Examinations of Three Eighteenth and Nineteenth Century Rice Plantations on the Waccamaw Neck*, Chicora

Foundation Research Series 31 (Columbia, S.C.: Chicora Foundation, 1993), 207–8. Percival Pawley had land nearer to the Vereen plantation, leaving that link as another distant possibility.

30. Schoepf, *Travels in the Confederation*, 157–62.

31. We do not know the specific names of these children. Although the children's ages are not listed, in different accountings of the slaves the number of children varies, suggesting that some might have been old enough to pass as adults.

32. William Bartram, *Travels Through North and South Carolina, Georgia, East and West Florida* (Philadelphia: James and Johnson, 1791), 471, 29, http://docsouth.unc.edu /nc/bartram/bartram.html; Mouzon, *An Accurate Map of North and South Carolina with Their Indian Frontiers*. Special thanks to Ben Burroughs of Coastal Carolina University's CCU's Center for Marine and Wetland Studies, who knew that the river was navigable in this area.

33. Charles Joyner, *Down by the Riverside: A South Carolina Slave Community* (Urbana: University of Illinois Press, 1984), 132; Sally Hadden, *Slave Patrols: Law and Violence in Virginia and the Carolinas* (Cambridge, Mass.: Harvard University Press, 2003), 73, 21–24.

34. William Bell Clark, William James Morgan, William S. Dudley, and Michael Crawford, eds., *Naval Documents of the American Revolution*, 11 vols. (Washington, D.C.: Naval Historical Center, 1964–2005), 8:81; 9:192–93; Frey, *Water from the Rock*, 92, 122–123; Schama, *Rough Crossings*, 107, 119.

35. "Dolphin" probably meant "mahi-mahi," which is also known as dolphin-fish.

36. Charles Connors, diary, 1779–80, manuscript, South Caroliniana Library, University of South Carolina, Columbia.

37. Board of War for *Massachusetts v. The Ship Victoria*, 1779, Records of the Court of Appeal in Cases of Capture, Revolutionary War Prize Cases, 1776–87, M162, Massachusetts, #59, NARA, Washington, D.C. Urezberoeta had just purchased the ship in South Carolina.

38. Board of War Letters, 1777–80, MAC, 153:229–30, Massachusetts Archives, Boston; Board of War Minutes, 1776–80, MAC, 151:292, Massachusetts Archives, Boston; Board of War for *Massachusetts v. The Ship Victoria*, 1779, Records of the Court of Appeal in Cases of Capture, Revolutionary War Prize Cases, 1776–87, M162, Massachusetts, #59, NARA, Washington, D.C.

39. Board of War Minutes, 1776–80, MAC, 151:167–71, Massachusetts Archives, Boston.

40. Records do not mention the British ships sailing into Boston. Either the British released the *Victoria* and fled, or the captains decided they could not keep control of three ships and just kept control of the ship with the booty (Board of War Letters, 1777–80, MAC, 153:229–30, Massachusetts Archives, Boston).

41. Joseph Des Barres, "Boston Harbor Seen from Castle William to Governor's Island," *Atlantic Neptune* series 2, no. 26, Harvard University Map Collection, Harvard College Library, Cambridge, Mass.; Christian Remick, *A Perspective View of the Blockade of Boston Harbor*, watercolor on laid paper, 1768, MHS, Boston; Boston; Board of War for *Massachusetts v. The Ship Victoria*, 1779, Records of the Court of Appeal in Cases of Capture, Revolutionary War Prize Cases, 1776–87, M162, Massachusetts, #59, NARA, Washington, D.C.

42. John Gray, diary, October 3, 1778–December 15, 1778, photostats, 1776–78, MHS, Boston.

43. Board of War to Paul Revere, June 28, 1779, Board of War Letters, 1776–83, MAC, 151:291–92, Massachusetts Archive, Boston; Board of War to Elbridge Gerry et al., June 29, 1779, Board of War Letters, 1776–83, MAC, 151:293–94, Massachusetts Archive, Boston; Board of War Minutes, June 28, 1779, MAC, 150:288, Massachusetts Archive, Boston.

44. Committee report, June 29, 1779, Revolutionary Council Papers, 1778–79, MAC, 175:360, Massachusetts Archive, Boston; Moore, *Notes on the History of Slavery in Massachusetts* (New York: Appleton, 1866), 167–68.

45. Board of War for *Massachusetts v. The Ship Victoria*, 1779, Records of the Court of Appeal in Cases of Capture, Revolutionary War Prize Cases, 1776–87, M162, Massachusetts, #59, NARA, Washington, D.C.

46. Clark, Morgan, Dudley, and Crawford, *Naval Documents of the American Revolution*, 10:930.

47. Clark, Morgan, Dudley, and Crawford, *Naval Documents of the American Revolution*, 10:930.

48. *New England Chronicle*, August 15, 1776; Massachusetts, *A Journal of the Honorable House of Representatives of the State of Massachusetts-Bay, in New-England, Begun and Held at Boston, in the County of Suffolk, on Wednesday the 26th Day of May, Anno Domini, 1779* (Boston: John Gill, 1779), 105; Abner Goodell, Ellis Ames, and Melville Bigelow, eds., *The Acts and Resolves, Public and Private of the Province of the Massachusetts Bay*, 21 vols. (Boston: Wright and Potter, 1869–1922); Moore, *Notes on the History of Slavery in Massachusetts*, 148–54.

49. Clark, Morgan, Dudley, and Crawford, *Naval Documents of the American Revolution*, 8:930–31.

50. Qtd. in Patricia Bradley, *Slavery, Propaganda, and the American Revolution* (Jackson: University Press of Mississippi, 1998), 13.

51. Board of War to Elbridge Gerry et al., June 29, 1779, Board of War Letters, 1776–83, MAC, 151:293–94, Massachusetts Archive, Boston; House of Representatives resolution, June 24, 1779, Miscellaneous Revolutionary Documents, 1777–81, MAC, 150:288; Board of War Minutes, June 28, 1779, MAC, Massachusetts Archives, Boston.

52. Resolve respecting captured negroes, Revolutionary Resolves, 1779, MAC, 223:307, Massachusetts Archives, Boston.

53. Henry Laurens to John Rutledge, July 17, 1779, Records of the General Assembly, #55, 11, SCDAH.

54. Harlow Giles Unger, *John Hancock: Merchant King and American Patriot* (New York: Wiley, 2000), 282; Thomas Cushing to council chamber on behalf of John Hancock, July 24, 1779, Revolutionary Council Papers, 1779, MAC, 170:270, Massachusetts Archives, Boston; Nathaniel Appleton to council, June 22, 1779, Revolutionary Council Papers, 1778–79, MAC, 175:53, Massachusetts Archives, Boston; Revolutionary council resolution, Henry Gardner grant, MAC, Revolutionary Resolves, 1779, MAC, 224:389, Massachusetts Archives, Boston; Miscellaneous Revolutionary Documents, 1777–83, MAC, 151:170, Massachusetts Archives, Boston.

55. Miscellaneous Revolutionary Documents, 1777–83, MAC, 151:170, Massachusetts Archives, Boston; Moore, *Notes on Slavery*, 167–68.

56. Paul Trapier to Henry Laurens, October 7, 1779, Charles Francis Jenkins Collection, Historical Society of Pennsylvania, Philadelphia.

57. Henry Laurens to Anthony Pawley, July 17, 1779, Records of the General Assembly, 1784–55–9 SCDAH, Columbia.

58. Committee Report, July 10, 1779, *Letters of Delegates to Congress: June 1,*

1779–September 30, 1779, ed. Paul H. Smith, Gerard W. Gewalt, and Ronald M. Gephart (Washington, D.C.: Library of Congress, 1996), 183–85, http://memory.loc.gov/cgi-bin/query/r?ammem/hlaw:@field(DOCID+@lit(dg013T000)).

59. Petition of Isaac Smith, John Codman, and William Smith, Revolution Petitions, 1779, MAC, 185:407, Massachusetts Archives, Boston; John Codman, Letterbook, July 3, 1783–June 4, 1785, manuscript, 1783–85, Harvard Business School Baker Library, Boston.

60. Petition of Isaac Smith John Codman, and William Smith, Revolution Petitions, 1779, MAC, 185:407, Massachusetts Archives, Boston; Petition of John Winthrop, Revolution Petitions, 1779, MAC, 185:409, Massachusetts Archives, Boston; Resolution, November 18, 1779, Revolution Petitions, 1779, MAC, 185:410, Massachusetts Archives, Boston; Lawrence Shaw Mayo, *The Winthrop Family in America* (Boston: Massachusetts Historical Society, 1948), 225–28; "Family Records from the Pawley Bible," Pawley Family File, South Caroliniana Library, University of South Carolina, Columbia.

61. Will of William Vereen, 1811, Horry County Will Transcripts, ST547, 1:45, SCDAH, Columbia.

62. Marriage did not confer freedom on a slave married to a free person. See Emily Blanck, "1783: The Turning Point in the Law of Slavery and Freedom in Massachusetts," *New England Quarterly* 75.1 (2002), 24–51.

63. U.S. census, 1790, Massachusetts, National Archives Annex, East Point, Ga.; SJC Record Books, 1783, reel 18, 177–78, Massachusetts Archives, Boston.

64. SJC, order to issue writ of habeas corpus, August 26, 1783, Records of the General Assembly, 1784–55–21, SCDAH, Columbia.

65. C. S. Manegold, *Ten Hills Farm: The Forgotten History of Slavery in the North* (Princeton, N.J.: Princeton University Press, 2010), 156–66; Alexandra Chan, *Slavery in the Age of Reason: Archaeology at a New England Farm* (Knoxville: University of Tennessee Press, 2007), 50.

66. Manegold, *Ten Hills Farm*, 192.

67. Chan, *Slavery in the Age of Reason*, 97, 148–49, 167, 143–44, 160–64.

68. Chan, *Slavery in the Age of Reason*, 168; Manegold, *Ten Hills Farm*, 226.

69. Will and codicil of Isaac Royall, 1781(?),US 919 MAS ROY Folio, 3, Law School Rare Books, Harvard Law Library, Cambridge, Mass.

70. Petition of Belinda to the general court, February 14, 1783, Revolutionary Resolves, 1783, MAC, 239:11–14, Massachusetts Archives, Boston.

71. Phillis Wheatley, "On Imagination," www.poetryfoundation.org/poem/236938; petition of Belinda to the Massachusetts General Court, February 14, 1783, Revolutionary Resolves, 1783, MAC, 239:11–14, Massachusetts Archives, Boston.

72. Melvin Wade, "'Shining in Borrowed Plumage': Affirmation of Community in the Black Coronation Festivals of New England, ca. 1750–1850," in *Material Life in America, 1600–1860*, ed. Robert Blair St. George (Boston: Northeastern University Press, 1988), 171–79.

73. Paul Cuffe's petition is reprinted in Sidney Kaplan, *The Black Presence in the Era of the American Revolution 1770–1800* (Washington, D.C.: Smithsonian Museum Press, 1973), 129–35.

74. Moore, *Notes on the History of Slavery in Massachusetts*, 196–99.

75. Olwell, *Masters, Slaves, and Subjects.*

76. *Nickels (Administrator of Sackee) v. Dunbar, 1768*, SJC Record Books, case no. 88589, Massachusetts Archives, Boston.

77. Percival Pawley, "Claims Against the Continental Army" RW2800, AA #5768, 3, SCDAH, Columbia.

78. Anthony Pawley, "Claims Against the Continental Army," RW2800, AA #5766, 2, SCDAH, Columbia.

79. Samuel Hasford, petition to Governor Hancock, August 25, 1783, Records of the General Assembly, 1784–55–17, SCDAH, Columbia.

80. "Negroes," Papers of Board of Trade and Secretaries of State: America and West Indies, Original Correspondence, Dispatches and Miscellaneous, 1780–83, CO 5/8/86–88, BPRO, London.

81. General Leslie to Guy Carleton, October 3, 1782, Papers of Guy Carleton, 30/55/ 51/5787, BPRO, London.

82. Agreement between Alexander Wright, John Johnson, Edward Rutledge and Benjamin Guerard, Cedar Grove, October 10, 1782, Papers of Board of Trade and Secretaries of State, 30/55/51/5844, BPRO, London.

83. Alexander Leslie, order of return of provisions, December 1782, Papers of Board of Trade and Secretaries of State, 30/55/97/10348, BPRO, London.

84. David George, a Baptist missionary who eventually moved to Sierra Leone, offers one of the most vivid depictions of the life of a black Loyalist in "An Account of the Life of Mr. David George, from Sierra Leone in Africa; Given by Himself" (*The Baptist Annual Register*, ed. John Rippon [London: n.p., 1794]).

85. Archibald Campbell to Guy Carleton, December 6, 1782, Papers of Board of Trade and Secretaries of State, 30/55/56/6342, BPRO, London.

86. Olwell, *Masters, Slaves, and Subjects*, 270.

CHAPTER 4. DIVERGING SLAVE LAW IN THE NEW NATION, 1783–1787

1. Robert Olwell, "Becoming Free: Manumission and the Genesis of a Free Black Community in South Carolina, 1740–1790," *Slavery and Abolition* 17.1 (1996): 1.

2. See chapter 1 for a discussion of the manumission policies of South Carolina.

3. *Ancient Charters and Laws of Massachusetts Bay* (Boston: T. B. Wait, 1814), 746; Abner Goodell, Ellis Ames, and Melville Bigelow, ed., *Acts and Resolves of the Province of Massachusetts Bay*, 21 vols. (Boston: Wright and Potter, 1869–1922), 1:519.

4. *Ancient Charters and Laws*; William Dillon Piersen, *Black Yankees: The Development of an Afro-American Subculture in Eighteenth-Century New England* (Amherst: University of Massachusetts Press, 1988), 48.

5. Essex Institute Historical Collections, 1908, vol. 44 (Salem: Massachusetts Historical Society, 1908), 89.

6. Charlestown Selectmen's Records, 1767–78, August 5, 1771, Henry Herbert Edes Collection, box 1, folder 14, MHS, Boston.

7. Henry Barnard Worth Collection, 1641–1905, book 4, Town Meeting and Court Records, November 27, 1773, back pages of book, Nantucket Historical Association, Nantucket, Mass.

8. Indenture agreement between Isaac Smith and Scipio Dalton, June 20, 1779, December 20–24, 1779, Smith-Carter family papers, MHS, Boston. The document is available at www.masshist.org/database/transcription.cfm?transcriptDir=masshist&transcript= lsta_4852.xml&queryID=728.

9. Henry Barnard Worth Collection, 1641–1905, book 4, Town Meeting and Court

Records, November 27, 1773, back pages of book, Nantucket Historical Association, Nantucket, Mass.

10. Nantucket Deedbook, 5:184, Nantucket Town Hall, Nantucket, Mass.

11. Nantucket Deedbook, 6:264, Nantucket Town Hall, Nantucket, Mass.

12. Dorchester Account Book, 1766–73, MSS C 2506 NEGHS, Falmouth Records, Falmouth Historical Society, Falmouth Mass.; Massachusetts Taxation Account, New Bedford, MSS 1926, 1771, N534, New Bedford, Harvard Baker Library, Cambridge, Mass.; Bolton Town Records, MHS, Boston; William Hurt Account Books, MHS, Boston; Rehoboth 1781 Tax Records, MHS, Boston; Sudbury, Massachusetts, *The War Years in the Town of Sudbury, Massachusetts, 1765–1781* (Sudbury, Mass.: Town of Sudbury, 1975); Edward Brandon, *The Records of the Town of Cambridge, Massachusetts, 1603–1703* (Cambridge, Mass.: Cambridge City Council, 1901); Robert Dunkle and Ann S. Lainhart, *The Town Records of Roxbury, Massachusetts, 1647–1730* (Boston: New England Historic Genealogical Society, 1997).

13. Dorchester had thirty-seven slaves (3 percent of overall town population), New Bedford sixteen (2 percent), Bolton four (.4 percent), and Sudbury twenty-seven (2 percent). See J. H. Benton, *Early Census Making in Massachusetts 1643–1745* (Boston: Charles E. Goodspeed, 1905), 74–99.

14. It is unclear why they did not collect these bonds. It is possible that they did collect them but that the records were lost or that they simply failed to record them. It also could be that these towns did not feel as though they could require a bond by the authority of an expired law or that they found other ways to ensure that the slave would not become a burden on the town.

15. Catharine M. Sedgwick, "Essay on Mumbet," Catharine M. Sedgwick I papers, box 6, folder 6, 2–6, MHS, Boston; Jon Swan, "The Slave Who Sued for Freedom," *American Heritage* 41.2 (1990): 51–55; Harold W. Felton, *Mumbet: The Story of Elizabeth Freeman* (New York: Dodd, Mead, 1970), 24, 40; Arthur Zilversmit, "Quok Walker, Mumbet, and the Abolition of Slavery in Massachusetts," *William and Mary Quarterly*, 3rd ser., 25.4 (1968): 614–24.

16. Several books and articles refer to Mum Bett. See, for example, François La Rochefoucauld-Liancourt, *Travels through the United States of America, the Country of the Iroquois, and Upper Canada, in the Years 1795, 1796, and 1797*, 2 vols. (London: R. Phillips, 1799); Swan, "The Slave Who Sued for Freedom"; Beth Zemaitis, "Elizabeth Freeman: Free at Last," unpublished ms., 1991; Zilversmit, "Quok Walker, Mumbet, and the Abolition of Slavery"; William C. Nell and Harriet Beecher Stowe, *The Colored Patriots of the American Revolution, with Sketches of Several Distinguished Colored Persons: To Which Is Added a Brief Survey of the Condition and Prospects of Colored Americans* (Boston: R. F. Wallcut, 1855); David Levering Lewis, *W. E. B. Du Bois: Biography of a Race, 1868–1919* (New York: Henry Holt, 1993), 14; and Harriet Martineau, *Retrospect of Western Travel* (London: Saunders and Otley, 1838), 1:246–47. An interesting tidbit is that W. E. B. Du Bois was related to her.

17. Catharine Sedgwick, "Slavery in New England," in *Bentley's Miscellany*, Charles Dickens, William Harrison Ainsworth, and Albert Smith (eds.), vol. 34 (London: Richard Bentley, 1853), 419–20; Sedgwick, "Essay on Mumbet," Catharine M. Sedgwick I papers, box 6, folder 6, 10, MHS, Boston.

18. George Henry Moore, *Notes on the History of Slavery in Massachusetts* (New York: Appleton, 1866), 210. For the legal importance of *Brom and Bett v. Ashley*, see Arthur Zilversmit, "Quok Walker, Mumbet, and the Abolition of Slavery in Massachusetts," 614–24.

19. Arthur Zilversmit, *The First Emancipation: The Abolition of Slavery in New England* (Chicago: University of Chicago Press, 1967), 112; Zilversmit, "Quok Walker, Mumbet, and the Abolition of Slavery in Massachusetts," 624; Richard E. Welch Jr., "Mumbett and Judge Sedgwick, A Footnote to the Early History of Massachusetts Justice," *Boston Bar Journal* 8.1 (1964): 13–14.

20. *Brom and Bett v. Ashley*, May 28, 1781, Inferior Court of Pleas, Great Barrington, Mass., SJC Record Books, Massachusetts Archives, Boston.

21. La Rochefoucauld-Liancourt, *Travels through the United States of North America*; Swan, "The Slave Who Sued for Freedom," 54.

22. In Peru, the actions of the enslaved abolished slavery as well. See Carlos Aguirre, *Agentes de su propia libertad: Los esclavos de Lima y la desintegratión de las esclavitud, 1821–1854* (Lima: Pontificia Universidad Católica del Perú, fondo editorial, 1993).

23. Although black slaves had been carried to other colonies before they arrived in Massachusetts, the Bay colony was the first (1641) to legally sanction slavery. See "Bond-Slavery," *The Laws and Liberties of Massachusetts Bay*, 3 vols. (Wilmington, Del.: Scholarly Resources, 1976), 1:4. Virginia and Maryland were the next mainland English colonies to enact slave codes (in the 1660s). See A. Leon Higginbotham, *In the Matter of Color: Race and the American Legal Process* (New York: Oxford University Press, 1978), 34–38, 61–62. Vermont freed its slaves through its constitution, but in 1783 it was not yet part of the United States. In addition, it should be noted that Pennsylvania passed a gradual emancipation act before Massachusetts in 1780, but Massachusetts' judicial decree ended slavery wholly, so that no master could claim a man or woman was a slave after 1783.

24. "Jennison v. Walker" (SJC case no. 153101), SJC Record Books, Massachusetts Archives, Boston; Zilversmit, "Quok Walker, Mumbet," 614.

25. The docket for the Worcester County Court of Common Pleas, June session, lists Walker's case before Jennison's, although Jennison's came before Walker's in the court record. The court clearly decided both practically alongside one another.

26. Robert M. Spector, "The Quock Walker Cases (1781–83): Slavery, Its Abolition, and Negro Citizenship in Early Massachusetts," *Journal of Negro History* 15.12 (1968), 15; Nathaniel Sargeant, a bill against slavery, Miscellaneous Revolutionary Documents, 1772–81, MAC, 142:58, Massachusetts Archives, Boston. Although Sargeant fought to end slave trade, it's not clear he was in fact sympathetic to antislavery. The slave trade was generally seen as reprehensible by a wide range of Americans, but not necessarily slavery.

27. Zilversmit, "Quok Walker, Mumbet," 614–15; William O'Brien, "Did the Jennison Case Outlaw Slavery in Massachusetts?" *William and Mary Quarterly*, 3rd ser., 17.2 (1960): 219–41; John D. Cushing, "The Cushing Court and the Abolition of Slavery in Massachusetts: More Notes on the 'Quock Walker Case,'" *American Journal of Legal History* 5.2 (1961): 118–44.

28. See chapter 1, pages 34–35 and 178n70, for a list of the freedom suits.

29. "Notes on Law Cases, 1783," 98, William Cushing Papers, 1664–1814, MHS, Boston; Higginbotham, *In the Matter of Color*, 95; "Declaration of Rights," Massachusetts State Constitution, 1780.

30. "Notes on Law Cases," 98, William Cushing Papers, 1664–1814, MHS, Boston.

31. "Notes on Law Cases," 98, William Cushing Papers, 1664–1814, MHS, Boston.

32. "Notes on Law Cases," 99, William Cushing Papers, 1664–1814, MHS, Boston.

33. Higginbotham, *In the Matter of Color*, 99.

34. U.S. census, 1790, Massachusetts, National Archives Annex, East Point, Ga.

35. Charles Cushing to Jared Ingersoll, draft, Boston, May 1, 1798, William Cushing

Papers, 1664–1814, MHS, Boston; Cushing, "The Cushing Court and the Abolition of Slavery in Massachusetts," 222.

36. *Jackson v. Phillips et al.*, 14 Allen (Mass.) 563–64 (1867); O'Brien, "Did the Jennison Case Outlaw Slavery?" 220, 238.

37. *Winchendon v. Hatfield*, 4 Mass. Reports, 128–29.

38. O'Brien in particular has been at the fore of the reevaluation of the legality of *Jennison* ("Did the Jennison Case Outlaw Slavery?" 220).

39. Joanne Melish, *Disowning Slavery: Gradual Emancipation and "Race" in New England, 1780–1860* (Ithaca, N.Y.: Cornell University Press, 1998), 3.

40. Moore, *Notes on the History of Slavery in Massachusetts*, 247n2; Spector, "The Quock Walker Cases (1781–83)," 25.

41. *Exeter v. Hanchett* (1784) demonstrated that the court would not protect out-of-state slaves.

42. Anne Baker Leland Bridges and Roy Williams III, *St. James Santee, Plantation Parish: History and Records, 1685–1925* (Spartanburg, S.C.: Reprint Company Publishers, 1997), 380–81.

43. Samuel Hasford, petition, August 25, 1783, 17, Records of the General Assembly, 1784–55–02, SCDAH, Columbia; Samuel Hasford, petition, July 20, 1784, Records of the General Assembly, 1784–55–02, SCDAH, Columbia.

44. Samuel Hasford, petition, August 25, 1783, 17, Records of the General Assembly, 1784–55–02, SCDAH, Columbia.

45. Samuel Hasford, petition, August 25, 1783, 17–18, Records of the General Assembly, 1784–55–02, SCDAH, Columbia.

46. SJC, order to issue writ of habeas corpus, August 26, 1783, 22, Records of the General Assembly, 1784–55–02, SCDAH, Columbia; Charles Cushing, writ of habeas corpus, August 26, 1783, Records of the General Assembly, Governor's Messages 307, 31–32, SCDAH, Columbia.

47. Thomas Crafts to jail keeper, August 29, 1783, Governor's Messages 307, 23, Records of the General Assembly, SCDAH, Columbia; Adele Stanton Edwards, ed., *Journals of the Privy Council, 1783–1789* (Columbia, S.C.: South Carolina Department of Archives, 1971), 82. For examples of slaves being imprisoned, see *Boston Gazette*, November 3, 1777. For other examples in 1777, see also March 10, 1777, March 17, 1777, May 26, 1777, and October 27, 1777.

48. Peter Edes, *Peter Edes, Pioneer Printer in Maine*, ed. Samuel Lane Boardman (Bangor, Maine: De Burians, 1901), 103.

49. Archibald Campbell's letter to George Washington, dated February 4, 1777, is reprinted in Charles Walcott, *Archibald Campbell of Inverneill, Sometime Prisoner in the Jail at Concord Massachusetts* (Boston: Beacon Press, 1898), 32.

50. Walcott, *Archibald Campbell of Inverneill, Sometime Prisoner in the Jail at Concord Massachusetts*, 32; Adam J. Hirsch, "From Pillory to Penitentiary: The Rise of Criminal Incarceration in Early Massachusetts," *Michigan Law Review* 80.6 (1982).

51. Charles Cushing, order to sheriff, August 30, 1783, 307–31, Records of the General Assembly, Governor's Messages 307, 31, SCDAH, Columbia; *Boston Gazette*, 3 November 1777. The slaves in the cases cited in n. 47 were likewise ordered to appear before the court.

52. Charles Cushing, report of case, Jack Philips, writ of habeas corpus, Records of the General Assembly, 1784–55–21, SCDAH, Columbia; SJC Record Books, 1783, reel 18, 177–78, Massachusetts Archives, Boston.

53. Thomas Crafts to jail keeper, August 30, 1783, Governor's Messages 307, 23, SCDAH, Columbia; Akhil Reed Amar, *America's Constitution: A Biography* (New York: Random House, 2006), 258.

54. John Winthrop to Pawley, September 1783, Records of the General Assembly, 1784-55-25-26, SCDAH, Columbia.

55. John Winthrop to Pawley, September 1783, Records of the General Assembly, 1784-55-25-26, SCDAH, Columbia.

56. John Winthrop to Pawley, September 1783, Records of the General Assembly, 1784-55-25-26, SCDAH, Columbia.

57. Edwards, *Journals of the Privy Council, 1783*, 82-83.

58. Benjamin Guerard to John Hancock, October 6, 1783, Records of the General Assembly, Governor's Messages 262, 7-9, SCDAH, Columbia.

59. Address of the council to Governor James Glen, *South Carolina Gazette*, February 19, 1756.

60. William Byrd, *Histories of the Dividing Line Betwixt Virginia and North Carolina*, ed. William K. Boyd and Percy G. Adams (New York: North Carolina Historical Commission, 1967), 5; "Letter from a Freeholder," *South Carolina Gazette*, March 28, 1743.

61. Benjamin Guerard to John Hancock, October 6, 1783, Records of the General Assembly, Governor's Messages 262, 7-9, SCDAH, Columbia.

62. Jeremy Boucher, "To the Hon'ble the Deputies in the Congress from the Southern Provinces, 5 August 1775," in *Reminiscences of an American Loyalist 1738-1739*, ed. Jonathan Boucher (Boston: Houghton Mifflin, 1925), 130.

63. William Cushing to John Hancock, December 20, 1783, Records of the General Assembly, Governor's Messages 307, 15-16, SCDAH, Columbia. A copy of this letter can be found in William Cushing Papers, 1664-1814, William Cushing 1783 folder, MHS, Boston.

64. William Cushing to John Hancock, December 20, 1783, Records of the General Assembly, Governor's Messages 307, 15-16, SCDAH, Columbia.

65. William Cushing to John Hancock, December 20, 1783, Records of the General Assembly, Governor's Messages 307, 15-16, SCDAH, Columbia.

66. William Cushing to John Hancock, December 20, 1783, Records of the General Assembly, Governor's Messages 307, 15-16, SCDAH, Columbia.

67. Mark Weiner, *Black Trials: Citizenship from the Beginning of Slavery to the End of Caste* (New York: Vintage, 2006), 6.

68. *Boston Gazette*, November 3 1777.

69. This subtle difference may indicate the start of Massachusetts' transformation into a free-market, free-labor economy.

70. Pennsylvania's gradual emancipation law of 1780 expressly excluded fugitive slaves from emancipation. Because the men and women in the *Tyrannicide* case were under charge of the owners' agent, they would not be considered fugitive slaves, although the South Carolinians began to call them such.

71. Article 4, paragraph 1, *Articles of Confederation*.

72. *Corfield v. Coryell*, 6 F Cas. 450 (1823); Paul Finkelman, *An Imperfect Union: Slavery, Federalism, and Comity* (New York: Lawbook Exchange, 2000), 10.

73. George Van Cleve, *A Slaveholders' Union: Slavery, Politics, and the Constitution in the Early American Republic* (Chicago: University of Chicago Press, 2010), 51-56.

74. Ira Berlin, *Many Thousands Gone: The First Two Centuries of Slavery in North America* (Cambridge, Mass.: Belknap Press of Harvard University Press, 1998), 320.

75. Twenty-one was a large number of manumissions for one year. Only one other year comes close, 1784, when twenty slaves were recorded in the Secretary's records. Other than these two years, the greatest number of slaves freed was thirteen.

76. Manumission of Jesse Donaldson, Miscellaneous Records, WW, SCDAH, Columbia.

77. Manumission of Betty, Miscellaneous Records, WW, SCDAH, Columbia.

78. Our only reliable record of black crime before 1800 in South Carolina is the records the legislature kept on payment of executioners. All slaves that were executed are listed, therefore, in the records of the South Carolina House of Representatives. See Lark Emerson Adams, ed., *Journals of the House of Representatives, 1785–86* (Columbia: South Carolina Department of Archives and History, 1979); Theodora J. Thompson, ed., *Journals of the House of Representatives, 1783–1784* (Columbia: South Carolina Department of Archives and History, 1977), 332; and Michael E. Stevens, ed., *Journals of the House of Representatives, 1787–1788* (Columbia: South Carolina Department of Archives and History, 1981), 157, 428.

79. Qtd. in Charles Lesser, *South Carolina Begins: The Records of a Proprietary Colony, 1663–1721* (Columbia: South Carolina Department of Archives and History, 1995), 240.

80. Lesser, *South Carolina Begins*, 240.

81. Robert Olwell, *Masters, Slaves, and Subjects: The Culture of Power in the South Carolina Low Country, 1740–1790* (Ithaca, N.Y.: Cornell University Press, 1998), 274.

82. Douglas Egerton, *Death or Liberty: African Americans and Revolutionary America* (New York: Oxford University Press, 2004), 155–57.

83. Egerton, *Death or Liberty*, 158.

84. *The Guardian of Sally (a negro) v. Beaty*, 1 Bay 260–63 (S.C. Superior Court 1792).

85. *Snow v. Cullum*, 1 Des. 541 (1797).

86. Sidney Kaplan, *The Black Presence in the Era of the American Revolution 1770–1800* (Washington, D.C.: Smithsonian Museum Press, 1973), 181; Amrita Chakrabarta Myers, *Forging Freedom: Black Women and the Pursuit of Liberty in Antebellum Charleston* (Chapel Hill: University of North Carolina Press, 2011), 11.

87. Indenture agreement between David Stoddard Greenough and Dick Morey, September 6, 1786, David S. Greenough Family Papers, MHS, Boston. The document is available at www.masshist.org/database/doc-viewer.php?item_id=701&mode=nav.

88. Indenture agreement between Isaac Smith and Scipio Dalton, June 20, 1779, December 20–24, 1779, Smith Carter Papers, MHS, Boston.

89. Indenture agreement between John Ashley and Mary, 1789, Miscellaneous Manuscript Bound Additions II, MHS, Boston; Indenture agreement between Theodore Sedgwick and Cato Freeman, 1802, Sedgwick II Collection, Box 3, folder 4, MHS, Boston.

90. Theodore Sedgwick to Henry Van Schaack, April 2, 1787, Sedgwick III Collection, box 1, folder 4, MHS, Boston; petition of Prince Hall to the Massachusetts General Court, February 27, 1788, Jeremy Belknap Papers, MHS, Boston (the document is available at www.masshist.org/database/710use-onview-id); Van Cleve, *A Slaveholders' Union*, 246; John Wood Sweet, *Bodies Politic: Negotiating Race in the American North, 1730–1830* (Baltimore, Md.: Johns Hopkins University Press, 2003), 246–47. The slave trade abolition did include a grandfather clause that would uphold contracts and insurance of ships that set sail before the enactment of the law (*The General Laws and Liberties of Massachusetts Colony* [Cambridge, Mass.: Samuel Green, 1672], 320–21).

91. *The Acts and Resolves of Massachusetts, 1786–1787* (Boston: Secretary of the Commonwealth, 1889), 625, 635.

92. *Massachusetts Mercury*, September 16, 1800.

93. *Winchendon v. Hatfield*, 4 Mass. Reports, 114.

94. Moore, *Notes on the History of Slavery in Massachusetts*, 196–99; Jeremy Belknap and St. George Tucker, *Queries Respecting the Introduction, Progress and Abolition of Slavery in Massachusetts* (Boston: Joseph Belknap, 1795).

95. Ruth Herndon, *Unwelcome Americans: Living on the Margin in Early New England* (Philadelphia: University of Pennsylvania Press, 2001), 18–20.

96. Sidney Kaplan, "Blacks in Massachusetts and Shays' Rebellion," *Contributions in Black Studies* 8.1 (1986): 5–14.

97. "Blacks in Massachusetts" is reprinted in Kaplan, *The Black Presence*, 10–11.

98. U.S. census, 1790, Massachusetts, National Archives Annex, East Point, Ga., Jack Phillips, 56 (index page number 193), George Pauley, 44 (index page number 188), Prince Hall, 47 (index page number 189), and Prince Hall, 57 (index page number 193).

EPILOGUE. FUGITIVE SLAVES IN THE CONSTITUTIONAL CONVENTION

1. George Van Cleve, *A Slaveholders' Union: Slavery, Politics, and the Constitution in the Early American Republic* (Chicago: University of Chicago Press, 2010), 48; Max Farrand and David Maydole Matteson, eds., *The Records of the Federal Convention of 1787*, 4 vols. (New Haven, Conn.: Yale University Press, 1966), 1:486. While the Congress debated taxation and representation, Pennsylvania and South Carolina previewed the sparring over power in the Constitutional Convention. Some other provisions in the articles touched on slavery, such as the privileges and immunities clause, but provoked little debate, affirming that the Congress did not seek to challenge slave property in the 1770s.

2. Please see chapter 2 for an in-depth discussion of slave resistance during the American Revolution. Some key works on the disruptions by the slave population are Sylvia R. Frey, *Water from the Rock: Black Resistance in a Revolutionary Age* (Princeton, N.J.: Princeton University Press, 1991); Robert Olwell, *Masters, Slaves, and Subjects: The Culture of Power in the South Carolina Low Country, 1740–1790* (Ithaca, N.Y.: Cornell University Press, 1998); Peter Wood, "'Impatient of Oppression': Black Freedom Struggles on the Eve of White Independence," *Southern Exposure* 12.6 (1984): 10–16; Jerome J. Nadelhaft, *The Disorders of War: The Revolution in South Carolina* (Orono: University of Maine at Orono Press, 1981); and Benjamin Quarles, *The Negro in the American Revolution* (Chapel Hill: Institute of Early American History and Culture, 1996).

3. At the time, many delegates, especially southerners such as Madison, described what we know as a North-South division as a diversion by the eastern states. This description might have been tactically important as well because the country was also grappling with how to deal with the western territories. Southerners felt that the western states had a greater affinity to their states than they did to the commercializing Northeast. Alexander Hamilton described this North-South division in terms of navigating states versus nonnavigating states. Other divisions existed as well. Within many of the states, divisions between east and west created social and political tensions. See Staughton Lynd, *Class Conflict, Slavery, and the United States Constitution: Ten Essays* (Indianapolis, Ind.: Bobbs-Merrill, 1967), and Alexander Hamilton, *The Works of Alexander Hamilton*, ed. John C. Hamilton (New York: John F. Trow, 1850), 433.

4. It is interesting to note that the phrase "provided always" would reemerge in southern documents. For example, when North Carolina ceded what would later be Tennessee, it used this phrase. "In the case of North Carolina's cession, however, the phrase was

meant to guarantee slavery eternally: The territory would be ceded so long as "no regula-tions made or to be made by Congress shall tend to emancipate slaves." This language returned in the U.S. Congress when the body accepted the first cession of southwestern territory and when it passed the ordinance for that territory in May 1790. See Lynd, *Class Conflict, Slavery, and the United States Constitution*, 192–93.

5. *Journals of the Continental Congress, 1774–1789*, 34 vols., ed. Worthington Chauncey Ford et al. (Washington, D.C.: Library of Congress, 1904–37), 28:239; *Letters of Members of the Continental Congress*, 8 vols., ed. Edmund C. Burnett (Washington, D.C.: Carnegie Institution of Washington, 1936), 8:622n5.

6. *Journals of the Continental Congress, 1774–1789*, 26:119; John Chester Miller, *The Wolf by the Ears: Thomas Jefferson and Slavery* (New York: Free Press, 1977), 27.

7. The provision lost by only one vote. New Jersey voted against the antislavery provi-sion because one of its most ardent antislavery delegates was too ill to attend the meet-ings (Miller, *The Wolf by the Ears*, 28).

8. Staughton Lynd and Peter Onuf attribute the change of heart primarily to the north-western focus of the ordinance. Eliminating slavery in this region had beneficial results for the South because it would eliminate competition in indigo and tobacco for the Up-per South and would keep prices of slaves low for the Deep South (Lynd, *Class Conflict, Slavery, and the United States Constitution*, 185–213; Peter S. Onuf, *The Origins of the Federal Republic: Jurisdictional Controversies in the United States, 1775–1787* [Philadel-phia: University of Pennsylvania Press, 1983], 169–71). Paul Finkelman has emphasized how ineffectual the article was because it was added at the last minute. The provision conflicted with various sections of the ordinance and provided no implementation plan. Finkelman also questions the connections that Lynd draws between the Congress and the convention (*Slavery and the Founders: Race and Liberty in the Age of Jefferson* [New York: M. E. Sharpe, 2001], 39–48).

9. Van Cleve, *A Slaveholders' Union*, 153–65; Lynd, *Class Conflict, Slavery, and the United States Constitution*, 185–213.

10. Lynd, *Class Conflict, Slavery, and the United States Constitution*, 189. Not only Coles thought that the fugitive slave clause was essential to the passage of the Constitution; Justice John McLean argued that the "constitution could not have been adopted without it" (Paul Brickner, "Reassessing Long-Accepted Truths about Justice John McLean: His Secret of Success," *Ohio Northern University Law Review* 38.1 [2011]: 193).

11. Farrand and Matteson, *The Records of the Federal Convention of 1787*, 2:443.

12. John P. Kaminski, ed., *A Necessary Evil? Slavery and the Debate over the Constitu-tion* (Madison, Wis.: Madison House, 1995), 65; Farrand and Matteson, *The Records of the Federal Convention of 1787*, 2:443, 46.

13. Paul Finkelman, "The Cost of Compromise and the Covenant with Death," *Pep-perdine Law Review* 38, special issue (2011): 847.

14. Darrell A. H. Miller, "The Stain of Slavery: Notes Toward an Attainder Theory of the Thirteenth Amendment," *University of Toledo Law Review* 38.3 (2007): 1033–34; D. Scott Bennett, "Chimera and the Continuum of Humanity: Erasing the Line of Con-stitutional Personhood," *Emory Law Journal* 55.2 (2006): 364n130.

15. Anthony J. Sebock, "Judging the Fugitive Slave Acts," *Yale Law Journal* 100.6 (1991): 1835–55.

16. Virginia is a notable exception because it had a large slave population and the larg-est overall population.

17. Farrand and Matteson, *The Records of the Federal Convention of 1787*, 1:35–37, 204.

Virginia delegates Madison and Randolph, although representing a southern state, did not protest this limitation to freemen.

18. Farrand and Matteson, *The Records of the Federal Convention of 1787*, 1:204–5.

19. Kaminski, *A Necessary Evil?*, 21–22, 43.

20. Farrand and Matteson, *The Records of the Federal Convention of 1787*, 1:580–81.

21. Farrand and Matteson, *The Records of the Federal Convention of 1787*, 1:581, 593.

22. Farrand and Matteson, *The Records of the Federal Convention of 1787*, 1:588.

23. Farrand and Matteson, *The Records of the Federal Convention of 1787*, 1:586.

24. Farrand and Matteson, *The Records of the Federal Convention of 1787*, 1:586, 206.

25. Farrand and Matteson, *The Records of the Federal Convention of 1787*, 2:566.

26. Farrand and Matteson, *The Records of the Federal Convention of 1787*, 2:566.

27. Farrand and Matteson, *The Records of the Federal Convention of 1787*, 1:204–5, 580–81, 586–88, 591–97.

28. Farrand and Matteson, *The Records of the Federal Convention of 1787*, 2:95; Finkelman, *Slavery and the Founders*, 19.

29. Farrand and Matteson, *The Records of the Federal Convention of 1787*, 2:220, 183, 188, 175.

30. Farrand and Matteson, *The Records of the Federal Convention of 1787*, 2:403–4; Christopher Collier and James Lincoln Collier, *Decision in Philadelphia: The Constitutional Convention of 1787* (New York: Ballantine, 1986), 301; Jack Rakove, *Original Meanings: Politics and Ideas in the Making of the Constitution* (New York: Vintage, 1996), 90–93.

31. Rakove, *Original Meanings*, 90–91.

32. Farrand and Matteson, *The Records of the Federal Convention of 1787*, 2:443; Finkelman, *Slavery and the Founders*, 27.

33. Farrand and Matteson, *The Records of the Federal Convention of 1787*, 3:601.

34. Farrand and Matteson, *The Records of the Federal Convention of 1787*, 2:467.

35. Farrand and Matteson, *The Records of the Federal Convention of 1787*, 2:378; Finkelman, *Slavery and the Founders*, 24; Chris Brown, *Moral Capital: Foundations of British Abolitionism* (Chapel Hill: University of North Carolina, 2006).

36. Farrand and Matteson, *The Records of the Federal Convention of 1787*, 2:220.

37. Farrand and Matteson, *The Records of the Federal Convention of 1787*, 2:221.

38. Farrand and Matteson, *The Records of the Federal Convention of 1787*, 2:364, 371.

39. Farrand and Matteson, *The Records of the Federal Convention of 1787*, 2:364.

40. Farrand and Matteson, *The Records of the Federal Convention of 1787*, 2:400, 415–16; Finkelman, *Slavery and the Founders*, 19–29.

41. Farrand and Matteson, *The Records of the Federal Convention of 1787*, 2:559.

42. Kaminski, *A Necessary Evil?*; Collier and Collier, *Decision in Philadelphia*, 189.

43. Jack Rakove (*Original Meanings*) and George Van Cleve (*A Slaveholders' Union*) describe this conflict in ways that are more sophisticated. David Waldstreicher has updated the Beardian economic analysis; he neglects the fugitive slave clause but reviews the integral nature of slavery in American economy as seen in the three-fifths clause. See his *Slavery's Constitution: From Revolution to Ratification* (New York: Hill and Wang, 2009).

44. Finkelman, *Slavery and the Founders*; John P. Kaminski, *A Necessary Evil?*; Lynd, *Class Conflict, Slavery, and the United States Constitution*; Rakove, *Original Meanings*; William M. Wiecek, *The Sources of Antislavery Constitutionalism in America, 1760–1848* (Ithaca, N.Y.: Cornell University Press, 1977); Don Fehrenbacher, *The Federal Govern-*

ment and Slavery (Claremont, Calif.: Claremont Institute for the Study of Statesmanship and Political Philosophy, 1984); Don Fehrenbacher and Ward M. McAfee, eds., *The Slaveholding Republic: An Account of the United States Government's Relations to Slavery* (New York: Oxford University Press, 2002).

45. Jonathan Elliot, ed., *The Debates in the Several State Conventions on the Adoption of the Federal Constitution*, 5 vols. (Washington, D.C.: published for the editor, 1836), 2:36–41.

46. Elliot, *The Debates in the Several State Conventions on the Adoption of the Federal Constitution*, 2:107.

47. Elliot, *The Debates in the Several State Conventions on the Adoption of the Federal Constitution*, 2:107–8.

48. Elliot, *The Debates in the Several State Conventions on the Adoption of the Federal Constitution*, 2:115.

49. Elliot, *The Debates in the Several State Conventions on the Adoption of the Federal Constitution*, 4:271–74.

50. Elliot, *The Debates in the Several State Conventions on the Adoption of the Federal Constitution*, 4:277.

51. Elliot, *The Debates in the Several State Conventions on the Adoption of the Federal Constitution*, 4:283–86.

52. Elliot, *The Debates in the Several State Conventions on the Adoption of the Federal Constitution*, 4:317–18.

Index

abolition of slavery. *See also* emancipation; slave trade

antislavery sentiments

before the American Revsolution, 37

of blacks, 7, 37, 72

and Loyalists, 44–45, 119

of whites, 32, 35–36, 38, 39, 62–63, 64, 67, 72, 74, 76, 77, 103, 105, 119, 181n103, 193n26

and Massachusetts, 116–31 passim, 150

abolitionist efforts, 6, 32, 37, 63, 68, 69, 116–17, 127, 150

dealing with becoming a free state, 150

first state to legalize and first state to emancipate all slaves, 122, 164, 193n23

protecting property ownership, 155–56

Southern opposition slowing Massachusetts efforts, 7, 8, 36, 64, 67, 80, 103, 127, 150

use of courts to abolish slavery, 117–27, 150. *See also* freedom suits; petitions for freedom

use of "free and equal" clause, 119, 120, 122, 124

and writing of Massachusetts constitution, 66–68

and South Carolina, 116–31 passim

abolitionist/anti-slavery sentiments in, 38, 39, 76, 77, 105

balking at antislavery positions in Continental Congress, 152–53

impact of *Tyrannicide* affair, 8, 103, 154

opposition to abolition, 6–7, 8, 63, 76

requesting removal of abolition language from Declaration of Independence, 63–64

seeing abolition as threat to economy, 79–80

as way to add soldiers to forces against British, 79

as a states' right issue, 63

and U.S. Constitution, 62–63

Act for Preventing All Riotous, Tumultuous and Disorderly Assemblies (in Boston), 15

Act to Prevent Profane Cursing and Swearing (in Boston), 15

Adams, Abigail, 4, 49

Adams, John, 35, 40, 45

and Boston Massacre trials, 50

and Constitutional Convention, 150

and Declaration of Independence, 61, 64

efforts to placate southern colonies about slavery, 6, 36, 64, 103, 127, 150

and Massachusetts constitution, 65, 67

Adams, Sam, 32, 33, 37, 65, 102

Affa (slave involved in *Tyrannicide* affair), 90, 93, 100, 107, 129, 145

Africa, blacks feeling identification with, 70, 109, 110, 143–44

African Americans. *See* blacks

African Lodge No. 1, 70

African religious practices, 25

Alison, Hugh, 39

Allen, John, 32–33

American Revolution, 34

Andrew (slave), 50

Anthony (slave involved in *Tyrannicide* Affair), 93, 99, 107, 129

Antigua (slave), 79

antislavery sentiments. *See* abolition of slavery

Appleby, George, 87

Appleton, Nathaniel, 32, 103

Articles of Confederation, 3, 129, 134, 148, 157, 158, 161

impact of taxing slaves as property, 64–65